"Most recall West Texan 'Claytie' Williams Jr. as the candidate who, in losing the 1990 gubernatorial race to Ann Richards, shot himself in the foot more times than a centipede with a machine gun. But Mike Cochran's biography of the colorful oilfield wildcatter, rancher, banker, born entrepreneur—a page-turner reading more like an adventure novel—introduces the philanthropist, loyal friend, honest and sometimes soft-hearted side of the bar-room brawling, hard-drinking, plain-cussing, fanatical Texas Aggie who has been a near-billionaire and also on the verge of bankruptcy in the boom-or-bust oilpatch. Claytie's life might be a movie—except I think it was shot in the 1950s as *Giant* with James Dean playing the Claytie Williams role, though they called him Jett Rink. A good read, for Texans or others."

—Larry L. King, author of *The Best Little Whorehouse in Texas*

"Claytie is quite the colorful man whose personality is bigger than the Permian Basin he hails from. George and I are both friends and fans of his."

—Barbara Bush, former First Lady

"Claytie Williams is a living symbol of the mythical larger-than-life Texan, sometimes down but never out, willing to back his judgment on a Hail Mary pass, win, lose, or draw. He is one of the most affable people I have ever met."

—Elmer Kelton, western novelist

"Clayton Williams's passion for making friends, making money, and making music is legendary. I've always admired Clayton. He's a genuine American—as tough as a boot but with a heart as big as Texas."

—Charley Pride, member of the Country Music Hall of Fame

"Clayton Williams—West Texas oilman, proud Aggie, and would-be governor of Texas—has lived life on a grand scale reminiscent of independent Texas oilmen of an earlier era. Mike Cochran has blended stories of Williams's personal, business, and political lives into a fast-moving, readable biography. Anyone interested in Texas history, petroleum history, or political history should enjoy this book."

—Joseph A. Pratt, Cullen Chair of History and Business,
University of Houston

"There is a forthrightness to his book that reflects Claytie's own basic honesty, his inimitable combination of straight talk, braggadocio, combativeness, and poking fun at himself."
— Dave McNeely, author and dean of Texas political reporters

"Clayton Williams defies the laws of physics — as an oilman/rancher he proves that oil and water DO mix."
— Bob Parker, chairman emeritus, Parker Drilling Company

"Clayton Williams looks across the Texas landscape and sees two things more clearly than most — where water will flow on the surface, and oil beneath."
— W. Herbert Hunt, Petro-Hunt L.L.P.

"In Mike Cochran's perfect-pitch account of the quintessential Texas wildcatter, the colorful life and multiple personae of Claytie Williams stand out for their true grit and integrity. This is an extraordinary biography."
— Davis L. Ford, adjunct professor of engineering, University of Texas, and past president of the Association of Former Students of Texas A&M University

"This book tells the story of the Claytie that his closest friends have appreciated for years."
— former Texas governor William P. Clements

"Clayton Williams's perfect counterpart is Col. Charles Goodnight. Their shared values and 'my word is my bond' reputation along with their pioneering accomplishments put them in the same category of remarkable leaders. Charles Goodnight, had he known Clayton, would have praised Clayton as the right man to join him on that last great trail drive."
— J. P. Bryan, former president of the Texas State Historical Association, sixth generation Texan, and descendent of Stephen F. Austin

Claytie

BY MIKE COCHRAN

Claytie

THE
ROLLER-COASTER
LIFE OF A
TEXAS WILDCATTER

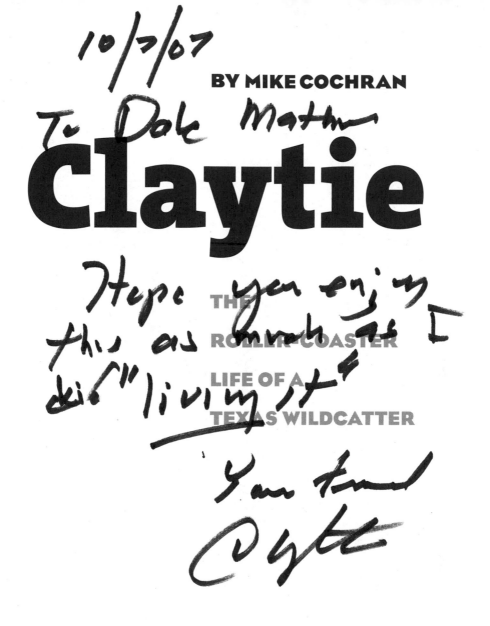

10/7/07

To Dale Mathew

Hope you enjoy
this as much as I
did "living it"

Your friend
Clytle

TEXAS A&M UNIVERSITY PRESS

College Station

The paper used in this book meets the minimum
requirements of the American National Standard for
Permanence of Paper for Printed Library Materials,
z39.48-1984.
Binding materials have been chosen for durability.
∞

Library of Congress Cataloging-in-Publication Data

Cochran, Mike.
    Claytie : the roller-coaster life of a Texas Wildcatter /
by Mike Cochran. — 1st ed.
        p. cm.
    ISBN-13: 978-1-58544-634-6 (cloth : alk. paper)
    ISBN-10: 1-58544-634-3 (cloth : alk. paper)
    1. Williams, Clayton, 1931–   2. Oil industry workers—
Texas—Biography.   3. Political candidates—Texas—
Biography.   4. Businesspeople—Texas—Biography.
5. Oil well drilling—Texas.   6. Governors—Texas—
Election.   7. Texas—Biography.   I. Title.
    CT275.W56517C63   2007
    976.4'063092—dc22
    [B]

                                2007018437

Contents

Claytie

The irrepressible Claytie, in kilt, sombrero, and Aggie boots

"I ran my company like Christopher Columbus. When he left Spain, he didn't know where he was going. When he got here, he didn't know where he was. When he got back, he didn't know where he'd been. And he did it all on borrowed money."

Introduction

OK, so he's a Texas Aggie who nearly burned down one West Texas town, forced the headline-grabbing evacuation of another—nothing personal, just business—and torched his own bid for Texas governor with some actions and brash words reflecting a political tin ear that a majority of voters found unnerving.

Yes, it's also true that his flag-waving manner, robust lifestyle, and shoot-from-the-lip openness reflect much of the best and a bit of the worst of America's storybook oil-field millionaires.

And there's no denying it was his own sister Janet who described him as "tender, sweet, loving . . . and ruthless."

Ruthless?

"She means tough," Claytie maintains, with a trademark ear-to-ear grin that would light up a brood of vampires.

Yes, indeed, with Clayton Williams Jr., what you see is what you get, and then some, for he is many things to many people, which is part of his magnetism, part of his enigma. Even elder daughter Kelvie speaks of the inescapable draw of his orbit: "He is the sun and we are all the little planets that rotate around him."

Who, exactly, is this Texas icon, the consummate West Texan and diehard Aggie, the rancher, farmer, wildcatter, conservationist, philanthropist, dedicated party animal, barroom brawler, benevolent dictator, family patriarch, wild-game hunter, and oil-patch visionary who doesn't just live life but attacks it? You're about to find out, because this book is designed to capture and showcase the full dimensions of the man—not just his public persona as a rowdy wildcatter, working cowboy, or would-be governor.

Under the watchful eye of wife and constant companion Modesta, Clayton Wheat Williams Jr. continues into his seventies to party hearty, punch cattle, climb mountains, fish, and hunt big-game animals around the world—all the while orchestrating a vast business empire that has included oil and gas production and transportation, real estate, ranching, banking, oil-field services and supply, alfalfa farming, an unprecedented African safari venture, and an equally innovative long-distance communications company. For several years into the late '80s, he even found time to teach a popular entrepreneurial class at his beloved Texas A&M—a course his students called "How to Make a Million Dollars." Claytie remembers that the course was better known as Bullshit 201 and, later, when elevated to an advanced offering, as Bullshit 489.

"That was one of the highlights of my life," he told me, just about the time he commissioned me to write this authorized biography.

"Bullshitting?" I asked.

"No," he frowned. "Teaching."

That exchange helped get us off to a rocky start and was the forerunner to dozens of lively and occasionally heated interviews, some of which his drop-dead gorgeous and long-suffering wife feared would end in fisticuffs. One of those climaxed when, red-faced and with eyes flashing, Claytie pushed back from the conference table and declared: "Cochran, sometimes you can be a real [blankety-blank, blankety-blank]."

A short time later we were knocking down shots of tequila, gnawing on lamb chops, and sharing risqué stories like a couple of good ol' small-town, West Texas boys.

I first began writing about Clayton Williams Jr. in the early 1980s as a roving West Texas correspondent for the Associated Press, and even then he was rocking princely boats with tsunami waves. He had adopted the maroon-and-white flags of his alma mater as a battle symbol, even hoisting one atop his Midland, Tex., office building in a defiant, go-to-hell gesture to an adversary. Aggie flags also flew daily above his oil rigs around the country. *Forbes* had recently listed him among its four hundred richest Americans—although the magazine did not mention he also had a debt load approaching $500 million. A paradox, you say? Later, when dismissed by many as a bumbling amateur in a madcap and haunting political drama, he was in fact reshaping and revitalizing the Texas Republican Party. Later still, with bankruptcy apparently the only option to rescue his company, he spurned that seductive solution and gambled everything on his own skills and those of a small, handpicked recovery team.

"Claytie's always at his best when his back's against the wall, when he's down and things are going tough," insists a former company president, Tom Moore.

In a long-ago interview, Claytie attributed his business success to his Aggie background and education as well as a feel he developed for the land and its subtle telltale geological formations. He also stated a conviction that would resonate in my mind for the next twenty-five years as I chronicled the business, financial, and personal ups and downs—the private and public triumphs and tragedies—of this remarkably unsophisticated and charmingly flawed West Texan.

"I think it's how you handle your failures that determines your eventual success," he told me. "It's the ability to retrench and regroup. It's not how many times you get knocked down, it's how many times you get back up."

That gallant Claytie doctrine would be tested repeatedly in 1990 when he ran for governor amidst the glaring spotlight of state and national media. In a reflective story written years later, AP political writer Michael Holmes described that election as "the biggest, bruisingest, costliest, craziest, nastiest, noisiest, wildest, woolliest Texas governor's race ever."

It was an election, filled with primary upsets and ultimately won by Democrat Ann Richards, that captured the fancy of not only the Texas media but also the national and international press. Yet it was through that campaign, punctuated by an off-color joke and a few other costly gaffes, that millions of Americans would come to know Claytie—or think they know him. In truth, few know the *real* Clayton Williams Jr. In the opinion of several of my journalistic colleagues and many of Claytie's friends, it would be an injustice if the political image that stuck to him during that campaign overshadowed his business, financial, philanthropic, conservation, and humanitarian accomplishments, as well as his bold and spirited adventures in the oil patch and on the cattle ranch—or even in the political arena itself.

John Gravois, whose coverage of Claytie's campaign for the *Houston Post* was often devastatingly critical, nevertheless called Claytie "a class act" and said it would be "a shame" if people formed their opinion of him based on his political miscues.

These are some of the more compelling reasons for writing this book. After what turned out to be a four-year commitment for me (starting with Claytie's upfront declaration that "I don't want a fluff book"); after hundreds of interviews with him and his family, friends, associates, and more than a few detractors; after perusing thousands of pages of books, magazines, and newspapers, I find Claytie an enigma still—a totally fascinating and domineering and combustible one. Almost everyone has an opinion about him, and not all opinions of Claytie are heartwarming. But I believe his loyal and longtime executive assistant, Denise Kelly, touched a lot of bases and perhaps said it best one day in a spirited defense of Claytie's little-known Bible study activities in Midland: "One of the most endearing and charming traits of Clayton Williams is his openness and willingness to point to his own human weaknesses without fretting about what someone will think of him. He is what he is. Take it or leave it. And one thing's for sure—he's no hypocrite.

He'll be the first to say he has room for improvement in any given area. He's still the boss, but he's not pretentious in any way. While he doesn't wear his feelings on his sleeve, he's transparent when it comes to his passion, his joy for life, his emotions, his affection, and his overall enthusiasm for doing the best job possible and enjoying the achievement."

Until the spring of 2003, despite the many interviews I had conducted, I had only a secondhand knowledge of the grand galas Claytie and Modesta staged intermittently at their Happy Cove Ranch near Alpine in the majestic mountains of far West Texas. That's roughly 450 miles west of Dallas, 200 miles east of El Paso, another 100 north of Big Bend country and Mexico. A long way from almost anywhere, this was a geographic setting designed for a Clayton Williams celebration. Many of Claytie and Modesta's famous bashes had already occurred there during the years they assembled one of the country's great ranch and cattle operations. These fabled events included record-breaking sales of Brangus cattle and celebrity-studded parties featuring country and western music's biggest stars.

My first experience there was over the 2003 Memorial Day weekend. I got a firsthand look at the couple's renowned flair for country-flavored elegance and dedication to good times with as many family, old friends, and business associates as they could gather. The occasion was the marriage of Claytie and Modesta's youngest daughter, Chim, an Aggie, to a fellow Aggie, Greg Welborn. Everyone there, family and guests, formed a tableau as fitting as it was telling: cowboys and oilmen, ranchers and bankers, fetching women and driven men; champagne and frozen margaritas, fine wine and cold beer; men in "black-tie optional" boots and jeans, suits and ties and tuxes; women aglow in sun dresses and party dresses and stylish gowns. It could have been a scene from the movie classic *Giant*. After all, the 1956 epic was filmed just over the mountains, hardly a ranch or two away.

And when the minister asked who it was that gave this beautiful young woman in marriage, Claytie stepped forward in his cowboy hat and boots and Aggie-maroon tuxedo and beamed: "My wife, Modesta, and I . . . and Texas A&M."

Six hundred guests, many of them Aggies, laughed and roared approval.

On that remarkable weekend in 2003, it would be son Jeff, then just months away from his thirtieth birthday, who best described Claytie and Modesta and the inseparable relationship that makes them so special in person and so fitting a subject for this book.

"My Mom's every guy's dream wife," he told this first-time visitor to Happy Cove in a casual conversation beside the Aggie-boot-shaped pool. "She's amazing. She's beautiful and she's strong, and you'd never have thought that little lady could do everything she's done. . . . Dad's amazing, too. They've had a wonderful marriage. Chim and I, and our brother Clayton Wade hope to mirror our marriages after theirs. They've been married thirty-nine years and they're more in love now than the day they first married."

Before nightfall, Claytie was serenading wedding guests in Spanish—no doubt dazzling the coyotes and cattle and maybe a rattlesnake or two as well. He was backed not only by a mariachi band but also by longtime party pal, rancher–musician–windmill man David Ligon. It was the inimitable Ligon who later confessed that he and Claytie, growing up together in Fort Stockton, discovered beer and women on the same evening. "It was a traumatic day in our lives and from then on we just weren't worth killin'."

With spotlights targeted on a giant American flag perched high atop a backyard mountain peak, Claytie's unfettered display of confidence and creativity that night would remind some guests of a passage from author Ruth Sheldon Knowles' oil-patch classic, *The Greatest Gamblers . . . The Epic of Oil Exploration*: "The minds who were born to seek and find oil are among the most fascinating and productive in all history. They changed the destiny of America and gave it the energy with which to build the world's greatest industrialized nation. Their imagination, courage, and ingenuity made the story of petroleum the greatest romance in industrial history."

That passage would come to mind again on a frosty winter night six months after the wedding when daughter Allyson's husband, Jerry Groner, stood quietly beside a campfire as Claytie entertained deer hunters on his Pecos County ranch, laughing and hugging his guests and singing along with guitarists.

"He's the last of a special breed of wildcatter," Jerry told me. "And that's really sad."

Who would have guessed that Clayton Wheat Williams Jr.—this Alpine-born and Fort Stockton–reared son of a prominent West Texas author-engineer-rancher-oilman-politician, this grandson of a pioneering, Harvard-educated lawyer-surveyor-judge, this Spanish-flavored tabletop troubadour and barroom brawler—could make an off-hand remark that would trigger a series of political events that forever changed the course of state, national, and world history?

Fifteen years later, with the country at war in Iraq and Americans coping with a staggering national debt and skyrocketing energy prices at home, former U.S. House Speaker Jim Wright of Fort Worth quoted a friend and fellow Democrat who put a clever spin on the global mess. If Claytie hadn't told "off-color stories to the press" during his 1990 campaign, the friend insisted, he would have been elected governor. And with a fellow Republican in that office, George W. Bush wouldn't have run for governor in 1994 and would have had no platform for a presidential bid in 2000.

"So just think," Wright's friend theorized, "whatever troubles we have today are all Clayton Williams's fault!"

That said, hang on. Like the dirt road winding through the harsh beauty of Happy Cove Ranch, riding shotgun with the irrepressible Claytie is a bumpy, serpentine journey . . . but also a magical and seductive adventure.

Mike Cochran
Spring 2007

One

Claytie at age five: a young buckaroo

"As a typical Aggie, I tried to drill my way out of trouble."

1

It was a silent, solemn group that boarded the company plane in Midland one fine spring morning in 1991 only months after a tumultuous Texas governor's race had sapped much of Claytie's strength and spirit—plus $8 million of his personal fortune.

If not the worst of times, it was a close second.

The destination that day: Houston. The purpose: a bankruptcy briefing. At stake: not only Claytie's oil company, and not only his reputation, but also his family legacy, which included pioneering forebears who for more than a century had helped settle and enrich far West Texas with sustained contributions to its land, law, and literature.

Now it had come to this: Claytie was smothering under nearly $90 million in debt, and his most prominent contribution to family legacy, his good name, suddenly was as vulnerable as bankruptcy was imminent and ugly.

Claytie's personal and professional woes had continued to mount since, a little more than a year earlier on Valentine's Day 1990, five close friends were killed in a company plane crash. After his narrow loss to Ann Richards in the governor's race, he discovered his energy companies were not nearly as healthy as he had been told during his twenty-two-month campaign hiatus.

"I was off balance and not thinking clearly," he said.

During his absence, and upon his return, the bulk of the company's activity was in South Texas in what was known as the Pearsall

Field, where the company started drilling in December 1989. "The problem was that the Pearsall reserves were overestimated and substantially devalued and not worth anywhere near what we thought—or what we had borrowed against," Claytie said. "We were in trouble, and we didn't realize it until the spring of '91."

The company drilled some sixty wells in the Pearsall Field while he was gone. "The ongoing drilling program averaged nearly $1 million per well," said Claytie. "And after my return we drilled thirteen or fourteen more before I came to my senses and realized that the Pearsall project was losing substantial amounts of money."

Worse, the company had borrowed millions against the reserves to continue drilling operations. Vendors such as Halliburton and drilling contractors such as Grey Wolf were squeezing the company for payment. But the wells weren't producing enough oil to allow the company to cover its debts, which were approaching $90 million. To compound the problem, the price of oil had dropped drastically.

"As a typical Aggie," Claytie said, "I tried to drill my way out of trouble, but just drilled myself in deeper. I was losing money on every well I drilled. It was a devastating time for me. Many drilling operations were curtailed across the country in the wake of falling oil prices."

Besides the negative oil environment and drilling problems, his Midland bank, ClayDesta National, was flirting with failure. Fourteen million dollars in car loans extended to poor credit risks would soon take the bank to the brink of insolvency.

Against this dark financial background, Modesta's mother—also named Modesta—had been diagnosed with cancer and had fallen fatally ill. Claytie and Modesta's elder son, Clayton Wade, added to the misery by getting busted on drug charges and sent to "boot camp." After pleading guilty to possession of LSD, the troubled youngster was sentenced by a Midland judge to six months at the federal camp in Lewisburg, Pa. The judge also ordered the twenty-year-old to spend an additional six months at an Odessa halfway house, assuming he satisfactorily completed the federal drug treatment program.

Claytie had been down before—during the fledgling business struggles in the 1960s, and the oil and gas busts of the 1980s—but never down *and* out. Given the exhausting governor's race, coupled now with the family and financial misfortune, he felt, as he told a friend, "whipped and whipped and whipped." While never one to wallow in self-pity, he had convinced himself that even Modesta had lost confidence in him, which was not true. But as he conceded later, he was not thinking clearly. His personal life was in shambles and his company was drowning in debt. Fellow Midland oilman Ted Collins always said nobody bounced back better from adversity than Claytie—"He defies gravity!" But gravity had now seized momentum.

Chapter 11 bankruptcy appeared the only way to escape his skyrocketing debts and buy time to reorganize and rescue the company.

Such was the backdrop that spring morning when Claytie, Modesta, and two of the company's top officers, Paul Latham and Mel Riggs, boarded the company jet and flew off to the state's largest city to confer with one of Texas' leading bankruptcy specialists.

Latham, Claytie's in-house counsel and manager, and Riggs, his top financial officer, shared similar thoughts as they settled in for the short hop to Houston. The atmosphere that morning was more conducive to a funeral than a business meeting—even Claytie wore a suit, although he didn't abandon his cowboy boots and hat.

Nobody spoke for long periods. Claytie, visibly distressed, was lost in his private thoughts. Modesta was quietly but deeply concerned about Claytie's emotional state. "He feels like everybody's down on him," she thought. She was aware that whereas bankruptcy offered a certain perverse appeal, Claytie dreaded it. Mel sparred mentally with a phenomenon he could not explain: a weird darkness, like a shadow, seemed to have descended on the group, although the skies were crystal clear. He grappled with a feeling one might have after losing something or somebody very dear to him.

Meanwhile, Paul studied the faces of both Claytie and Modesta and sensed that the bankruptcy issue was perhaps more personal than legal, that the consequences of this trip extended beyond monetary considerations. The pending decision, he knew, was crucial and would affect many people's lives in many ways, some unknown. Paul, who had been with the company nearly ten years, realized perhaps better than anyone on board that a bankruptcy filing would make a lot of money problems go away and buy the company critical time. But it would assuredly torpedo Claytie's lofty entrepreneurial status and jeopardize his reputation for integrity and ethical behavior.

When the bankruptcy discussions first surfaced weeks earlier, someone raised the possibility of shielding assets through the wives and children of family members and others. But Modesta said Claytie shot down that idea before it ever flapped a wing, let alone took flight.

"No," he snapped, according to those present. "I've never done that before and I'm not going to do it now." He conceded that in a crunch it's difficult to avoid such thoughts, but "I'm not that kind of person. I'm not going to hide my debts. I'm gonna try to pay everyone I owe."

Still, he suspected he might end up losing his company and his reputation, as well as besmirching his historic family legacy. No, this was more than about money, he decided, more than about reputation. This was deeper.

This was family.

It would be a stretch to describe Clayton W. Williams Jr. as a chip off the old fatherly or grandfatherly block, but no doubt both forebears proved to be powerful influences on the feisty youngster who grew up in the far West Texas hamlet of Fort Stockton and began working as a young boy on the family ranch and farm.

"My dad had a ranch of about thirty-five sections and an irrigated farm of about three hundred to four hundred acres just outside the small Pecos County town," related Claytie. "Sometimes I'd go spend the night on the ranch and other nights I stayed at the farm when baling hay. The ranch and farm—they were as much my home as Fort Stockton."

The elder Williams, Kentucky-born lawyer-surveyor Oscar Waldo Williams, was a marvelous writer and a noted historian. He never wrote a book, but he was the widely admired subject of several. Claytie's father, Clayton W. Williams Sr., was an Aggie, an oilman, and a county commissioner who wrote a number of essentially historical books—his first, *Never Again,* about his beloved Pecos County, was not published until he was sixty-five years old. Clayton Sr.'s literary ties to Texas A&M University Press would foreshadow Claytie's philanthropic relationship with the university.

Both sides of Claytie's family were historically intriguing, sometimes amusingly so. His grandmother's family, the Grahams, fought in the Civil and Revolutionary wars. The Williamses, particularly grandfather O.W., were on the scene during the exploits of a number of legendary figures of the nineteenth century. "Before coming to Fort Stockton, my grandfather traveled to Silver City, N.M., to prospect for silver and gold but wound up serving as assistant postmaster because nobody else in town could read or write," Claytie said. "He was in New Mexico when Geronimo was active, and he was there during the days of Billy the Kid. In fact, there were rumors and some writings that my grandfather *was* Billy the Kid. Well, he was not."

O.W. also was one of five suspects in the shotgun slaying of a rogue sheriff named A. J. Royal, who some suggest deserved killing.

"My daddy told me my grandfather was not the killer, but the killer was never caught," Claytie said.

A truly grim episode occurred as another of Claytie's forebears rode with a young Kit Carson on a wagon train carrying merchandise from St. Louis, Mo., to Santa Fe, N.M. "I remember as a boy my grandfather told me that a fellow somehow injured his arm in an accident, and Kit Carson and another man sawed off the arm to save his life," Claytie said. "Carson was probably a teenager, but he had the guts to saw off a man's arm and cauterize the wound."

Claytie's father recounted in one of his books how Christopher "Kit" Carson, then seventeen years old, made the cut with a sharp razor. The "amateur surgeons," he wrote, "used a common saw to sever the bone, after which the cut was seared with a red hot king bolt." The man eventually recovered.

Of Carson, Williams wrote: "More stories of frontier adventure have been built up around his name than can be claimed for any frontiersman excepting Daniel Boone [a distant Williams relative via marriage]."

As a frontier lawyer and early surveyor in 1876 and 1877, O.W. surveyed on the Staked Plains—a forty-thousand-square-mile extension of the Great Plains in West Texas and southeastern New Mexico and known widely as the Llano Estacado.

"In fact," Claytie said, "he surveyed the original town site of Lubbock, located in Block O, which bears his initial for Oscar."

O.W. arrived in Fort Stockton in 1883 as the county surveyor and, as one of the few educated men in town, was soon elected county judge. He served in Pecos County in the same era as Roy Bean, the Val Verde County judge known far and wide as "The Law West of the Pecos."

"He never met Judge Bean," Claytie said, "but he didn't think much of him from long distance."

O.W.'s wife, Sallie, sprang from the musical Wheat family of Dallas, and her piano reputedly was the first in a home west of the Pecos River. "The early pictures of the Williams family are of Sallie at the piano, Daddy with a trumpet, and all the other family singing and joining in," Claytie said.

While Judge Williams seemed drawn to the eye of the storm, his son Clayton Sr. rarely traveled the wild side. The son was not, however, inclined to sidestep a good fight, even at an advanced age. Claytie's namesake nephew Clay Pollard delights in telling the story of an incident that occurred in 1979 at his brother Scott Pollard's wedding in Dallas. All the family members were staying at the trendy Stoneleigh Hotel, whose desk clerk had impressed some as a smart ass—and a rude one to boot. Clayton Sr. had exchanged words with him a couple of times.

"Right before we're supposed to leave for the wedding, I'm in my tux and taking things to the car, walking through the lobby, and I see my grandfather leaning on the front desk," Clay recalled. "He shouts, 'Clay, come here! Clay, come here!' I walked over and said, 'Yes, sir?' He says, 'This man is dialing the police. He says I hit him. I didn't hit him. I reached over to take his glasses off so that I *could* hit him.' I think to myself, 'I can't have PaPaw arrested right here before the wedding.' So I grab him by the arm and take him to the elevator and we go upstairs. I get the family and say, 'Look, the police are coming for PaPaw, so you all just surround him. Go get in the car and go on to the church.' And they got him out of there.

"That was 1979, and he was eighty-something years old!"

Claytie's sister, Janet Pollard, often compared their father to Atticus Finch, the noble and compassionate lawyer in the Academy Award–winning movie *To Kill a Mockingbird*. A charming romantic, Janet likewise found a hint of Hollywood in their mother, Chic, whose personality reminded her of the actress Claudette Colbert, especially when she smiled. "She was uplifting, happy, inspirational, the kind of person you wanted to be around all the time," she once told a reporter. "Mother had this wonderful joy over the smallest things. Every day was a happy new day, and every day she smiled. She was a good mother, who told us every day how much she loved us."

Claytie's executive assistant, Denise Kelly, who joined the company in 1985, remembered Chic's excited response to the frequent invitations she received to social events. "Many times, when Chic was invited to be at an event that she was enthusiastic about, I heard her say, 'Oh, I'll be there! If the creek don't rise and the Good Lord's willing—and even if He's not, I'll slip off.' I thought that was so true and representative of her reverent but also feisty spirit."

The *Odessa American* did a lengthy profile of Chic as she approached her ninetieth birthday and described her as "an adventurer and world traveler, teller of stories, hostess par excellence,

Claytie with mother Chicora and sister Janet, 1935

and a constantly moving eighty-nine-year-old, almost five-feet-tall package of vitality."

In his own way, their father was every bit as special, Janet maintained. "Our dad was wise and gentle and unconditionally loving," she said. "He was very fair and just, and he was one of those people who listened, really listened to you when you talked. He listened to everybody, and he was beloved in our town, both by the whites and the Hispanics."

Clayton Sr. had the heart of a teacher and the soul of a writer, poet, and musician, she said. He played the piano, studied opera, and provided the family a cultural aura that was rare in the small, gritty towns scattered across the Texas plains.

"We had loads of books and music, and my mother and dad and Claytie and I sang," Janet said. "We each had parts. You know that old-time musical: I sang soprano, Momma sang alto, Claytie sang tenor, and Daddy sang bass. We would sing in the house and we'd sing when we took trips and we'd sing at Christmas, and music was just part of our life."

Mexican cowboys at the ranch taught the family Spanish songs, exposing Claytie to mariachi music at an early age. He sharpened this talent with the young Mexican boys whom he hired during his teenage farming ventures.

"As Claytie got older, we'd have mariachi music instead of Christmas carols," said Janet.

Although Clayton Sr.'s other accomplishments tended to overshadow his oil exploits, Claytie's father was inducted into the Permian Basin Petroleum Hall of Fame in 1986. Some considered him one of the petroleum pioneers of West Texas and assigned to him a major role in the development of the region's Big Lake Field.

"Wouldn't he be proud to know that his son would follow him into the hall and that their photographs would one day hang side by side?" Janet said. "He found some oil wells, but just like Claytie, he always thought the next wildcat was going to be the big one," she told a Midland reporter in 1987. Janet (whose late husband, Bob Pollard, was a Midland oilman) said her mother never really understood the oil business. "But she knew how to make a loving, happy home." Claytie said their mother probably inspired their father to abandon the nomadic oil business during a time when wildcatting was at its most sinfully alluring or despicable, depending on one's point of view. "He didn't feel like he could raise a family with all the hell-raising, drinking, and whoring so common among the 'boomers' bouncing from one oil boom to the next."

Clayton Sr. opted to settle down in Fort Stockton and raise a family instead of following the booms and the booze. "He was a fine man, patriotic and caring and honorable, and he loved to go to the coffee shop and tell stories and entertain people," said Claytie, who had an unusually close relationship with his father. "Dad always said I was at the heights of glory or the depths of hell," he remembered fondly. Often, he said, his father would inquire of Claytie if, on any given day, he considered himself a corporal or a general. The dichotomy reminded Claytie of Lord Beaverbrook's comment about British Prime Minister Winston Churchill: "One of the characteristics of this great man was his incapacity for dwelling anywhere but on the peaks, or in the abyss. Gloom or glory, near-despair or complete triumph—these were the opposed climates of his being."

A Claytie bull's-eye, that.

One characteristic Claytie definitely did not inherit from his elders was his father's more sedate lifestyle and his grandfather's disdain for the devil's grog. Said one researcher about O. W. Williams: "Whiskey he regarded as the root of all evil on the frontier, and a saloonkeeper as a man without a soul."

On those occasions when O.W. came to the house, Claytie's father would hide the whiskey. Once Clayton Sr. was plying two potential oil-well investors with liquor when he glanced out a window and saw the old gentleman on his way over. Claytie's dad snatched up bottles and glasses and poured everything down the sink. "He didn't care what those investors thought but he damn sure cared what my grandfather thought," Claytie laughed.

The *Odessa American* profile of his mother recalled that his father learned in 1983 that he had terminal cancer and accepted the news

Claytie's parents at his 1983 cattle sale

with typical stoicism, saying, "All is well. I am not afraid." A few days before his death, the family attended a cattle auction and barbecue at the Alpine ranch and Clayton Sr. was determined to join them, even though confined to a wheelchair.

"That's just the way he was," said Chic. "So we got him out of bed, and we went down there, and he was wearing his Stetson, and when Claytie said, 'I'd like to introduce my dad,' he tipped his hat, and . . . everybody stood up and cheered, and it was just wonderful!"

He died a few days later, at home, on September 10. It was their fifty-fifth wedding anniversary.

Shortly after his father's death, Claytie played a key role in a historical Texas literary milestone that remains a source of Aggie pride even today. Inspired by the noted author James Michener and

The Three Amigos: Claytie with James Michener and Joe Hiram Moore

honoring Claytie's dad, the project came together with the help of a visionary A&M figure, Joe Hiram Moore, along with Lloyd Lyman, director of the Texas A&M University Press—and a victorious Aggie football team.

The stage had been set in 1982 when A&M Press published a well-received book by Clayton Sr., *Texas' Last Frontier: Fort Stockton and the Trans-Pecos, 1861–1895,* edited by historian Ernest Wallace. That same year   Michener had arrived in the Lone Star State to research his novel *Texas* and was greatly impressed by Clayton Sr.'s book.

"While at work on *Texas,* Michener lived in Austin and focused his research efforts on the library and archival resources at the University of Texas," historian Henry C. Dethloff wrote in a book about A&M Press, entitled simply *A Bookmark.* "In the course of his research, he became acquainted with Joe Hiram Moore and Clayton Williams Jr., both of whom provided personal insights into the evolution of Texas' petroleum industry."

During his research, Michener became enamored with Claytie, and later proclaimed, "He's not just a breath of fresh air . . . he's a typhoon!"

Moore, a Midland oilman and staunch Aggie supporter, and Michener once flew out to Alpine with A&M president Jack Williams to attend one of Claytie's fabulously popular Brangus sales. Later, the author visited the A&M campus, and inspired by the publication series on Texas art that Joe Moore and his wife, Betty, had funded, he came up with a provocative idea. "Michener suggested . . . that TAMUP consider publishing a series of books devoted to aspects of daily life during the various periods of Texas history, from the time of the Spanish missions to the present," Dethloff wrote. Michener himself agreed to serve as consulting editor for the proposed twelve-book series, which focused on everyday life in the Lone Star State from the beginning of recorded history to modern times.

"At the Texas–Texas A&M football game in College Station in November 1983, press director Lyman and others discussed the Michener proposal with Clayton Williams Jr.," Dethloff related. Afterward, Claytie agreed to support the Texas Life Series. A few days after the game, Claytie wrote to Bob Walker, director of the Office of University Development. "Thanks to you and the Texas A&M football team," he said, "Modesta and I had one hell of a weekend, even if it was expensive."

That was a minor understatement.

Claytie committed $150,000 that weekend to fund Michener's proposed series, and an anonymous donor, actually Michener himself, tossed $100,000 into the pot—and thus was born the Clayton Wheat Williams Texas Life Series. Said Claytie: "I know my dad would be absolutely delighted at such a perpetual and ongoing acknowledgment in his memory to the history of Texas."

"As kids we learned we had four ancestors who were with George Washington at Valley Forge."

Judge O. W. Williams was immortalized in a 1966 book, *Pioneer Surveyor—Frontier Lawyer,* assembled and edited by S. D. Myres for Texas Western College, now the University of Texas at El Paso. Myres described O.W., a relative by marriage to legendary frontiersman Daniel Boone, as a scholarly reporter who had a Harvard law degree and college training as a surveyor. Myres recounted how Williams moved across the High Plains of Texas, worked in the mines of New Mexico, and covered the lower reaches of the Big Bend of Texas from 1877 to 1902, a time known to some as part of the Heroic Age of America. His field notes and diary would one day provide perhaps the most dependable firsthand account of that period, Myres asserted.

Myres, born and reared in the West Texas town of Sweetwater, emphasized that O.W. not only reported the facts objectively but also captured the spirit of the times, what he called the dynamism and adventurism that generally prevailed.

"And, not least of all, he delineates the character of the Southwestern frontiersman—his boldness, self-confidence, basic integrity, ironic humor, near fatalism," Myres wrote. "With an insight that is almost uncanny, Williams goes directly to the heart of each subject he discusses. A combination of vital subject matter and clear, forceful style makes Williams's account unusually readable."

A splendid example of this style surfaced in a letter O.W. wrote in 1925 to his son, Jessie Caleb Williams, Claytie's uncle, in which he recounted witnessing a Missouri bank robbery in 1866. It was a milestone because the notorious Jesse James led the gang that committed the first bank robbery during business hours in U.S. history. For Williams, the experience proved terribly personal.

"When I heard the first shots, fired by the bandits in front of the [bank], I little knew that one of them sounded the death knell of one of my schoolmates, whose name I believe was George Wymore, but who was known to his playmates as 'Jolly' Wymore," Judge Williams wrote in a poignant segment of his letter.

> I had the aversion to the appearance of death, which is so fixed in youthful minds before custom has staled the soul with its constantly recurring suggestion, yet somehow I had the courage to join some of my schoolmates the next day in going to view the dead boy's body before the ceremony of burial. I shall never forget the feeling that stole over me as I looked into the boy's face cribbed up in the black coffin. I had expected to see something repulsive, distorted, ugly with the agony of death. In life he was a slender boy of about 15, with curly hair and fairly cut features, but with a complexion marred by freckles, pimples, and sunburn. In death I saw a snow white face, like a statue cut in the whitest Pentelic marble, beautifully marked and accentuated by the dark fringed outline of long eyelashes and curved eyebrows. I had not thought that death could show so much beauty and distinction. But it was the beauty of a polar night, cold with the front of an everlasting zero, bright with light from the eternal spaces.

Expanding on Myres's theme in an introduction to the book, author C. L. Sonnichsen said O.W. was one of the few writers with firsthand experience of the frontier Southwest who could and did reveal, "expertly and vividly," what those eventful times were like.

"As the slender, white-haired old man in the rumpled business suit went about his legal and personal chores in Fort Stockton, he did not seem much different from other pioneer citizens," Sonnichsen wrote. (Claytie does not remember seeing his grandfather wearing

Grandfather O. W. Williams, left, surveyor and judge, with R. T. Bucy and W. D. Twichell, on survey in south Pecos County

anything but a coatless suit, accompanied always by gray suit pants, a gray vest, and a white shirt and tie.) "His rather stately manner and his excellent spoken English entitled him to respect, but his real distinction was appreciated by very few indeed," Sonnichsen said, observing that O.W.'s relative obscurity was his own fault.

"He was innocent of literary ambition," said the author, "and it seems never to have occurred to him to try to sell his stories to a commercial publisher. He paid country printers to set his letters and essays in type, and he 'published' them by handing them to his sons and grandsons and to a few friends who might be interested."

Later, as his children grew older, he began sharing memories and observations in letters to them.

"But he never tried to 'write' in the ordinary sense of the word," Sonnichsen reported, "and while he was alive only a few specialists realized what a good writer he was."

Among them was the famous Texas author J. Frank Dobie, who said of O.W. in his 1943 *Guide to the Life and Literature of the Southwest:* "Few men have known and understood the natural features of the Southwest as well as he. Some day his scattered writings will be put into an enduring book."

Claytie's grandfather enjoyed remarkable recall, and Sonnichsen pointed out that O.W.'s earliest memories were fond recollections of life in and around the prairie community of Carthage, Ill., where the family moved four years after his birth on March 17, 1853. To this day, his descendants delight in recounting the judge's recollections of an appearance by Abraham Lincoln in the courthouse square in 1858.

"A platform was erected against the building and covered by a brush arbor from which small limbs and branches projected out and down," O.W. wrote seventy years later. "Father and I were standing on the southeastern edge of the crowd, near some large trees, cottonwoods, I believe. We saw Mr. Lincoln come out from the crowd and step up to the platform. He presented a long, angular figure, dressed in a long-tailed black coat, and topped by a tall, stiff hat which was known in those days as a stovepipe hat because it had a narrow brim and a long upper story. As Mr. Lincoln stepped up to the platform, this stovepipe hat struck one of those projecting branches and in trying to catch it, he made an awkward grab for it, which made it extremely funny for my young eyes. I do not remember a word that he said, but the picture of that frantic grasp for the wandering stovepipe will remain in my mind to my dying day."

O.W. was twenty-four and freshly graduated with his law degree from Harvard when, for health reasons, he moved to the Southwest in 1877, arriving that spring in Dallas, a city of some seven thousand described as the "Queen of the Prairies" and the gateway to the Texas plains.

"Possessed of superior intelligence and a burning curiosity, he reacted at once to the unique character of the Southwestern frontier; and for his remaining sixty-nine years he manifested an ever-growing interest in the area he had chosen for his home—in the land itself, in its animal and plant life, in its people and their history," Sonnichsen wrote. Still, O.W. was not much taken with Dallas, in part because it was even then "overdone in the line of lawyers."

Claytie was particularly fond of that comment. "If a lawyer couldn't get a job in Dallas," he joked, "Texas was a better place then than it is today." O.W. signed on as a land agent, and soon he and his colleagues were off to West Texas and the Panhandle to survey much of the region's virgin public lands, a prelude for their sale to homesteaders.

Said Sonnichsen: "This decision was one of the most important of Williams's life. It introduced him to the unexplored Southwest—to its rawness, vitality, and challenge. It led to experiences that few men have lived through and recounted. These experiences broadened his horizon as only life on the Plains of Texas could. They matured him and made him more tolerant of his fellowman, while they confirmed and strengthened his deep moral convictions."

It is not so much expected as endearing that life on those same "Plains of Texas" would in time provoke similar assessments about both Claytie and his father.

Although O.W. was never enthusiastic about Dallas, it was there he met Miss Sallie Wheat, the attractive and multitalented daughter of a prosperous Kentucky couple who had come to Texas a few years earlier. With O.W. off surveying and prospecting and recording his experiences in the Wild West, theirs was in no small part a long-distance romance linked by frequent letters.

"This is not the best country in the world for personal safety," O.W. said in one undated letter to Sallie; he then described in a diary note his fellow frontiersmen's cavalier approach to death. "People will jest and laugh over a dead body here with the most charming indifference. Sitting up with a corpse, when such a thing is done, the watchers will vie with each other in telling good jokes on the deceased, and the story goes that one fellow was so absentminded after telling a good story as to poke the ribs on the corpse in a jocular manner, as if to remind it to laugh at that stage."

That also reminded Claytie that his grandfather talked about a tough, mean "half-breed" named Muddy Wilson whom he encountered on the plains. Muddy was a loner and a crack shot who once picked off the head of a duck at perhaps three hundred yards. "That made me think that *Lonesome Dove* author Larry McMurtry got the idea for his character Blue Duck from O.W.'s writings," Claytie said.

The romance of Oscar and Sallie culminated in marriage December 15, 1881, and a Dallas newspaper's breathless account of the wedding said of the bride that "a sweeter, more intelligent girl is rarely met." It concluded: "And thus one of the loveliest of our social garden withdraws from us the golden sunshine of her presence, leaving but the silver dew of memory to sparkle in the tide of unforgetting love and friendship."

Although departing Dallas on such a lilting note, the couple returned to Dallas, more out of financial necessity than choice. The first two of their five children were born at Sallie's parents' home, where the couple stayed while O.W. struggled to a fresh start. In 1883, he heard of an opening in Pecos County for a deputy surveyor and was hired. He was barely thirty years old when he moved his young family to Fort Stockton, and it was in and around that frontier outpost that Claytie's father and O.W.'s other two children were born. It was also where the elder Williams would serve ten years as Pecos County judge, earning the title he carried the remainder of his life.

The fort was named for Commodore Robert Field Stockton, a naval officer who distinguished himself during the Mexican war. According to the Fort Stockton Web site, the first site was southwest of the present location and the post protected travelers and settlers on the numerous roads and trails that made use of the abundant water supply of Comanche Springs.

"It was here that these trails crossed the Comanche war trail," states the Web site. "The U.S. Army withdrew from Texas during the Civil War and abandoned Camp Stockton in 1861. Confederate troops briefly occupied the site until they, too, withdrew. By the end of the war, nothing remained of this first post."

Fort Stockton then became garrisoned by companies of the Ninth Cavalry, known as "Buffalo Soldiers" and the subject of modern-day books and movies. Historians note that in 1867 a commander of the Ninth Cavalry returned to the area with one of the new regiments created for the black men who sought security in the U.S. Army after the Civil War. It was the Indians who christened them the Buffalo Soldiers because of their coarse hair, and the name stuck. The black enlisted men were commanded by white officers, and the postwar fort was occupied from 1867 until 1886.

"My dad was born in one of the old fort houses in Fort Stockton in 1895 and grew up as a child there," Claytie recalled. But unimpressed with the Fort Stockton schools in those early days, "Judge Williams sent my dad's older brother and older sister back East to Illinois to get their education."

Claytie's father, traveling via stagecoach to Monahans and then by train to Dallas and College Station, enrolled at Texas A&M in 1911. He left A&M before graduation to attend Officers Training School, and he entered World War I as a field artilleryman in France. After the war, he and Claytie's uncle, J. C. Williams, returned to Paris

Claytie's father, Clayton Wheat Williams Sr., Texas A&M Cadet, 1915

to help form the American Legion. By the late 1920s, he was back at A&M to complete his degree, then attended a year of law school at the University of Texas.

"He grew out of that," laughed Claytie, and soon, armed with degrees as both a civil and an electrical engineer, his father returned to Fort Stockton to work at several jobs including a total of eighteen years as an elected Pecos County commissioner. An enthusiastic reader and writer, he also authored four well-received historical books and a lively hardback epic entitled *Animal Tales of the West*. But, as his daughter, Janet, notes, "He not only wrote history, he made history."

The elder Williams spent several years actively involved in the oil business before it cratered, and he later shared many compelling tales of those early days with Claytie. "His stories infatuated me," he said, "but it would be misleading to suggest that I followed my dad's footsteps into the oil field."

Still, it was there, in Fort Stockton, that the elder Williams's watermelon-stealing, girl-chasing, football-playing, goat-rearing, hell-raising, Aggie-bound son—Clayton W. Williams Jr.—would launch the multitude of mostly money-making enterprises that would, in the prophetic words of his father, propel Claytie to "the heights of glory or the depths of hell."

As one might expect, Claytie's childhood was hardly ordinary, beginning with his birth during the Great Depression: "I was born in Alpine because my dad couldn't pay the light bill at our home in Fort Stockton." Shortly before Claytie's arrival, his father had moved Chic into the Alpine home of his maternal grandparents, O. H. "Oscar" and Mernie Graham, and Claytie was born in an Alpine hospital on October 8, 1931.

"It took my dad two or three weeks to get the money together to pay the light bill," recalled Claytie, "so then we went back to Fort Stockton."

Claytie described his grandfather Oscar Graham as something of a dreamer whose ambitious schemes seldom worked out; but "he was a sweet guy, and I loved him." After Oscar's death in 1949 at age eighty, Mernie, whose Christian name was Evie Lee, lived with Claytie's family full-time in Fort Stockton until she died at age ninety-four in 1972.

"Mernie was a grand and supporting grandmother and was convinced that I never did anything wrong in my life," said Claytie, who adored her. Mernie's homemade bread, pastries, and cookies remain family lore to this day.

"Her father was a surgeon from Waxahachie [Texas], and after she and Oscar married, they moved to the Osage Indian reservation in Oklahoma where Mernie gave birth to Chicora, whom everybody called Chic. Oscar was raising cattle—with Mernie's inheritance—but he soon learned that the Indians were eating the cattle faster than he could raise them. The Indians were stealing them blind. They lost all of her inheritance and moved back to Texas."

They were so poor that when Mernie sent Chic to the grocery store to get a loaf of bread the storekeeper wouldn't give it to her because they'd used up all their credit. "Chic was always very frugal because of that period when they couldn't even buy bread," Claytie said. "That stayed with her forever."

Those close to the family maintain, not always in jest, that Chic's frugality was passed on to her son along with more obvious lifelong traits. Referring to the mother's influence on her son, Claytie's executive assistant, Denise Kelly, said: "They had some good times, sang songs, loved life, and she passed on that love of life to him. And they are very similar in that they are antsy, antsy, antsy, always moving, always doing something."

In a 1987 feature story in the *Midland Reporter-Telegram,* Claytie's mom related the colorful tale behind the family name Chicora. "My grandfather, Capt. Joe Graham of the Confederate army, was a prisoner of war in a Yankee prison," she said. "The only way he survived was by the good graces of a little Indian girl, Chicora, who used to slip him bits of food." Captain Graham vowed if he lived and made it home, he would name his first daughter for the little Indian girl.

"My aunt was the first Chicora," she said. "I am the second Chicora and Claytie's daughter [Chim] is the third Chicora." Chim's middle name is Modesta, also making her the fifth with that name on her mother's side of the family.

Claytie's mother attended Trinity University, located then in Waxahachie, and Sul Ross College in Alpine, and taught school in nearby Gail even before obtaining a college degree. Chic married Clayton Sr. immediately after graduating from Sul Ross in 1928 and, accompanied by Mernie, the couple honeymooned in the Grand Canyon.

"Those were the days that nobody ever lived together or even slept together ahead of time," Claytie said, "so you know they both were getting pretty damn impatient to get on with the program."

The *Reporter-Telegram* article noted that Fort Stockton had already played a major role in the history of West Texas, serving as a "protective military harbor deep in hostile Indian and bandit country."

Though never burdened by an abundance of money, Claytie's childhood overflowed with happy memories, many differing slightly from those of his sister, Janet, four years younger. Both looked upon life as though the glass were half full, never half empty, but Janet enjoyed the comfortable notion that someone was always standing nearby to refill the glass when necessary.

"They called Janet the 'Gold Dust Girl' because she sprinkled happiness everywhere she went," said Claytie. "She made everybody happy and everybody loved her. It was a wonderful childhood."

He relished the joys of small-town, ranching-farming West Texas, and even as a youngster absorbed the lessons that guided him into adulthood. For instance, his father, whom he idolized, built the family home on the grounds of the old Fort Stockton, using rocks from the abandoned fort.

"His time in France influenced him because our house would have a little bit of a French look to it," Claytie said, adding that his father built the house as he looked at life: "Solid. Build it solid. I've tried to follow that through life."

One need travel no farther than Claytie and Modesta's Midland home today to see how faithful he was to that vow. "Dad's house was solid rock with oak floors and walls that could withstand bombardment," he said proudly. "I wanted a solid house. I wanted a solid office. When I moved to Midland, I wanted a solid foundation and I wanted a solid reputation." To that end, he bought the fifteen-story Gulf Building out from under a prominent banker and promptly got himself involved in a lawsuit. Later, striking another blow for solidarity, he built his own office building, which would become the premier business address in Midland.

Unlike most kids, even West Texas kids, Claytie took to manual labor before most youngsters learned to avoid it, and the influence of his father and grandfather surfaced time and again through those formative years. He spoke once to a reporter of the "memories of my grandfather coming over and watering the lawn, of my dad playing football with me, of times at the ranch and farm, of high school, of friends and family in a rather typical small town full of warmth but not without problems."

Besides the influence of his father and grandfather, his mother's two brothers were cowboys, "and pretty good cowboys, at that," he said. The two uncles worked the early ranches and cattle drives, and used their cowboy wages to help pay his mother's way through college. They also shared their stories with him, and Claytie was drawn to cattle and ranching almost before he was big enough to climb atop a horse. And both he and Janet were more than casually patriotic, at least in part because the families of both their mother and father were warriors of a sort, dating to the Revolutionary War.

"As kids we learned we had four ancestors who were with George Washington at Valley Forge," Janet said, identifying the quartet as John Collyer, Jesse Williams, Adam Files, and David Sydney Files. "Our great-great-grandmother, a descendant of the Files family, arrived in a covered wagon while Texas was still a republic." She noted also that other forebears fought in World Wars I and II and one was even wounded in the French and Indian War. Referring to the latter episode, she said the wounded ancestor escaped and took refuge in a hollow log. "His wife saddled up, got the ox and the wagon, and went looking for him in the war zone," she said. "So they were adventurous people. . . . I think in all our family, fear is just not an [operative] word."

During World War II, the Williamses shared their home with several civilian flight instructors from the primary pilot-training base at Gibbs Field, which was located nearby on land formerly owned by Claytie's father but not affiliated with the historic old fort.

As a thirteen-year-old, Claytie even cosponsored a "carnival" to raise money for the cadets. "Classmates Walter and James Scudday

The young patriot, Claytie, with his favorite "rifle," 1937

and I decided we would give a benefit for the cadets that were in primary flight training," remembered Claytie. "We put on a carnival with all sorts of stuff, like darts and pitching horseshoes and little games, and people came and spent money and we gave it to the cadet fund."

Claytie was quite proud of that endeavor, especially so when the *Fort Stockton Pioneer* published a story about it—his first brush in a lifelong but sometimes rocky romance with the media.

"There were a lot of air bases in West Texas because of the generally good flying weather," Claytie explained, "and it was not uncommon in Fort Stockton, with no motels, for families to open their homes to the instructors. A couple of the guys who lived with us became kind of part of the family."

So despite their youth, Janet said, "We really were very aware of the war. Every night at a certain time we listened to the radio, because we had an uncle in China and cousins scattered across Italy, France, England, and elsewhere."

Though much younger than Claytie, neighbor Dan Bullock remembered those childhood days for the warm and comforting times spent in the Williams home. "My father, Maurice Bullock, moved to Fort Stockton in the mid-'30s as an oil and gas attorney and met Clayton Williams Sr. there," said Bullock, now an Austin civic leader, activist, and financier. "We gathered together as families, and Claytie was sort of an older brother that maybe I wished I'd had. I can picture myself so many times being in their living room on holidays, listening to the A&M-Texas football games at Thanksgiving, and just seeing a family gathering that was cheerful, loving, and sharing. . . . I can see those smiles, those hugs . . . the infectious good will and spirit."

So impressed was he by Claytie and his dad that years later Bullock named his son after them, and invited Claytie to give the eulogy at the elder Bullock's funeral. "Claytie's dad was conservative and thoughtful and more reserved, but had a gleam in his eye and was a great family man," Dan Bullock said. "Claytie, on the other hand, was a lot more gregarious and outgoing and, as some might say, even reckless. But Claytie had the values of his dad and the good heart and the work ethic that I really admired, and I wanted my son to learn how to work hard and to play hard, and to do so as they did, with integrity."

Meanwhile, as a small boy, Claytie and his lifelong friend Jane Dunn, now prominent Austin socialite Jane Sibley, and a neighborhood buddy they called Little Al, spent endless hours playing cowboys and Indians. "That's all we ever played," she said. "We would play among the ruins of the officers' homes at the north end of the fort."

The three had a great many young years together, she recalled. "We didn't know we were poor, because everybody was poor. It was the Depression. We still had parties and barbecues, and of course everybody went to church on Sunday, and usually everybody went to the Stockton Hotel for lunch after church. Lunch was fifty cents, which included your drink and your fruit cocktail or maybe a congealed salad and dessert."

Janet says Claytie had a pet baby calf that he cleverly named "Baby Calf," and "Oh, how he loved it. The calf would just bawl when he saw Claytie. One day he brought the calf in the house and it pooped on the whole kitchen. Grandmother Mernie was the one who cleaned it up because Claytie and I had such weak stomachs."

When not romping with Baby Calf or dispatching Indians with Jane and Little Al, Claytie was fighting the Germans and Japanese with mud balls from crude bunkers he and his preteen "Scudday Buddies," James and Walt Scudday, fashioned from the ruins of the original fort. "During the war," recalled Jim Scudday, "we'd get out there and we'd build up these little fortifications, and after it rained and the ground was wet enough, we'd make bombs out of mud and throw them at each other. We even had little plastic helmets that we'd wear."

When the Scudday Buddies and Claytie weren't bombing one another, they busied themselves stealing watermelons, hunting, camping, poaching ducks, swimming and dancing at Comanche Springs, playing poker, and chasing and teasing girls—particularly two feisty youngsters named Susie Chriesman and LaFerne Nance. To-day Sue is Mrs. Walter Scudday of Georgetown, Tex., and Fern is the wife of Dr. James Scudday of Alpine.

Claytie's former schoolmates remained lifelong friends and were among the members of the old childhood gang who attended the wedding and party for Chim and Greg Welborn at Happy Cove Ranch in May 2003.

The Scuddays, David Ligon, and others shared "growing up" stories that day and night and revealed that their watermelon capers once came to a halt after the owner discovered the thefts and figured out who the culprits were. "They got the word out that they had poisoned some of the watermelons because the raccoons and coyotes were getting into them, and they wanted to kill the coons and the coyotes," Jim Scudday recalled.

"Did that stop it?" Sue Scudday asked.

"That stopped it," Jim said.

Truth be told—which happened once in a while—there were two endings to the watermelon capers. Claytie's mother caught 'em red-handed once with the ill-gotten bounty and marched the embarrassed culprits back to the owner to return the melons and apologize.

It was not one of Claytie's fonder memories.

"They said about the Panthers: They're small, but boy are they slow."

3

The most detailed account of Claytie's childhood emerged from the least likely of places—a momentous 1997 African hunting trip with Modesta, son Jeff, and daughter Chim. Freed from his frenzied work pace, Claytie slowed down long enough to record in a daily journal his recollections, experiences, and lessons from what he described as a "typical" West Texas boyhood.

"I had such an active high school life," he explained. "I was president of Thespians, acted in all of the plays, loved the dances, the football, the girls and the partying, loved my ranch work and summer activities."

So this is how, while hunting big game in Botswana, he remembered that childhood—his youthful reflections perhaps mellowed by the taking of a magnificent trophy elephant just hours earlier. Well, that and a generous number of rum and Cokes required to celebrate his jungle trophy—one with a hefty seventy-two-pound tusk.

I came from pioneer stock, both sides of my family being the third generation from the settlers. I believe my life was typical, a small boy growing up in a small town during the Depression. Memories of Pioneer Club picnics, ice cream socials with lots of aunts and uncles and cousins coming and going because both sides were extremely family-oriented. We were always going to visit kinfolks in the closest town or next door.

Our home was across the old fort grounds from the guard house where the Boy Scouts had their weekly meetings. At the age of seven or eight, I remember intensely yearning to "one day" be a Boy Scout. I envied their activity, their games, and their achievements, and from that early start, achievement has been the most important word in my vocabulary. . . . I was an overly aggressive young man and worked very hard to achieve all the merit badges for my Eagle Scout rank. I did so but somehow displeased the Scout Master [an Aggie, no less] and he denied his signature for me to get the rank of Eagle.

It angered me and it hurt me, and it could have crushed my spirit.

After he left, the next Scout Master granted it to me, but by then I was a sophomore, active in football, dating girls, and the badge meant less to me than it would have two years earlier when I earned it.

The lesson was that disappointments come, and you take them and go forward. I dearly loved Scouting and was probably overly enthusiastic in pursuit of my goals. A second lesson: when someone has worked hard to accomplish a set goal and has earned it, recognize him now; don't wait! Timely praise is warranted and does more to boost a person toward further achievement than if he doesn't get the praise when he earned it.

The Fort Stockton schools were filled with loving teachers such as Laura Walker and Rhoda Kelly, and I remember the rhythm band and lots of good friends, both boys and girls. I remember being selected high school "King," president of Thespians, and president of the senior class. I lettered in football three years. In a small community, we were all very close-knit. Working sheep and cattle and irrigating the farm in the summers started at age seven or eight, and work was always as important to me as play. At that age, the "work hard/play hard" attitude seemed to make sense to me.

When I was twelve or thirteen, my dad had a herd of 1,500 goats. They sheared them, and then came a very bad cold and rainy spell, and all the goats that were sheared died. The kid goats did not die because they still had their hair, so I went out and got some of my buddies and we captured all of them by hand. Then I took them to the house and bottle-fed them. I recall we were able to rescue about 250. I grew them out, sold them, and made my first money—$1,500, which was a nice hunk of change for a thirteen-year-old kid in the mid-'40s. I benefited from my dad's misfortune.

The summer before my freshman year in high school, I was able to lease a cotton farm from a neighbor who had drifted into financial trouble. Between my mother, Chic, and Aunt Mary Graham, we had a partnership, one-fourth each for them and half for me as operator-manager-worker. It was a grand experience for a fourteen-year-old boy. I learned about engine trouble, labor problems, bollworms, insects, pests, and hail, and I was thrust early into the world of management. I used "wets" [illegal immigrants from Mexico commonly known as wetbacks for their crossing of the Rio Grande to get into the United States] for farm labor at the time. I'd sit down at lunch with them and I learned to speak Spanish. I became good friends with the wets. That's also where I learned to sing Mexican songs. I loved the mariachi songs—it's "let's go conquer the world" kind of music.

My ongoing problem was the "immigrantes" in the form of the Border Patrol. They'd come by and pick up my wets. Then I'd be irrigating a double shift between myself and some generally lazy town boys. I'd eventually have to fire them and do it all myself. So early on I learned that labor and good people are very, very important to a successful venture.

I also learned how fate can deal you dirty.

Bollworms developed in my cotton and I knew I needed to spray. I went to the coffee shop, talked to the old-timers, and on the day they all said it wouldn't rain, I hired an airplane, sprayed at noon, and by 2 P.M. it had rained and washed the spray off. Thus I learned about the vagaries of farming and weather forecasting.

I gained management experience and learned about problems firsthand at an early age. Uncle Oscar Graham helped me bring in the crop while I was playing freshman football. At the end of the football season, there was a lot of cotton stalks to graze in a high yield crop, so I went with Raymond Hale, a local trucker and the father of one of my buddies, to San Angelo. He was delivering cattle to the San Angelo sale and was looking for a backhaul to make money both ways, going and coming. I was looking to buy some cows to graze the stalks. After watching in amazement all the exciting activity at the auction, I started buying the cows that were the cheapest, and I had so much fun. Then Raymond reached over and tapped me on the shoulder and said, "That's a truckload, Claytie." So then we walked out and looked at what I bought, and I lost some of the confidence. They didn't look near as good outside in the sun as they did going through the auction ring with the auctioneer playing up to me. He'd spotted a mullet.

I got them back to Fort Stockton, unloaded 'em at the stockyards, and my dad and Uncle Oscar came out. Daddy walked up, looked at 'em, and then turned and walked away without saying a word. But Uncle Oscar said, "Well, blankety-damn, there were millions of cows before you were born, there are millions of cows now, there'll be millions of cows after you're dead and gone, and you don't have to buy a blankety-blank one of 'em."

With my spirits sagging, I got some of my buddies, and we drove 'em from the stockyards to the farm where I put them to grazing the cotton and hegari stalks. I grazed them three months, the market went up 20 percent or so, and I carried 'em back to San Angelo and wound up losing one dollar.

I learned a couple of things: one, a trucker's always looking for a backhaul, and, two, the cheapest is not always the bestest.

Still, my cattle-grazing experiences were more successful than my short-lived animal-trapping career. The Scudday Buddies and I went out to my dad's place, about a mile and half west of town, and set four traps, which we had to pay for. We planned to finance the operation with raccoon and fox furs, which brought a good price. Instead, we captured three skunks, putting an odorous end to our trapping career.

Proud boy Claytie with his father and his first deer, 1944

The summer after my freshman year, I worked for Schlumberger Seismic, an oil-field service company. They were working around McCamey and later around Rankin. I started as a brush cutter and later moved my way up to head chainman through the summer. The older boys were working with us, one of whom was a guy named Wes. Wes would go out partying every night, get up at 4:30 or 5 A.M., ride to Rankin, and start work at 8. He always had a hard time, but he always seemed to feel good enough to go back and do it again. I later did some of that myself.

The lesson was clear: you pay the next day for howling at the moon the night before! Particularly if you're riding in the back of a pickup truck.

I was feeding lambs as a 4-H project, and I did well at the local show, so I went with the big boys in a group to El Paso for the "big show." We camped outdoors on the baseball field, and I remember vividly the big boys so generously offering us little boys some free chewing gum. The chewing gum turned out to be a strong laxative, Feenamint, and we were busy crawling in and out of our bedrolls all night long.

We went across to Juarez, and I bought what I thought was a beautiful decoration for my mother. It was a whiskey decanter with lots of jiggers on it. My mother smiled when she received it, but she didn't drink.

My lamb won first, though it was not the grand champion, and I sold it for a very good price. But I remember being very sad to part with it. This was in the winter, and the county agent and the big boys rode up in the front of the cattle truck on the way back to Fort Stockton. They put me in the back of the open cattle truck with the cattle. There's no way I could've had enough cover with the wind blowing through and the cows messing on me, but the county agent was teaching me to "be tough."

Well, I made it—250 miles at night, and it was cold! But I learned a lesson: even at an early age, it is best not to be on the bottom of the totem pole.

High school was grand. It was an ongoing social event with good teachers, football in the fall, athletics through the year, lots of dances, and lots of friends—both girlfriends and boyfriends. And in the summers I ranched and worked cattle and farmed, which I dearly loved. I lettered in football my sophomore year, was second team all-district halfback my junior year, and co-captain of the team my senior year. Years later, when I ran for governor, I would relate how I played fullback and strong-side linebacker for the Fort Stockton Panthers. They said about the Panthers: they're small . . . but boy are they slow. Our record wasn't all that bad, five and five—lost five at home and five on the road.

Actually, it wasn't quite that bad. We won about half our games, but it's a better story that way. I had great enthusiasm for football, and I wanted to win. I was a scrapper, and by the time

I was a senior, we were a bunch of little wild asses. And we paid for it. My buddy Robert Huckaby's dad, J. B. Huckaby, was the high school principal and a wonderful man, but he was tough as nails. He would give us "licks" with a belt when we misbehaved, and it was macho to go take your licks. He'd really put it to us, leaving the window open so the kids outside could hear us getting whipped. We were being nurtured, but like I said, he was tough as nails.

Although my senior year was memorable for lots of reasons, it was the end of my junior year when I got my first lesson in politics.

The class before us campaigned and won the office of president of Student Council of Texas for the entire state, a grand accomplishment for a small school such as ours. So I decided to run for president. In the primary, there were three of us, and I lacked one vote beating both my opponents, who were good friends. Then I find out that my campaign manager, Bryan Hale, did not vote. If he had voted, I would have won without a runoff. I was defeated in the runoff and was thoroughly devastated. It became a major turning point in my life, because for the next several years my decision was "to heck with people and to heck with politics."

I decided right then and there that I was going to A&M, get an education, and to heck with anything else. I wanted to learn how to solve problems that I'd encountered in farming and ranching these last four high school years.

Claytie celebrated his trophy elephant deep into the African night, secure in the knowledge that campsite rum and Coke is not a volatile mix. At least not like gin and gunpowder. But, alas, he committed to his daily log only a single notation that next day.

DAY 10—Had a bad hangover.

He did not recover sufficiently to resume his journaling at once, although he did venture out the next two days in a futile search for a trophy leopard. He also encountered another elephant, but the experience was less memorable. Early on the morning of Day 12, the beast ambled into the campsite and discovered bedrolls, vegetables, and eland jerky stored in the pickup bed. The nosy elephant proceeded to unload the bedrolls, eat the vegetables, and dump the jerky, which was gobbled up by a pack of pesky hyenas.

"Such is life in an African hunting camp . . . ," Claytie noted, before resuming his jungle dictation on Day 13:

> Graduating from high school in the spring of 1950 was an exciting time for me. I made plans to attend Texas A&M and was admitted in to study Animal Husbandry, now called Animal Science. I had decided that my days of being "All-Around Boy" and an athlete were over. I was taking dead aim at a good education. I intended to learn how to solve the many problems I had encountered in managing the farms and ranches at Fort Stockton, and I wanted to take advantage of the opportunities that existed in agriculture.
>
> But a major problem unexpectedly loomed on the horizon. North Korea invaded South Korea, so after several years of peace at the end of World War II, we were again at war. The future of any nineteen-year-old was uncertain. The draft was still in effect, and so was my tendency to experience extreme highs and extreme lows. Like my dad said, I was at the heights of glory or the depths of hell.
>
> I suffered the lowest day of my young life when Mother and Daddy and Janet left me at the dorm at A&M and drove away. I never had been so blue as when I began that lonely walk into the dorm knowing the happiest and most wonderful period of my life had now come to an end and another chapter—an unknown chapter—was beginning.
>
> I was immediately thrust into the structured military life at A&M.
>
> I played the coronet in the high school band, so I was placed with the Aggie Freshman Band. We were the first freshman group back on campus after World War II. Prior to that, the freshman

classes had been housed at the old Bryan Air Force Base to avoid such intense hazing of freshmen.

The campus had its own form of boot camp with an early rise, the company lineup, the march to breakfast, the march back, the march to classes, the march to lunch, and the march to classes in the afternoon. Then band practice and more marching, then a return to quarters for study sessions at your desk. The end of the day was 11:20 P.M.

The days were full of upperclassman "princes," particularly the sophomore princes, who we called "pissheads," bringing you down to ground zero so that over the four years they could mold and build you into a leader.

The more I saw of military discipline, the less I liked it.

When we lined up in the company, the tall guys were placed at the front and short ones at the back. I was almost always at the back and I didn't like it and I didn't like being short. Of course, that wasn't A&M's fault.

We were told that only one of four of us sitting there would actually obtain a degree from Texas A&M. There were five of us from my graduating senior class at Fort Stockton who chose A&M, and I was the only one who would finish. And I spent most of my freshman year quitting—or thinking of quitting. In retrospect, I believe it was fortunate that I was by myself in the band while the other four were all together in another outfit. They could get together in their spare time and commiserate and feel sorry for themselves, and probably that is one of the reasons they didn't finish.

Also, in that first year, I tried out for the freshman swim team and made it, but I didn't stick with it because the chlorine in the water irritated my eyes and I couldn't study at night.

Most of that freshman year I was "campused"—confined to campus—and walking the "bull ring." Walking the bull ring was an hour-long tour, walking square tours for fifty-five minutes with a five-minute break. Shortly after I had arrived at A&M I got in some kind of trouble with an upperclassman and was given demerits and bull-ring tours. Later I was involved with a group *that went to steal the Baylor University bear. One carload actually got the bear. I was in a group that got lost, but we got campused anyway. So after that, I had full bull-ring tours for the remainder of the year. Also, I was campused, which meant I had to sign in at frequent intervals during the weekend, including every hour on Saturday and Sunday afternoons. So you could not even go enjoy a movie without leaving every hour to go sign in.*

It was pure misery, and it didn't help that one of my early phone calls was from my dad reporting that "the town dogs got into your sheep and killed thirty-four of them!" I had about 120 yearling ewes, and they were paid for. One of the few times in my life I had no debt. The next call I got informed me that while moving the sheep away from town, they encountered a patch of the poisonous yellow weed and another twenty-five or thirty died. So I said, "Sell 'em! I need to get an education."

Despite everything, trips home were great during Thanksgiving, Christmas, and the semester break. And I had a very close-knit group of high school friends who would get together once a year in Dallas for the Oklahoma–Texas football game. One time we even had a group of girls come to A&M from TCU, and we went out drinking beer and found an old, abandoned farm house and started playing "kick the can."

Unfortunately, there was no romance involved, just good friends having a good time. In those early A&M days, it didn't take much to entertain us.

Even though there were weekend Corps trips, the football games, work on the bonfire, nonmilitary activities, and making new freshman friends, I continued to dislike the military process.

Obviously, I was spoiled. I had a loving family and great freedom managing the farm and the ranch. In high school I had rarely opened a book, and mostly just went about the process of enjoying my life. A&M was all work, detail, military, hazing. I started seriously thinking about quitting school in October. I would get through week by week by saying, "Well, I may quit next week, but I won't quit now."

All the while, the war went on. Would we be deferred? Should I enlist?

One morning in early November I forgot my overcoat when I left a math class. When I went back to get it, it was gone. Someone had stolen it. I was furious. "I'm quitting this place," I vowed. "Nothing but a bunch of thieves. I don't like the band. I don't like the military. I sure as hell don't like the upperclassmen."

I didn't like anything about it.

So I called my dad and told him I was going to quit. And he said OK. I think if he'd argued with me I might have quit. But he didn't argue, so I didn't quit. I decided I would stay until Thanksgiving, take the holiday vacation, then quit school and enlist in the army. After Thanksgiving, I came back and thought maybe I should wait until Christmas, then quit and join the army. I made it through the Christmas holidays and thought it would be helpful in the army if I had one semester of college. I'll quit after the semester. Of course, after the semester I thought it would be helpful if I had a full year of college before I quit.

In the meantime, the Chinese Communists entered North Korea and that made the future look even more ominous for young men our age.

At the end of the school year, I actually flashed an obscene gesture at the campus when I departed and said aloud, "I'll never see you again."

And I meant it.

Little did I know that my first year at A&M would turn out to be the most miserable year of my young life!

It would be so bad, in fact, that Claytie later told the *Dallas Morning News* exactly how he felt about his alma mater that first year: "I hated it. I spent my first year quitting. I felt like I was in jail."

I spent the summer working on the farm and ranching. But then I got to wondering how some of my Aggie buddies were doing. So I decided to go back to school again.

Some of my classes were very difficult for me, particularly chemistry because I had taken no high school chemistry. I was totally lost. I just couldn't grasp it. I went to another student, a chemistry major named Fred Haney, for help. But then one pivotal night I became very angry with myself. I became determined, and I just sat there at my desk with that chemistry book and I studied. And studied. And studied until I began to understand it. It was a crucial point. I realized that instead of relying on someone else, sometimes you've got to do it yourself.

This was critical also because I learned that if you stop and really apply yourself, you could solve almost any problem. It was another turning point in my life — a turning point in developing self-confidence.

The beginning of my sophomore year, I left the band and enrolled in a military air force squadron, and I felt more at home in this outfit. And I at least had worked through that horrible freshman year. I now realized I was there for a purpose, and that my studies came first. I did participate in intramural boxing and made it to the quarterfinals in my weight division. I've always liked to fight; something I inherited from my dad.

I also learned how to study, to really study. I would sit at my desk until 12:30 or 1 A.M. — beyond the mandatory "call to quarters" from 7:20 P.M. until 10:20 P.M. I really worked at it. After I got past the first part of the sophomore year, and was no longer walking the bull ring, I would head out on the weekends. In those days we called A&M "Sing-Sing on the Brazos," and I wanted to get away. I wanted to get back to my philosophy of "work hard/play hard." Then, the second part of my sophomore year, I spent so much time with a friend at the Sigma Nu fraternity in Austin that they once sent me a house bill as a joke. That was my good friend, Karl "Buddy" Butz.

One thing I knew for certain: it was always fun when you left A&M!

By my junior year I was in the Agricultural Honor Society, but I laid out the first semester of my junior year in order to improve the irrigation system on my dad's farm. I did love farming and going to help Dad. I returned for the spring semester as a junior and really got into the swing of things. About this time, Dad began selling off parts of the ranch and farms to cotton farmers, and I could see there was no future for me there. Oddly enough, in retrospect, I seriously considered a career in dentistry. I knew I wanted to make more money than country agents or soil conservation agents, and I had the basic medical background to go forward in dentistry due to my science and agricultural courses.

But fate intervened. I recalled at the time a trip to Oklahoma City to visit with a great-uncle, Charles Garnett. "Young man," he told me, "the problem with going into dentistry or law and other such things is that you are limited to your own work. That is, your hands or your mind. If you could somehow become an entrepreneur, you'd make money from other people's work while still using your mind."

That conversation stuck with me, and over the years I came to realize that it was probably one of the most important lessons in my life. There's little doubt the entrepreneurial path was personally more productive than dentistry.

What's more, I was coming to love A&M and recognizing what it was doing for me. That summer, after my junior year, I took two courses at Sul Ross College in Alpine.

But because I had laid out a semester, I was out of sync with the military schedule, and that triggered a chain of events that resulted in my not getting a commission as a second lieutenant. If I had received my commission, who knows where fate would have led me? I was disappointed about the commission, but looking back now at my whole life, it started me on the path to the oil business, and that was a great thing.

What it boiled down to was, in the end, I had two choices: I could stay at A&M for an extra six months, or I could drop out of

Claytie in his sophomore year as a Texas A&M Cadet

Claytie (second from left) at final review, 1954: a day both happy and sad

the Corps and pay back the money they had advanced me my junior year. I made the decision to drop out of the military for my last year so I could finish early.

For a few years I regretted that decision, particularly since my buddies were officers and I was not. But in hindsight it turned out for the best. I finished A&M in three and a half years plus one summer semester. In the final semester of my senior year, I took twenty-four hours and got sixty-nine grade points, making all A's and one B. At the time, that was the most grade points ever posted in the School of Agriculture. With my checkered history as a student, I've always been very proud of this.

Right before my senior year, my high school sweetheart, Betty Meriwether, and I decided to marry. And while I finished my senior year as a nonmilitary, it was still great being at A&M.

There is a photograph of my classmates and me at the "Final Review," which is the last march by seniors before they graduate from A&M. I stood with my company in a shirt and blue jeans while they all had on their uniforms and senior boots. Obviously, at that moment, I regretted very deeply my decision not to go ahead and spend the extra time to get a commission.

After graduation, I returned to Fort Stockton to help my dad campaign for county judge, but he lost by a narrow vote. I remember his telling me, "Give me a few days to lick my wounds and I'll be all right and I'll go forward."

At that point he started writing his book, History of West Texas, *which was a greater contribution than he would have made as a county judge. I always marvel how things generally work out for the best in this life.*

Thirty-five years later, Claytie would see this maxim put to a supreme personal test.

Claytie wasted no time volunteering for the draft after graduating from Texas A&M in 1954, and the normally dreaded basic training proved to be a snap.

"It was old hat to me and not near as tough as A&M," he said.

Claytie, A. W. Bishop, and David Ligon—the boyhood buddy who claims he was with Claytie when they discovered beer and girls—invaded Fort Bliss in El Paso together. Ligon befriended a former roper and rodeo hand who worked in the eye, ear, nose, and throat clinic and periodically provided bogus medical notes to free them from training exercises.

One of Ligon's fondest memories of basic training was hearing the first sergeant announcing in front of the troops on those special mornings: "Ligon and Williams . . . Report to the EENT clinic. There's a bus outside."

According to Claytie, all those frivolous days spent drinking beer with Ligon took its toll. "He wore me out. Basic training was tough, but drinking beer with Ligon every day was tougher. I finally realized I couldn't go drink beer with Ligon and his powerful jolly personality anymore."

"Never happened," Ligon insisted.

The Fort Stockton terrors also had a crony named John who brewed a lethal grain alcohol and juice drink called "Shady Ladies" in a fifty-five-gallon container with a gas pump attached. Ligon says when they weren't drinking the stuff they were bottling and selling it to their army pals to finance their trips across the border to Juarez, Mexico.

"Never happened," Claytie insisted.

"We would go to the houses of ill repute, but we didn't go there for the girls," Ligon maintained. "We'd just party and sing and play the guitar with the mariachi bands."

"Never happened," Claytie insisted.

In spite of all the titillating events that "never happened," they somehow survived basic training. Although Claytie hoped to join the Veterinary Corps, he was sent to Fort Lee, Va., and wound up as an army engineer attached to the air force. The Korean War had ended with an uneasy truce, and he served out his army time as an engineer supply specialist with a company in Mineral Wells, Tex.

"I was bored to death," remembers Claytie.

With wife Betty and newborn daughter Kelvie, he was living in cheap army housing, receiving a corporal's pay of $198 monthly, and "basically killing time." He launched a secondary career as a waiter after hours at the NCO Club, but he got himself fired when he dumped a tray of drinks on a group of noncommissioned officers. His dismissal was a blessing, because he landed another job waiting tables — at the Brazos Club in the fashionable Baker Resort Hotel. Working nights and weekends, he saved his money and tips in a Mason fruit jar. The savings gave him a start for his future after his discharge, and his time spent waiting tables was itself a valuable experience. Says Claytie: "I learned that high-quality people treat an underling with dignity and respect even while being waited on, while lesser people treat you like dirt to puff up their own self-image."

It was a lesson he would carry with him up and down the peaks and valleys and through the periods of rags and riches — *the heights and depths*. He also learned that the great drives and desires in life come not so much from your successes but more often from your failures.

"It's not from what you have but wanting what you don't have," he said. "One time Betty and I drove over from Mineral Wells to meet her parents in Fort Worth where friends of theirs took us out to the Ridglea Country Club. I was quite impressed with such a fancy layout and the wonderful food. I remember saying to myself, 'Some day I'll be able to belong to a club like this.'"

Claytie also looked back on those days as a time of discovery, among the foremost revelations being that he had a natural flair for business. He learned this in a most unusual manner. He and his wife had befriended another military couple, R. J. and Betty Campbell, graduates of Hardin-Simmons University in Abilene, and the four would play Monopoly at night after Claytie got off work. He loved the wheeling and dealing.

"I don't think I ever lost a Monopoly game," he says with not the slightest trace of modesty.

One night while waiting tables and hustling tips at a sales convention at the Baker Hotel, Claytie was approached by a representative of New York Life Insurance Co. The executive wondered if Claytie might be interested in selling life insurance after his discharge, and invited him to Fort Worth to discuss the proposal.

"I had studied agriculture but Dad had sold the farm and ranch, so my future was not there," Claytie said. "I was unemployed."

Claytie had toyed with the idea of law school when the possibility of an early release from his A&M military obligation arose. "The Korean War had ended by then and the military considered releasing people early if they would go to school," Claytie explained. "I applied to the University of Texas Law School and was accepted. I thought, 'Man, I'm gonna get out early and I'm gonna go to law school — even if it was UT.' But the military killed that early-out option before I could act on it."

Even then, he found his glass half full. "Look what fate did for me there," he grinned. "If I'd gone to law school I'd be just another damn lawyer."

In the meantime, he had found the insurance offer interesting and figured he should look into it as a means of supporting his family. Right away, he realized the value of selling, not just insurance but himself. According to Claytie, "The best training in the world is learning to sell, and if you can sell life insurance, you can sell anything." His rationale for such a statement was pure Claytie: "Imagine, if you can talk some old boy into taking his beer money, and instead of drinking beer he buys a life insurance premium so when he dies, his wife can live happily ever after with another man. That's selling!"

His immediate concern, however, was not selling insurance but whipping a supply company warrant officer whom he felt had mistreated him throughout his Mineral Wells military service. "I had made up my mind to go whip his ass when I was discharged. I actually started out there to do it when I realized that, one, I was out of the army, two, I had a bright future ahead of me, and, three, I would probably go to jail if I did it.

"But the guy still needed an ass whippin' pretty bad."

Instead of pummeling his adversary, Claytie took his discharge pay and Betty to New York City, where they celebrated amid the sights and sounds of the Big Apple, all the while pondering his new career selling insurance to enlisted men in Mineral Wells. Returning to Texas, he and Betty stopped over in Fort Stockton to visit his parents. They were seated around the dining-room table when Claytie stunned everyone. "I don't want to go to Mineral Wells to sell life insurance to soldiers," he announced. "I want to stay in Fort Stockton and figure some way to make a living here."

And he did—but not by ranching or farming. With West Texas crippled by a record drought, his father had sold the ranch and leased the farm, thwarting his early plans to be a cowboy. Later, Claytie joked about the sale, quoting ranchers around Fort Stockton as saying, "The country gets better any direction you go from the Clayton Williams ranch."

Working out of a local insurance agency, he obtained both a general insurance license and a real estate license. And in 1957 he busied himself by peddling life insurance to mostly friends and kinfolks and hail insurance to cotton farmers. When he ran low on friends, family, and farmers, he began working the "real estate angle" with limited success.

In a Fort Stockton coffee shop one day, he heard of a farm for sale and arranged a meeting with the owner, John May. Hoping to get a listing and a commission on the sale, he got much more. Almost overnight, a partnership developed, hurtling him to the doorstep of a new, exciting, and lifelong career.

In the oil patch.

Two

Claytie down in the ditch, 1965

Johnny May and Clayton Williams Jr. hit it off at once, quickly deciding to partner in the oil and gas business as lease brokers and well promoters. Claytie knew nothing about his new venture, but both his dad and his grandfather had represented landowners in oil and gas leases, and May and his father were already promoting money for drilling wells.

"Johnny grew up in Pecos and we complemented one another in that he had ties to the existing oil business and I had a good solid agricultural background and a good family reputation with two generations who had lived and done business in Fort Stockton," explained Claytie. "This enabled me to communicate easily with farmers, ranchers, and landowners when negotiating for oil and gas leases. And Johnny and his dad's contacts with oil people in Midland helped us from the oil side."

Claytie's grandfather had built offices near Comanche Springs, later shared by Clayton Sr. "After O.W. died, my dad moved into my grandfather's office, leaving Dad's vacant. Johnny and I cleaned it up, painted it, built a map room, and moved in on July 7, 1957. And thus the partnership was born."

Significantly, the partnership would ride out a bumpy couple of years and build a small pipeline to carry gas to farmers from a well in Pecos County thirty miles northwest of Fort Stockton. That opportunistic little enterprise would become Clajon Gas Co., which years later, with Claytie at the helm, would morph into the largest independently owned gas company in Texas and form the cornerstone of his first great fortune. His battle cry: "Bustin' ass for Clajon Gas!"

Williams and May quickly emerged as an interesting and engaging team, although not always a financially solvent one. Brick manufacturing, rare minerals, and oil-field trucking were imaginative but ill-fated ventures, and a fling with a paper-products corporation fared only marginally better.

Even their oil and gas enterprises, though eventually successful, got off to an erratic start. May became the field man, the well driller, and Claytie the broker, the dealmaker, and they bonded as a team. They enjoyed not only working and partying together but also hunting. "Johnny and I were probably as good a pair of blue quail hunters as ever came along."

Working with information from the county clerk's office on filings of oil and gas leases and mineral and royalty deeds, they developed a plan: call on ranchers, negotiate a price on a lease for a certain period, determine royalty, tack on their commission, and present the package to the oil companies.

"Using our map as an information center, we started approaching all the local land and mineral owners to obtain listings," Claytie explained. "Then we typed a written submittal to all the oil companies who had recently bought leases in our two-county area."

By necessity, they spent many hours in coffee shops and bars, gathering leads on drilling locations and leases from land men and geologists—an oil business tradition called "swabbing." Then he and May would attempt to acquire listings on mineral interests on surrounding properties.

They started with high expectations, but six months sped by with no sales.

"We pushed forward with stars in our eyes, but for lack of contacts and experience we were unable to make any deals," Claytie said. "The only money I'd made was fifty dollars for checking re-

Johnny May and Claytie in costume for the Fort Stockton centennial

cords for my dad. I was able to provide for my family by selling life insurance on nights and weekends. To stay afloat, working weekends was a normal part of my life for several years."

Nine or ten months into the partnership, Maurice Bullock, the Fort Stockton attorney close to the Williams family, enlisted Claytie as a notary public on an estate he was closing and paid him $220 for affixing his notary seal on 440 documents. The experience became one of the many lessons Claytie would collect and nourish through the years.

"Of the five different heirs present, only two were speaking to each other," he said. "All were in separate rooms and had their own lawyers. It was a lesson for me to realize that a person can leave his heirs great wealth, but if not properly done, it can do more harm than good. They will fight over land in particular, and in this case it was an undivided interest in land. I learned that minerals, stock, royalty, and money can be evenly divided, but an undivided interest in land will guarantee a family fight. Do not leave your heirs an undivided interest in land!"

Before the end of the first year, the fledgling partnership compiled all its listings and mailed them to companies, touting a "Fall Clearance Sale." The leases were listed for ten years, one-eighth royalty, and a ten-dollar bonus per acre. All seemed hopeless.

"It was our last shot and we were about to admit failure," said Claytie. "Then one afternoon around 4:30, Johnny and I were sitting there all down and depressed, not believing we were going to be able to make a go of our business. The phone rang. By 5:30 we had made two different deals, which gave us two commissions of about $1,000 each."

Breathing room.

Shortly afterward, the May-Williams combine bounced back from a dry hole and promoted itself a free one-sixteenth interest in a well that briefly boosted spirits.

"I thought we were rich until I got the first check, which I remember as being about thirty-five dollars," Claytie said. But they soon struck a deal with Great Western Drilling Co. Admittedly nervous during negotiations, Claytie nevertheless closed the deal, and eventually the partnership drilled six producing wells and one dry hole in an area two miles west of Fort Stockton.

A couple of the early May-Williams investments produced expensive "lessons" but little else. Creative, yes. Profitable, no. The first, Delaware Transports Inc., was an oil-field and trucking and water-hauling company designed to provide services for area drilling activity. The idea sprung from the fertile mind of one of Johnny's Pecos friends, a "good ole boy" called McDougal, who was carried for a quarter of the deal. May-Williams purchased two trucks and a trailer house and hired a truck driver. Unfortunately, the driver had a fetching wife who distracted McDougal to the detriment of his responsibilities to Delaware Transports, and the sexually endangered trucking scheme blew up in a few months.

The lesson, said Claytie: "Be careful of good ole boys."

Then there was a fanciful strategy for making adobe bricks, using a "secret formula" acquired from an acquaintance of Johnny's step-father. Claytie and Johnny purchased a brick-making machine from a failed venture in Arizona, brought it to Fort Stockton, and put the "secret formula" to work producing faster, cheaper, and higher quality adobe bricks. Or so they thought. To cut costs, the operation was moved to Marfa's cheaper labor market. They contracted with an early-day oilman, Lee White, to deliver their wares at eighteen cents a brick for his Fort Stockton home.

"When we fulfilled our commitment, we added up the cost," Claytie said. "The bricks and transport to Fort Stockton cost us thirty-two cents a brick. End of venture."

The lesson? "Beware of secret formulas."

A third venture involved an investment of twenty-five thousand dollars in a company called Rare Minerals of New Mexico. "Johnny's dad had invested in the venture," Claytie said. "It sounded really good." The target was tantalum, a corrosive-resistant metallic chemical element used in missile and electronic components. Early assessments reported the ore as 90 percent tantalum and 10 percent waste. In fact, the percentages were reversed.

"We later came to believe the mine was salted; that is, someone had taken a shotgun and fired pellets of tantalum into the walls of the mine," Claytie said. "The lesson: when deals appear too good to be true, they generally are."

Still another venture, Stockton Paper Products Inc., involved making paper-based twine for binding wool fleeces. The key to this operation was a young twine-making expert from Michigan named Tom Phelps. But, alas, after two years Tom grew lonesome for his girlfriend in Michigan and quit. The partnership managed to sell the business to wool growers in San Angelo, and broke about even.

This time the lesson was a stretch: "A manager won't stay a long way from his girlfriend unless he finds a new one."

Unquestionably, the most delightful of their early acquisitions involved not bricks or trucks or even oil or gas, but a tart-tongued office assistant named Wynona Riggs. "Sometimes she was as mean as a snake," Claytie said, while admitting that she probably had to be to cope with him back then.

"There were some lean times," Wynona said, who insisted with an enigmatic smile that her toughest job was keeping Claytie in line, financially and otherwise. "If Claytie had a nickel to his name, the man would go buy bubble gum. He just cannot stand prosperity. We've been totally major outfits three times, and every time we'd go back in debt and start a new company."

"Never happened," said Claytie, laughing.

Wynona would spend thirty-five years working for Claytie and only begrudgingly and privately admit that she loved "almost" every minute of it. "He never thought small, and he was never afraid to dream. And there were a lot of things we did that seemed like a good idea at the time." She called Claytie "ol' M.I.H," an abbreviated version of his favorite phrase: Make it happen. "Just because you didn't know how to do something was never a reason not to get it done," Wynona explained, mockingly quoting Claytie: "Make it happen. Just make it happen. Don't bother me with details. Just make it happen." Handling Claytie was a handful, she said. "He wanted everything yesterday, and he wanted it perfect."

Back then, Claytie intermittently grew a beard for the Fort Stockton centennial celebration, evoking guffaws from Wynona: "We always thought he looked like Fidel Castro with this beard. We also thought that might be why he acted like him a lot — like a dictator."

Under Wynona's skeptical and sometimes cynical eye, Claytie and Johnny rebounded handily from each financial misadventure. Their energy-related reputation as competent and honest operators and brokers gathered steam, and their oil and gas lease-commission business prospered.

"In looking back, I see that all my significant moves forward were like stair steps, some larger than others," Claytie said, "and the Great Western deal was the first stair step."

The next step involved 960 highly sought after acres northwest of Fort Stockton, near a discovery well outside Coyanosa that was drilled by a well-known oilman named Ralph Lowe. The prize

Wynona Riggs, 1965: perky and enthusiastic, the glue that held Clajon Gas together

acreage was owned by a Pennsylvanian named Robert J. Merrick, whom Claytie's dad had known when he and Merrick operated a Fort Stockton movie theater in the 1920s. At Claytie's and Johnny's urging, the elder Williams called Merrick in Pennsylvania and arranged a meeting on behalf of the partners at Merrick's suburban Philadelphia home.

Abundantly aware of the meeting's importance, Claytie was hardly confident during his trip. Further, when he arrived in Dallas to connect with his flight to Philadelphia, he learned that a new Electra turbojet had just crashed and all Electra flights were delayed.

"So I stayed in the airport all night long, the plane finally departed the next morning, and I got to Pennsylvania late that afternoon with virtually no sleep. I called Mr. Merrick and told him what had happened and that I needed to get a few hours' sleep. He said, 'Boy, you better hurry, because there's some other people hot after it and they're here in town.'"

Merrick was about to close a deal with an oilman Claytie knew named John Blake. After meeting Merrick, Claytie sensed he needed to first gain his trust, which he did, aided in part by Merrick's respect for Claytie's father. As Claytie meticulously explained every detail of the oil and gas deal, the good and the bad, Blake and his partner showed up at the door. What then unfolded stunned Claytie. Merrick ordered Claytie to run upstairs with him and hide while his wife told Blake that Merrick was not home. "I knew then we had the deal done," Claytie said. "We did close the deal, and we proceeded to knock out the competition."

Eventually, the May–Williams–Robert J. Merrick #1 was drilled with money raised from an El Paso man named W. R. Weaver, a brilliant manufacturer and a savvy businessman with whom Claytie would become deeply involved. Weaver was known outside the oil patch for his telescopic rifle sights, called Weaver Scopes, a name that attached itself to two of Claytie's early and profitable investments, Scope Oil and Scope Royalty. Along with two other royalty companies, Coyanosa and Century Productions, these entities represented early investments totaling $1.9 million that would over the years reap more than $43 million.

Their Merrick #1, meanwhile, came in flowing fifty barrels an hour, and with May-Williams getting a half interest, Claytie was ecstatic: "Our first well! It was an exciting time. We thought, man, we've really hit it. It was so much fun. There were rumors and talk all through the oil patch about the May-Williams well."

They rushed out and bought their wives nearly identical 1960 Oldsmobiles. "This was a big event for both families," Claytie said.

Even though the well turned out more flash than substance, it did generate a certain notoriety that helped move May-Williams forward. "It gave us more credibility, more recognition, because we bought the lease when everybody in the Permian Basin was looking at the area," Claytie said. "Then we got name recognition as May and Williams from the discovery of the flowing well. We offset this well with one dry hole and a couple of noncommercial wells, so it was not as big a boom as we thought.

"But it was a step forward."

The Merrick well story didn't end there. A year or so later, Mobil Oil drilled the Sibley #1 in the same area. Named for the mineral owner, a prominent Fort Stockton family, it was a deep well that turned out to be a major discovery—the Coyanosa Field.

One day while Mobil was drilling this well, Claytie and his lawyer friend Maurice Bullock drove out to look it over. The well, located in a cotton field, was obviously having trouble, and a hundred or so roughnecks and service company workers were fighting the drilling problem. Also at the scene were a number of farm laborers picking cotton. Because Bullock represented the Sibleys, he and Claytie had access to the well, and they walked the rig floor and inspected the well from top to bottom.

"It was really stupid, because the well was having major pressure-control problems." Claytie said. "It . . . was threatening to blow out from the Wolfcamp Formation at about ten thousand five hundred feet. But we were satisfied by what we found and felt pretty good because it looked like it was gonna be some kind of discovery."

Returning to Fort Stockton, they met fire trucks and ambulances. Fifteen minutes after they had left the well, the casing collapsed, ignited, and touched off a huge explosion. Five people died, two of them cremated. Nearly one hundred workers, including those picking cotton, were burned, many severely.

"The injured filled up the hospitals in Fort Stockton, Kermit, and Pecos with burn victims," Claytie said. "Had we been at the well when it blew, we'd have been killed. Cremated. No question about it. Fifteen minutes. That close. *Fate.* That was another time I felt the Lord was looking after me."

Fate and Claytie. They kept the Lord busy, many believed.

"Clayton and I did lots of partying and drinking, chasing girls and whatever."

Despite the tragedy, the Sibley #1 discovery well foreshadowed development of the Delaware Basin's Coyanosa Field, where May-Williams would be successfully involved. The Mobil-Sibley also kicked off the hottest play in the United States and significantly enhanced the budding May and Williams enterprise. Moreover, the well became another forerunner of Clajon Gas, the little company with the big future.

Almost as important during this period, Claytie ran across a former Aggie named Bill Haverlah, a landman working for Mobil. He was not quite as colorful or nearly as sanguine as Claytie, but he was equally hardheaded. Lured into the aggressive Williams business complex, he eventually became a key player in Claytie's activities, professionally and socially.

"I had met Claytie at A&M," said Haverlah, who was two years ahead of Claytie, and remembered that "he managed to stay in trouble with his upperclassmen a lot."

Haverlah also remembered somewhat grimly the early days of the Fort Stockton operation—recollections that Claytie contends were more artful than accurate. "Clayton was so poor back then he paid me about once every three or four months," Haverlah said. "He couldn't pay his bar bills, either. They cut off our water and electricity and sewer and everything else at the office, and back then our office was horrible. It was one of those old fort buildings in Fort Stockton, and the wood was so old, Wynona [Wynona Riggs, the

1964, Claytie with Johnny May, left, and Weaver representative John St. Clair

inimitable and fearless office manager] would wear those high-heeled shoes, and every now and then she'd poke through the floor. She'd get mad and stomp across that floor and that heel would go right through the linoleum, wood and all, and she'd be stuck. We were so poor we couldn't even pay our gasoline bills."

Claytie merrily argues that Haverlah's complaints were grossly exaggerated, and that he did pay the gas bills and water bills and most assuredly the bar bills. "Sometimes it took me a while, but I always did it," he said, adding that the office was not all that bad, either. "The building was constructed by my grandfather in 1906, so it was *just* fifty years old."

When not fretting over bar bills and such, Haverlah contributed handsomely to the early success of Clajon Gas. Before Haverlah's arrival, the company supplied fuel gas for irrigation engines via a three-inch pipeline from the Merrick discovery to only three area farms. "The Mobil-Sibley added depth and reserves to our small gas company," Claytie said. "Along with the Weavers and Humble, we drilled a Devonian-Ellenberger well that offset the Mobil-Sibley and added substantial reserves for May-Williams and particularly promising reserves to Clajon to expand its system."

After Clayton bought Johnny May's interests in 1964, and with Haverlah's help, Clajon grew to deliver irrigation fuel gas to most of the farmers in the Coyanosa area and subsequently to farms in Belding and the city of Fort Stockton. All played important advances in Claytie's energy-based career, and he took great pride in winning contracts with both the farmers and the city. His first battle was in 1965 with Pecos Growers Gas Company, founded by Billie Sol Estes, the infamous West Texas wheeler-dealer and con man who built the first gas system in the Coyanosa farm area.

Texas Oil and Gas bought out Pecos Growers in 1966, and in 1967 Claytie outmaneuvered this group to build the pipeline from Coyanosa to Fort Stockton and Belding. "Williams is on a rampage again," one of his old adversaries complained.

For Claytie, winning the Battle of Belding resulted in an early affirmation of Clajon's potential, and foreshadowed a life's work, in style and substance, of its young owner.

"I built it from the first piece of pipe and I did it with my hands, working from early in the morning until late at night. We worked fast and hard, delivered better-quality gas at a better price, and ran an honest meter. We weren't fancy; we were achievers. We delivered lots of gas to a lot of farms and I'm very proud of that."

To understand Clayton Wheat Williams Jr. and his success as an oilman over a half century, the founding of Clajon can provide textured insights into the man: the grit, moxie, high energy, creativity, and knack for a deal that soon would propel him into prominence as one of America's leading independent oil and gas producers. In many ways, Clajon would become a model not only for his business success but also for his business ethic, style, and personality. When Claytie says he still gets emotional about Clajon, there's good reason, even two decades after the sale of the company. More than any undertaking of his career, Clajon emerged from nowhere when few noticed, went somewhere when many doubted,

Bill Haverlah, Wynona Riggs, and Claytie celebrate termination of the Pecos Growers contracts and the beginning of Clajon Gas

and trail-blazed when none could deny the strategic brilliance and unbridled passion of its maverick owner. Clajon would make Claytie a credible force in the industry, one to be reckoned with, and more than a wee bit wealthy.

In 1962, the May-Williams team hooked up with Jack McCall, a former president of Louisiana Land & Exploration, and that relationship propelled May-Williams another big step forward. After resigning from the Louisiana company, McCall came to

Midland because he foresaw a boom in the Delaware Basin, which embraced Pecos, Fort Stockton, Monahans, and Kermit. Claytie was fond of telling folks that the big, deep gas wells were in the basin, and that he cleverly had been born in the right place.

"We made a good team in that I knew the landowners, the royalty owners, and was a good buyer, and Jack knew the buyers and was a good seller," Claytie said. "We made many, many deals and our area of interest expanded into Ward and Loving counties as well as Pecos and Reeves. We were most active in the Coyanosa Field, and it was fun buying, dealing, and selling."

But as the partnership moved forward, storm clouds loomed. Not surprisingly, Claytie's marriage to Betty had begun deteriorating in the early '60s. Those close to her described his childhood sweetheart as lovely, kind, and funny, but said the two were as different as noon and midnight in their lifestyles.

"My mother loved opera, the symphony, art museums, antiques, and traveling," daughter Kelvie explained. "No two such different people than my mother and father have ever existed."

Before the divorce, the couple separated for six months. Claytie blamed himself for the split and even took a shot at reconciliation. "It didn't work," he said, despite the pending birth of a second daughter, Allyson. "I wanted to go a different direction." The divorce turned bitter, though not over money. Betty emerged from the marriage with roughly half a million dollars. "She got the assets and I got the liabilities," Claytie said with a hollow laugh. That was no exaggeration. Wynona Riggs says he did give Betty much of the producing properties, but he still was forced to go to court to gain visiting privileges with his daughters.

"I got to see my kids one weekend a month, and then a month in the summer," he said. He was not happy with the arrangement, but he became a better parent. "When Allyson and Kelvie were with me," he said, "my time was totally devoted to them." Recalling those monthly trips to see her father, Kelvie noted that the bitterness caused considerable stress for both mother and daughters.

Family music time with daughters Kelvie and Allyson, 1964

Daddy did know, however, the path to his daughters' hearts. "We looked forward to visiting him—we'd always have leftover birthday cake or pizza for breakfast," Kelvie said. Eventually, she said, her mom mellowed toward Claytie. When Claytie's father died in 1983, Betty and her own ailing father traveled to Fort Stockton to attend the funeral, and she went out of her way to express condolences to Claytie and the family. "This was a big step for her," Kelvie said. "I was so proud of how gracious she was."

On Super Bowl Sunday of 1994, Betty suffered critical injuries in an auto collision with a drunken driver in Austin; she died ten days later.

Following the separation and divorce in '64, Claytie found solace as a swinging single in the saloons of West Texas with his rowdy friends, male and female. "I dated a whole bunch of cute girls in Midland and Odessa," he said somewhat grandly. "I was also very active in the Jaycees. I made many good friends and went to several Jaycee conventions." He would later make a spirited bid for the presidency of the Fort Stockton Junior Chamber of Commerce, losing narrowly. Despite the loss, his affection for the group never wavered. "The Jaycee creed," he explained, "ranks right along with the Boy Scout Oath and Scout Law in my book as a road map to an honorable life."

Though a debatable issue, Claytie's mid-'60s interval as a free-wheeling single allegedly was tougher on his landman Bill Haverlah than anyone.

"We drank lots of beer together," Haverlah told a visitor to his ranch outside Santa Rosa, N.M. "I went dove and quail and deer hunting with both Johnny and Clayton, and Clayton and I did lots of partying and drinking, chasing girls and whatever. He damn near ruined my health." A fighter since boyhood, Claytie changed little through the years, stressing always the psychological and physical virtue of throwing the first punch. He found a certain enjoyment in his barroom brawling and revelry until he came to realize his life, if not spinning out of control, was headed in a treacherous direction.

"I did not like who I was. I was drinking too much, and I saw lots of misery in those bars, lots of unhappy people," he said. He awoke one morning after a particularly harsh night of revelry and decided changes were in order. "I told myself I was going to be better or worse, but I could never be the Claytie I was before the divorce."

He opted for better, contending that his walk on the wild side had been necessary to get a little "sorry-ass" out of his system. He continued as always to work hard and play hard, remaining fast friends with cold beer and warm women while tempering his helter-skelter lifestyle.

Unfortunately, though, the divorce had an unexpected impact on the already frayed business partnership—one that neither he nor May could control: Johnny's wife, Sue, and a hefty portion of the

Fort Stockton populace understandably sided with Betty. "It was terrible," said Haverlah. "Half the people in Fort Stockton hated Clayton, though half the people still liked him. And since I was with him, and oil-field trash to start with, I wasn't too well thought of, either."

The spousal pressures brought on by the divorce contributed to a decision to end the partnership of May-Williams; but that wasn't all. Because Johnny and Claytie were equal partners, neither was actually running Clajon, which both realized was unwise. Fashioning a unique arrangement, they dissolved the partnership with no lingering personal acrimony and remained friendly.

"We divided the real property, with each taking half, and we bid between ourselves on every single office item: each file cabinet, each typewriter, everything," Claytie said. "That way, whoever quit bidding could never say the other one took advantage of him. It took all the manipulating out of it. We split the office equipment that way."

Then came the Clajon deal.

"I was always fascinated by having a gas company, a retail company, and Johnny and I each owned half," Claytie said. "I made him an offer and he turned it down. So then I made him another offer—I think it was twenty-five thousand dollars—give or take; I'll sell it or you sell it. He decided to sell, and that's how we solved that. I raised the price a little above what I thought it was worth because I wanted to buy it. It was just a three-inch gas pipeline to three farms with eight irrigation wells, but I believed it had potential for growth."

He was, in gambling parlance, betting on the come.

"It was a hell of a good way to dissolve a partnership," said Claytie, who moved forward with Bill Haverlah, Jack McCall, and Clajon toward an uncertain future.

Haverlah remembers those days with Claytie and McCall in the early and mid-1960s as both horrible and humorous, perhaps more of the former. He had spurned several offers to work full-time for Claytie, but finally acquiesced when both Claytie and McCall, although not formally partners, urged him to do, exclusively, all their land work.

"Jack would tell me one thing and Clayton would tell me another," he said, smiling at the recollection. "Both of them were very domineering, and it was like trying to work for two bulls. . . . I finally said, 'Clayton, I'm through with this thing. I'll work for you or I'll work for Jack, but I'm not going to work for both of you. That's an impossibility, and nobody can do it.'"

With Clajon, it was always personal for Claytie, always emotional: he and Johnny May had opened their business with no money but a reputable family name that squared with hard work and integrity. "I never felt guilty about using my family's reputation, my dad and granddad's good name," Claytie said. Even the idea to start Clajon had roots in the family. Claytie's father-in-law, Jimmy Meriwether, owned a small but money-making gas company that convinced Claytie an integrated retail gas operation—production, pipelines, sales—made good business sense.

Expanding its pipelines beyond the original three farms and the city of Fort Stockton, Clajon soon developed a reputation for laying lines quickly—sometimes in days, not weeks—to neighboring farms. Defying all odds, including a right-of-way obstacle, he once completed a pipeline to Sinclair's sulfur plant in seven days, silencing the doubters with one quick stroke. Then, in a major step forward, Clajon contracted to lay temporary lines to supply gas to drilling rigs in the Gomez and Coyanosa fields. "We developed a kind of cowboy/farmer work ethic," Claytie said. "We could do things others couldn't because we were head down, ass up, let's go get it. We built pipelines, and we were good. In fact, there wasn't anybody our size any better." How did they do it—become so successful so fast? Primarily, they charted their own business plan and developed their own work ethic, as evidenced by how they built their early pipelines.

For instance, Clajon, if facing a dire deadline, was not always encumbered by conventional pipe-laying protocol, which included the timely securing of proper right-of-way permits. Such was the case when Clajon built the pipeline to supply gas to Sinclair's sulfur plant. Clajon had to either make its deadline or lose its contract after Texas Oil and Gas undercut Clajon with a last-minute bid. Sinclair proposed a counteroffer to Claytie: "Since you've started [right-of-way work], we'll give you seven more days to flow the gas to our sulfur plant." Or lose the contract. "We plowed on," Claytie said, "then could not get the right of way for the San Pedro or Leonard Simon lands. We had the construction right up to San Pedro when we had to stop. But we were next to the county road. I went to County Commissioner Bill Moody and asked if we could build the pipeline up the county road to the sulfur plant. 'I can't tell you not to,' he said.

"On we went. We built seven miles of three-inch pipe-line—through ditching, laying, and welding of pipe from the Gulf pipeline—to Sinclair in seven days."

Claytie attributes the Sinclair pipeline success to his employees' work ethic. "We were able to do this because we had construction crews at work on the Belding/Fort Stockton pipeline and just shifted them over to the Sinclair line. We could not have done it if we were not fresh from building the Fort Stockton/Belding pipeline. I was really proud of our people and our accomplishments."

But all did not end well: "The price of raw sulfur dropped, Sinclair closed its plant, and the pipeline only partially paid out."

It was one of Claytie's early lessons: "Maybe it ain't over till it's over."

Many considered Clajon and its pipeline successes a mere extension of its leader's drive and personality. Employees often worked until nine or ten o'clock at night, with Modesta making their evening beer runs.

"The real work story of Clayton Williams, who he was and what he was doing, can be found in those long days and long nights," Modesta says. "What he was doing was building three companies. With Clajon he would be down at the coffee shop before daylight, and then he would be out with the working men putting that pipeline together. And then come in maybe at ten that night and get on the telephone with Jack McCall making business deals. His life wasn't just fun and games."

Claytie says he always believed a good boss had to be a good leader, and that the boss and employees had to be a team. He learned this at A&M when he was a member of the Corps of Cadets. Some upperclassmen gave him a piece of cotton string one time and told him to push it to the other side of the table.

"No, you can't push it," Claytie said. "It wads up."

"OK, now, Williams. Pull it to the other side."

"Well, you can pull it real easy," Claytie said.

"Williams, leadership means you have to be out front, pulling. Not behind, pushing."

That, Claytie maintains, is what the Corps taught him about leadership, and that's how he has tried to lead his company.

Claytie believed in recruiting good people and then letting them do their jobs, but he hardly followed a conventional path in hiring. Rather than recruit an established—and expensive—engineer to design one of his early gas systems, Claytie checked out and hired a young graduate from A&M, Bob Bayless of Odessa, who was trained as an air-conditioning specialist. Both Claytie and Bill Haverlah remembered his work fondly. "It was flawless," said Haverlah.

In another creative example of expense reduction, Clajon spurned the traditional ditching machine in favor of a maintainer, or road grader, with its blade set at a high angle. "The operator could build a two-foot ditch and cover it at a tenth of the cost of a ditching machine."

Ever cost-conscious, Claytie himself joined workers in the ditch to help install cumbersome, eighty-pound gas meters. "One fell on my face and left a scar," he said. "Maybe that's why I like that Mexican song, 'Juan Charrasquedo' [Scarface], so much." Claytie believes it is good for workers to see the boss working alongside his men, whether down in the ditches, in the cattle pens, or on horseback.

Claytie also put a premium on how Clajon dealt with customers. Because of escalating gas prices, Clajon lost considerable money for five years on its contract to supply gas to Fort Stockton. "I was paying $2 or more per thousand cubic feet for gas and selling it for 21.75 cents," he said. "It was painful, but I honored my commitment." And it helped solidify his reputation for integrity.

The incredulous mayor, Howard McKissack, told Claytie, "We'll always trust you."

Though modest by any measure, Clajon's beginning proved as visionary as it was resourceful. Within two decades it would gross $700 million in annual revenues.

Not bad for starting from scratch, Claytie says. Zero to $700 million. Enough to make *anyone* emotional.

The pipeline era of the mid-1960s indeed took a toll on Bill Haverlah — and not just the deadline pressure. "Claytie had a habit of calling me when I was in bed — eleven or twelve at night or two in the morning — it made no difference," he said, chuckling at the memory. "It was like he owned me."

Usually it was the boss wanting a ride home from some bar. "He wouldn't call Modesta," says Haverlah, "he'd call me." One night Haverlah rebelled. He and Claytie had driven from Fort Stockton to Midland to attend a landmen's party. When Haverlah was ready to go home, Claytie of course was just getting started.

So, recalled Haverlah, "I go home, and about two in the morning he calls and says, 'Bill, would you come to Monahans and pick me up at the intersection. Ol' Charlie Perry [an oilman friend of both] is going to bring me halfway.

" 'Come pick me up. I'm scared to call Modesta.' "

"Well, you sorry son of a gun," Haverlah remembers saying, "you had plenty of opportunities to go home with the rest of us."

"Aw, do me a favor," Claytie pleaded, "I'll be waiting at the intersection."

After he hung up, Haverlah called Modesta. "Modesta, Claytie wants me to pick him up at the Monahans cutoff. You want to go up there and get him?"

"You bet I do!" she snarled.

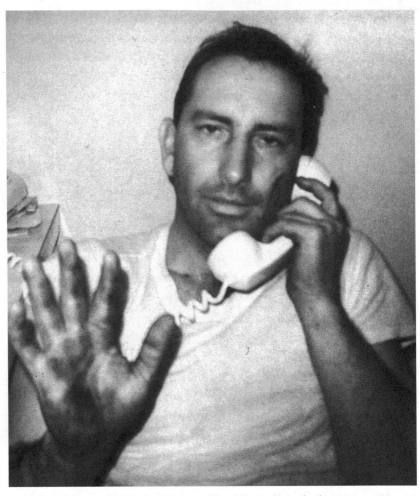

"Scarface" Claytie, 1965: working deals at night while pipelining by day

It was not a pretty sight. There sat Claytie near the intersection, alone in the cold darkness, accompanied in the vast West Texas loneliness by only a small campfire. Meanwhile, Modesta was smoldering fury when she reached the intersection.

"He was like a hobo," she recalled, "sitting there warming his hands. I just said, 'Get in the car.'"

Claytie: "I think I went to sleep while she was chewing on me all the way home."

Modesta: "I bet you didn't. Not for long anyhow."
Claytie: "No, I bet I didn't."

The only thing Haverlah liked less than working for the "two bulls," Claytie and McCall, was riding in a vehicle with one of them. "I mean you got a death wish when you ride with Claytie," he said, recounting one of his more infamous escapades behind the wheel. Preoccupied as always and accompanied by a terrified Mexican pipeline worker, he drove his new Oldsmobile at high speed off the end of a farm road and into a muddy cotton field. Claytie remembered they were building the first pipeline at the time and his mind was on a simultaneous money-making deal with Jack McCall when his passenger, Cipriano Velasquez, began screaming, "*Quidate! Quidate!*" [Look out!]

"Here I am going eighty miles an hour and I look up, and here comes the dead-end road," Claytie said. "I hit the brakes as much as I could, but my reflexes were good and I didn't try to turn. That's how people get killed. I just sailed out into the cotton field and bent the frame on the Oldsmobile."

"He'd had so many wrecks," Haverlah said, "we couldn't afford to report it to the insurance company because they were gonna cancel us. So he had to fix it himself, and from then on it limped down the road kind of like an old dog trotting sideways. He finally collected so many tickets he had to get somebody to drive the car for him."

Predictably, Claytie countered with a disclaimer: "It wasn't that bad." However, legions of witnesses—family, coworkers, law enforcement types from multiple cities and agencies—would respectfully beg to differ with Claytie's assessment. Those who know him well give testament to an otherwise commendable soul who for more than half a century has terrorized human and jackrabbit alike in his addiction to speed and inattention when he mounts anything on wheels.

Claytie even believed he best could teach his children how to drive, a curious fatherly confidence considering his universally recognized reputation for ineptitude behind the wheel; to some, Claytie teaching driving evokes the same leaping logic of a frog that preens in a mirror and sees Prince Charming. Nonetheless, daughter Kelvie's driving lessons commenced at the tender age of thirteen. "I thought I was doing good, but he said, 'Now that is just not the right way to pass. Let me show you,'" recalls Kelvie. Claytie slipped into the driver's seat, sped up, illegally passed a car on a hill, got pulled over by the cops, and gravely accepted a traffic ticket.

"Maybe that's *not* the right way," he grumbled as he drove off.

Claytie's most persistent driving talent? Speed. It came as naturally to Claytie as laughter and barroom song. When troopers clocked him once between Fort Stockton and Midland, running between eighty-five and ninety miles an hour, he decided a little fun was in order—at Modesta's expense.

"Now I'm on driver's probation, so I said, 'Modesta, get behind the wheel.' We changed drivers while waiting for the cop to catch up; I'm sitting in the right seat when the cop walked up and said, 'Miss, we had you clocked at eighty.' And I said, 'No sir, she was doing closer to ninety.' We already had a ticket; I thought we ought to have some fun out of it. We did that twice."

Allyson actually witnessed an infrequent occasion when her dad was driving less than eighty or ninety miles an hour. She was home from college—she swears Claytie "bribed" her to go to A&M after attending Texas Tech for a year—and she and Modesta were awaiting his arrival from a bar where he'd been cutting an oil deal. Modesta spotted him creeping through the gate and "putt, putt, putting" slowly up to the house in his maroon-and-white Bronco.

"He was all bent over and driving real slow," Allyson noticed, and when he pulled up to the house, she said, "Daddy, why are you driving so slow?" His response would become a classic Claytieism: "Do not ever drive faster than you can see."

Putting aside his misgivings, Haverlah soon wound up not only working just for Claytie but also sharing a "little chicken house" with him after the marital split with Betty. "Clayton was divorced so he didn't have a house, and of course I didn't have one in Fort Stockton," said Haverlah, who had a home and wife in Midland. "So we rented a little old adobe shack. I think it had one bedroom, one bath, and a living room, and we had a bed in the living room that I used during the week when I was in Fort Stockton. Then we'd go and party every night at those little local bars and beer joints, and 'course Claytie, being single, it was proving time for him, but I was married. I couldn't really ramble around quite like he did."

At that point, no one could have guessed what lay ahead. Certainly Claytie could not know that he was on the threshold of the most important discovery of his career.

And that discovery would not be made in the oil patch.

"I couldn't understand what this beautiful woman saw in me, but who was I to question her taste?"

"The first time I saw Claytie was in 1963," Modesta said with a mischievous grin lighting up her face. "I didn't meet him then, but I saw him.

"My mother and my brother Wade and another friend and I had all gone out to dinner at the old Monterrey Kitchen in Midland. There was a guy sitting over there with his date, minding his business pretty well. There was a guy, a drunk guy, at another table who just kept nipping on him . . . really acting pretty stinky. We were too far away to hear what was happening, but the drunk walked over to the other table, and just as he got there, the guy with the date came up with his right fist and just knocked him back across a table. They got in a wrestling match, broke the table, and knocked a light off the wall. The guy got his legs wrapped around the drunk and — pow, pow — knocked him back and forth.

"We were all sitting there just stupefied because this was a nice restaurant, not some barroom. They were going to call the cops when the drunk's buddy broke up the fight and got him out of there."

A year later, in 1964, Modesta was in the same restaurant with a girlfriend and spotted some gringo singing Mexican songs with the mariachi band; she didn't recognize him as one of the brawlers from the fight night. "When he was singing those mariachi songs, I thought he was the cutest thing in the whole wide world," she recalled.

Claytie had spotted her, too.

Meanwhile, Joe Luther, one of Claytie's geologist buddies from Fort Stockton, slipped into the table with Modesta and her friend, Sandy Hyde. After his gig with the band, Claytie ambled over to their table and introduced himself. One of the women struck him as petite and beautiful, the other buxom and sexy. Following dinner, he opted for petite and beautiful and invited Modesta to go dancing at a popular nightspot called the Penguin Club.

"We danced the night away until they closed everything down," she recounted. "Then we went over to my apartment and I started making him Black Russians [a potent vodka-based concoction]. Now, he tells the story a little differently, but this is actually what happened: We were lying in the middle of the floor, and we literally passed out from those Black Russians. The next morning my room-mate, Nancy Renfro, comes running down the stairs and she's yelling, "'Modesta, Modesta, what are you doing?'"

Modesta's only response: "Ohhhhhhhhhh."

Claytie's version is a little more titillating, asserting that it was a honky-tonk where they met, not a café, that she picked him up, took him dancing, then to her apartment, and that they slept together that very first night.

"And he tells it with such gusto," a friend joked with Modesta.

"Yes, my mother really loved the way he told it, too," Modesta said. "She could have strangled him!"

When pressed, Claytie laughingly admits he might have exaggerated his version a little bit and that while they hit it off immediately, they mostly just annihilated a few Black Russians and talked into the wee hours of the morning.

"I learned she was a ranch girl, went to high school in Big Spring, attended Texas Tech and TCU, had been a model, ran her own model and charm school, and that we had much in common."

Among the most important things they shared was a love of the land, for ranching and farming — everything outdoors. Like Claytie's grandfather, O. W. Williams, Modesta's paternal grandfather had been a surveyor, in San Angelo, and the two knew each other. Her maternal grandfather, T. J. Good, had homesteaded the family ranch north of Big Spring, and it was he who took her and her young friends hunting—but for birds and rabbits, not trophy sheep and elephants.

"It was a wonderful childhood," she said. "I was a cheerleader, and I played volleyball and did all those kinds of things. It was a real special high school, and I made good grades. I was proud of my grades. It was just fabulous because we lived in town during the week so my brother Wade and I could go to school, and then we'd go back to the ranch on the weekends. I spent many of my fun days—before I grew up into a bad teenager—at the ranch having a good time. My two best friends were Mary Reed and Sherry Lurting, and we're still very dear friends."

Another "best friend" was her horse, Leebe.

"I rodeoed some when I was young, and I'd go see my horse every afternoon. He was my best friend, my solace, and everything else. I just loved that horse. When I would have a bad day, I'd go out and cry on his shoulder."

Her idyllic childhood ruptured on occasion because her parents, who met at Texas Christian University, periodically divorced and re-married each other. "They couldn't live with each other and they couldn't live without each other."

When they finally did call it quits for keeps, after four divorces, Modesta's mother married a Snyder rancher, Aubry Stokes. "They got married in 1970 and he was a dear man and really sweet to my mother. He took good care of her and they had a good life for many years."

Modesta's own youthful fling at marriage was an admitted mistake. "I was married right out of high school and ruined a nice friendship. We didn't have children—no animosity, no meanness. He was a nice guy and we were just young and in love."

Actually, she smiled, it might have been more lust than love.

After spending a semester at Texas Tech, she transferred to TCU, where she studied business. In Fort Worth, she enrolled in the John Robert Powers Modeling School. Her modeling career included opening her own school in Midland. "I had a nice little modeling

Wooing Modesta, 1964: love is in the air

school, but the girls that really wanted to go to modeling school would go to New York or Dallas."

At the time of the meeting at the Mexican restaurant, she was consumed with making a go of the charm and modeling venture. "Claytie and I started dating, and I didn't work quite as hard after I ran into him. But I gave it a try anyway."

During one of their early dates the subject of Claytie's penchant for fighting reared its ugly head. Modesta volunteered that she'd once seen a *real* fight in the café where they met.

"Where?" Claytie asked.

"The Monterrey Kitchen."

"When?"

"About a year before we met," she said, providing him blow-by-blow details.

"That was me," Claytie confessed. Modesta was relieved at least to learn her new friend was the gallant brawler, not the rowdy drunk.

While theirs was not a case of love at first sight, an early, mutual infatuation blossomed between the budding Aggie oilman and the dark-haired fashion model, a passion that surprised but delighted Claytie. "I couldn't understand what this beautiful woman saw in me, but who was I to question her taste?"

The courtship was brief, exciting, and fun, Claytie said.

He drove her through the Davis Mountains to show her the distinctive beauty of the country after a rainstorm, and they agreed they would love to own a ranch in those storied mountains some day.

The courtship included bass fishing with her father at Falcon Lake in South Texas and quail hunting with her mother at her ranch in Borden County.

"In those days I carried a guitar, a shotgun, a case of shells, my fishing rod, and a blanket and pillow in the trunk at all times," Claytie reminisced. "They were wonderful days, and I was ready for whatever occasion arose."

Claytie's introduction to Modesta's mother made a lasting impression. He told Modesta he would stop by her Midland apartment on his return from a Jaycee convention in Sweetwater. He did so, but with a hangover. "If you didn't have a hangover after a Jaycee convention, you probably weren't there," contends Claytie.

And so it was that a Sunday in 1964 mother and daughter were seated on a couch, talking, when Modesta noticed a sliding glass door quietly opening behind her mother.

"I just kind of looked over Mom's shoulder and here comes this guy in a black Beatle wig and sombrero crawling across the floor on all fours. He crawls up behind her, looks up over the couch, and says, 'Boo!' And that was my mother's introduction to Claytie, this man I'd been telling her about who was so *wonderful!*"

After recovering from the initial shock, her mom laughingly embraced Claytie's sense of the weird, and the two developed a hearty relationship as her daughter and Claytie reluctantly fell "deeper and deeper in love."

Reluctantly?

"When we started dating, neither one of us was ready to get married again," Modesta said. In fact, their special song while dating was "We'll Sing in the Sunshine," Gayle Garnett's hit tune of the '60s that includes lyrics about a warm and cuddly but no-strings-attached romance.

Of course, it didn't turn out quite that way. Always the romantic, Claytie decided to propose on Valentine's Day 1965, and like everything he did, he planned a major production. After first secretly telling her parents of his intentions and asking their permission, he shared his plans with his artistic sister Janet, who insisted that his proposal be not only romantic but fun. So here's how he did it:

"As a little girl and a young adolescent, Modesta had a favorite spot on a hill right behind her ranch house. It was where she would go to contemplate and philosophize and have some quiet time. I told her mother and her grandmother, Mrs. T. J. Good, when and where I was going to propose so they could be watching out the window of the ranch house. I knew they would be happy. The day before Valentine's, I got two bottles of champagne and a champagne holder. I put it on ice in the car trunk along with a dozen roses and the engagement ring.

Wedding Day, 1965

"At the prearranged time, I told Modesta, 'Let's take a little drive,' so we drove in my car out to the top of the hill. I told her to lie down in the back, and when she balked, I said, 'Just do what I say.'"

He then removed the champagne, roses, and ring, invited her out of the car, dropped to his knee, and asked for her hand in marriage.

"How could she turn me down?"

She couldn't. Afterward, they drove down to the ranch house for a grand celebration. "I stored up a lot of points with this proposal and this approach," Claytie bragged afterward. "And it stood me well over the years when sometimes I was on thin ice. Lord knows, there were times in our marriage when I had to draw on those points."

Three months after his hilltop coup, on May 22, they were married in the First Presbyterian Church at Big Spring, forty miles east of Midland. His rowdy friend Bill Haverlah was best man and Sherry Lurting was the maid of honor.

"When I first took Modesta to Fort Stockton she was received coolly by some of the establishment and by my mother," Claytie recalled. "My dad and my Jaycee friends liked her immediately, and in a very short time she was better loved and more accepted in my own hometown than I was."

Not long after the wedding, Claytie decided to run for president of the Fort Stockton Jaycees, inspired in part by the issue of permitting Mexican Americans into the organization. He had met a young Hispanic named Frank Velasco and supported his membership.

"There was a lot of racial prejudice back then, and it was a close vote," Velasco remembers. "Claytie lost the presidency, but I got in by maybe one or two votes."

They would become lifelong friends.

Claytie hired Velasco in the early 1970s to oversee his farming operations, and he has spent much of his adult life as foreman at the Fort Stockton farm. "Claytie's very demanding, but he's been very good to me," said Velasco. "He loves the land, and he's always looking for ways to improve the ranches or increase production at the farms. And he gives me a percentage of this or that and permits me to invest in his deals."

After the election, Velasco and his wife, Carmen, accompanied Claytie and Modesta to a Jaycee convention in Houston. "I took him to a raw oyster bar and it was the first time he'd had raw oysters," Claytie recalled fondly. "He loves them to this day."

A friend once asked Modesta if, during those early years of marriage, she ever thought, "My Lord, what have I gotten into?" Chuckling softly, she replied: "Probably about once a week."

Claytie himself, never one to mince words, wisely or otherwise, described those early marital years as turbulent. "We had terrible fights . . . and they would usually happen when we were out partying and drinking. We never had sober fights."

"Hardly ever," Modesta added, eyes atwinkle. It may have been about this time a sign appeared in her office: "Men are God's gag gift to women."

Occasionally, one or the other would huffily leave "forever," then return in a day or two. Later, as they mellowed, they would simply take silent refuge in different parts of the house. Sparring over those early disputes, Modesta laughingly recalled the time her boozed up, freshly married mate grabbed up his bedroll and announced, "'I'm leaving for good.' And away he went, out to the caliche pit west of town."

Claytie awoke the next morning with a hangover and asking himself, "What am I doing here, you dumb shit?" But, in defense, he said, "Modesta left a few times, too."

"Yes," she cooed, "but I didn't go to the caliche pit! I was a little higher class."

The truly turbulent period lasted only about three or four years until, according to Claytie, "I finally realized I wasn't gonna get to be the boss anymore. I became resigned to my fate, and it got smoother after that."

Exceptions arose—some more notable than others—but Claytie was generally too busy building his first couple of pipelines during those early years to get in too much trouble. "We were growing and building," he said, and Modesta would make those popular nightly beer runs to the pipeline work sites for Claytie, Haverlah, and the crew.

Overcoming or simply ignoring periodic setbacks, Claytie and his fun-loving and hardworking gang continued to rack up marginally more wins than losses in an assortment of mostly energy-related ventures. By 1965, the year he and Modesta married, he had formed several oil and gas partnerships, beginning with May-Williams in 1957. However, the wheeling and dealing and routinely cashless operation was taking its toll on Haverlah. He was uncomfortable with Claytie's renowned but risky operational OPM credo, "Other People's Money."

"Bill was just a habitual worrier," recalled Wynona Riggs, whose job it was to oversee the Fort Stockton office in those wild and restless days. She said his first demand upon arriving each morning was to examine the mail, which he knew to be virtually all bills.

"Nona," he asked her time and again, "how are we going to pay for all this stuff? Clayton hasn't even gotten a loan on it yet." She would tell him she had mentioned it to Claytie and his stock response was, "Not to worry. When I get time, I'll get a loan."

And he did, eventually, although only enough to barely cover the rapid expansion.

The oil and gas partnerships had grown beyond Scope Oil to include Scope Royalty, Coyanosa Company, Century Royalty, and of course Clajon, the hand-crafted pipeline and gas company that was slowly emerging as the backbone of Claytie's empire.

Another major step came in 1967 with the building of the second pipeline, from Fort Stockton to Belding, a chancy undertaking in which success depended not only on completing the line but also on persuading the big drilling contractors in the active Gomez Field to buy from a start-up gas company. "I was betting that we could sell gas to the drilling rigs in the Gomez Field and expand the system, so I was willing to take the risk," Claytie explained. "I was also betting that I could make enough money cutting deals to cover the shortfall in the meantime."

The Fort Stockton–Belding project encountered problems almost from the outset, and as the evils escalated he turned for help to another former teammate on the Fort Stockton football teams of the late '40s. Claytie previously had tried unsuccessfully to hire Clint Atkins, an honors graduate in petroleum engineering from the University of Oklahoma, to manage the gas system.

"As my troubles deepened, I approached him again and said, 'Please help me. I'm really in trouble.'"

Atkins agreed to hop aboard. "Clint was just what the doctor ordered: bright, methodical, and organized. He soon had all systems humming, and we completed the pipeline on schedule and on budget. I decided to turn over the administrative and managerial work for all my other operations, and he handled them beautifully."

When the pipeline system became operational, Claytie tackled the next huge hurdle: selling the gas to the drilling rigs. He pulled it off, but only after some truly inspired Claytie-like finagling to overcome reluctance by the big drilling contractors to purchase a small operator's gas. He did this by persuading a friendly landowner, Gene Riggs, to refuse the contractors permission to lay their pipe across his strategically located land unless they used Clajon gas. Riggs, coincidentally, was a member of a solid pioneer family and his wife, Wynona, was the indomitable fixture in Claytie's Fort Stockton office.

With no choice, the reluctant contractors surrendered. Claytie quickly hooked up most of the rigs in the Gomez Field and more than doubled his Clajon gas sales. Additionally, he won the respect of the contractors with quality performance and attractive prices, delivering gas to the drilling rigs and saving them money.

"We sold gas to probably seventy or eighty different drilling operations," Claytie said. "We made more money from the rigs than we did Fort Stockton farmers. That paid out the pipelines."

By the time Claytie really got rolling, Haverlah was long gone, having bailed out after helping complete the second pipeline.

Claytie's work demands coupled with his fast-paced nocturnal activities had taken their toll. "When we get through over there at Belding, I'm leaving," he had told the boss.

"Aw, you can't do that," Claytie said dismissively.

Once the pipeline was hooked up and the gas flowing, Claytie tossed another of his early beer and barbecue celebrations. Gene Riggs, Wynona's husband, barbecued the goat. As the festivities drew to a close, Haverlah approached Claytie, shook hands, and said, "Good-bye, Clayton. Tomorrow morning I'm cleaning out my office and I'm gone."

"You're not really gonna do that," Claytie argued. But he did, never dreaming that after a few years of ranching in South Texas he would return to the Williams financial merry-go-round.

And if anything, it would be even wilder the second time around.

Another key addition to the Williams expanding energy circle during the tumultuous 1960s was Wayne Roye, a former Mobil Oil geologist who was consulting for Claytie's business associate Jack McCall. Heavy-set, rusty-haired, and square-jawed, Roye was a University of Texas graduate Claytie described as "bright, strongly opinionated, and hardheaded as a mule." While Haverlah performed his magic as a trader, Roye's geological expertise in the Delaware Basin proved brilliant.

"These two guys played very important roles in my career during the '60s and '70s," Claytie said. "Wayne not only brought the mapping of the Coyanosa Field in that area but did regional mapping for us. With Wayne, I had access to real, solid geology for the first time."

Claytie also was gaining access to a growing line of credit, due not only to his increasing credibility but also to a fast friendship with banker Karl Butz, whom friends called Buddy. He was Claytie's classmate at Fort Stockton High School and his teammate on the Panthers football team.

"Buddy and I were born in the same bed in the same town, but I was born four days earlier, so we were friends from birth," he liked

Buddy and Connie Butz in Mexico

to remind associates. "He went to the University of Texas when I went to A&M, but we always remained in touch."

Buddy, like Claytie, hailed from pioneering stock. "His grandfather settled in this area right after my grandfather," Claytie said. "We played sports together—he was an all-around athlete. Our mothers were best friends, and we dated the same girls. I even dated his wife, Connie, before they married."

Claytie had quietly turned to Buddy and Connie for consolation and support during the difficult days of his divorce from Betty. It was also Buddy, then a loan officer at the Bank of the Southwest in Houston, who recommended that Claytie move his banking to the reputable First National of Midland.

"In fact, First National was almost like God to the oilmen of Midland," Claytie said. The bank was run by John Butler and C. J. Kelly, the latter a powerful and prominent Midland figure with whom Claytie was later destined to clash in a most unforgettable fashion. In the meantime, as Claytie moved toward the go-go 1970s, he was content to work with a First National loan officer named Charles Frazier, a former engineer for Mobil Oil.

"I had a fine relationship with Charlie and the First National," he said, "though Charlie, like many good bankers, did enjoy the power he held over his customers. We were great friends and took some grand fishing trips together."

As oil and gas prices fluctuated, so did Claytie's fortunes, but they tended to improve as he rolled through the '60s and into what loomed as the spectacular '70s. Not everything he touched turned to gold, but an impressive amount did.

It would be a peculiar but inspired mix of black gold and black cows.

Hardly had the 1970s blossomed when a young Fort Stockton man named Sam Pfiester appeared at Claytie's yearly winter wingding known as "deer camp." Under the spell of cheap peach brandy, he decided it would be great fun being part of the Williams empire—which consisted then of six employees. "You gotta be two out of three," Claytie told young Sam. "You gotta be shorter than me, you gotta be from Fort Stockton, and you gotta be a Texas Aggie." Pfiester was two out of three: "I ain't no Aggie."

Soon there was an opening, sort of. The tempestuous office manager Wynona Riggs, fresh from another clash with Claytie, "had quit for the fifth time," he said. Claytie threw Wynona a big going-away party, then escorted Pfiester around the office, gave him a desk, and outlined his duties.

Two hours later, Sam recalled, Wynona stormed in, spotted him working at his desk, and said, "Who in the hell are you and what are you doing at my desk?"

With Wynona back in charge, Claytie shuffled Pfiester off to Florida to open a new Pensacola office, which, Sam said, consisted of renting some space and buying some furniture. "By the way," he remembered Claytie saying, "I've got a bass boat on Falcon Lake. Go get that and get you a trailer hitch. Here is a new car, and here is five hundred dollars cash."

Pfiester was speechless. "I thought, OK, five hundred dollars cash, a new car with a trailer hitch, go get a bass boat and open an office in Florida. It doesn't get any better than this—and the truth is, it didn't. That was the peak. . . . But he was a shooting star and I hitched onto it."

The first rude awakening, aside from the abrupt return of Wynona to her desk, came at Falcon Lake when an older fellow confronted him while he was hooking up Claytie's bass boat.

"What in the hell are you doing?" the man asked.

"Isn't this Claytie's boat?" Pfiester replied.

"Yeah," said Modesta's father, Dick Simpson. "He gave it to me."

"Well, I don't think so, because I'm taking it to Pensacola, Fla.," said Sam, realizing belatedly that Claytie had sent him to reclaim the boat without telling his father-in-law.

"I was the messenger without the message," he sighed.

"Well, I guess we'll have to buy this damn ranch!"

On an early spring day in 1972, Claytie and Modesta drove from Fort Stockton to look at a Davis Mountain ranch north of Alpine. They had visited the area previously, and Claytie knew the Willie Henderson Ranch was under grass lease to one of the Southwest's most exceptional cattlemen, Ted Gray of Alpine. Gray had given them permission to take another look as potential buyers.

They drove along the top of Black Canyon and stopped to gaze at the dazzling panoramic view below. Spotting a windmill rising from the starkly beautiful ranchland, Modesta's eyes began to tear. Claytie spotted the teardrops and said with a sigh and a smile, "Well, I guess we'll have to buy this damn ranch!"

With Ted Gray's assistance and cooperation, they did, agreeing to pay it out in monthly payments over ten years.

"We had the ranch under contract almost a year before we actually took possession, and that allowed Modesta and me to spend a lot of time roaming around and camping on it, hiking over it, riding over it, and spending a great deal of time with Ted," Claytie said. "He was one of the best cowmen and cowboys that I had ever known, and he taught me the workings of the ranch and how he operated it."

For both Claytie and Modesta, ranching was a joyful endeavor, one they had dreamed about. "When we were dating, we always hoped that we could make enough money so that we could buy a ranch," Modesta said. "Well, finally we made enough money to

Claytie's mentor, cattleman Ted Gray

Modesta and Claytie on the Alpine Ranch

make a down payment. For us, ranching is one of the basics of life. It's the love of land, sky, and animals. Once you've had a taste of it, it's awfully hard not to go back to it."

Not all of Claytie's attempts at improvement succeeded, but most of his grassland and water-spreading systems and storage innovations did. Some of his pioneering water developments could be traced to the techniques learned when he built the Coyanosa and Belding pipelines and irrigated his dad's Fort Stockton farm.

"To me, there's true joy and happiness in stopping erosion and improving the productive capacity of the land. Growing up on my dad's ranch, with its poor land, always left me wanting something better. I do love the oil business, but I also love the land and seeing what I can do to make it better. This ranch and the friends and acquaintances that grew from it have been one of the great joys and a source of happiness to Modesta and me and our families."

Range improvements at Alpine Ranch, 1978: Claytie loves his grasses!

In an interview with *Texas Business* magazine, Claytie said that having embraced many phases of the highly chancy petroleum industry, he felt an investment in land was more secure. "After being in oil so long, I had enough assets to buy a ranch. When you're an oilman [and facing depletion of your oil reserves], you ultimately want to own something that's permanent. We all know that someday the wells will run dry, which makes you somewhat insecure. Conversely, the ownership of land is something solid and permanent. Because of my agricultural roots, I was dying to own my own ranch."

Soon after he acquired the ranch—the first of more than a dozen he would eventually own—Claytie added two new companies to his burgeoning oil and gas operations. With Clajon Gas the evergrowing and flowing flagship of the financial fleet, Claytie formed Williams Partnership in 1975 and Williams Exploration in 1976. But, with Happy Cove Ranch in the mix, he also flirted with serious involvement in the ranching and cattle business. Williams Ranches, a cow-calf operation launched in 1975, preceded Williams Brangus, a Texas-registered purebred cattle operation that would establish him as a major player in something other than energy.

The goat-raising, insurance-peddling, wildcatter-in-training was about to become a real-live cowboy.

Although not yet rolling in dough, Claytie's far-flung companies were on the upswing when a dynamic young woman named Sandy Jones joined the Williams merry-go-round in 1973. Her husband was fresh out of the army, living in Midland, and working for Phillips Petroleum, which was how she met geologist Wayne Roye, one of Claytie's closest friends and executives and a dedicated party animal. Sandy told Roye she knew nothing about the oil business except how to spell *oil,* but he hired her anyway for the Midland office. A month later, she still had not met the boss, who was living in Fort Stockton, and when Claytie did schedule a visit to Midland, Roye neglected to tell her. Such was the background when the boss arrived at the office unannounced and unknown to his company's first secretary.

"I'm sitting at the reception desk feeling so important learning how to do all this oil business stuff and in comes this little guy walking right past my desk telling me to do this, this, this, and that," recalled Sandy. "He just never stopped, never introduced himself, just went right into Wayne Roye's office. I'm like, 'What in the world? Who in the world is that?' So I kind of sat there for a minute, and I'm thinking, 'Who are all these people he named off to call?' I don't know who these people are! There were all kinds of people coming in anyway, and I thought, 'I'm not going to do what that guy told me to do; I don't know who he is.' But I am looking through this Rolodex and in a few minutes he comes storming out of Wayne's office and says, 'I thought I told you to call so-and-so.' I thought, 'Now this is ticking me off just a little bit; who does this guy think he is?' I stood up and said, 'For one thing, I do not know who so-and-so is, and who the heck are you, anyway?' About this time I see Wayne Roye standing behind Clayton, just laughing like crazy. I thought, 'What's so funny?' And then I guess it hit Clayton, too, because he said, 'I forgot to introduce myself; I'm Clayton Williams.'

"Could I have died? I thought, 'Oh, my Lord, I'm going to be fired. I haven't even been on the job long enough to get my first paycheck and I'm going to be fired.' But it didn't bother him a bit. He slowed down and said, 'OK, here's who I need you to call,' and he gave me this list of people and let me write the names down. I thought, 'Oh, my gosh, I can't believe I've done this.' Eventually, I got used to it, but that first introduction was a doozy."

The year 1973 rivaled the mid-'60s in Claytie's hectic landmark series of decisions, acquisitions, and activities. He and Modesta moved from Fort Stockton to Midland, where they kept an apartment until they built a home. Having adopted his father's philosophy that a person needed a "solid" place to live and work, he set about finding a suitable office for him and his growing staff. He learned the Gulf Building was for sale and struck a deal with the out-of-state owner with financing through his bank line of credit.

"Trouble soon arose," Claytie recalled in an understatement. The same seller had given a letter of intent to sell to First National, the local banking institution headed by C. J. Kelly.

Claytie brought in Midland attorney Tom Scott to help resolve the issue. Scott talked with Kelly's lawyers and was convinced their client would not sue. He advised Claytie to pursue the purchase. "I went over to see Mr. Kelly to thank him for being so considerate in letting me buy the building," Claytie recounted. "He blew his top and ran me out of his office. Even an Aggie could realize he had not intended for me to have the building. He wanted it for his own expansion."

Hoping to avoid making the "God of the oil field" angrier, Claytie tried through lawyer Scott to reach an accommodation. That failed, and Kelly sued.

"I quickly acquired the largest A&M flag I could find and raised it from atop the Gulf Building's flagpole—directly across from the First National," said Claytie, his defiance bristling. "It was my battle cry and my response to the lawsuit." The confrontation between "the big bank" and the "country boy" generated much whiskey talk in the Midland clubs and honky-tonks. Claytie took possession and moved his people in, and, after additional haggling, the lawsuit was dropped.

Claytie admitted later he regretted the incident because it did nothing to endear him to the bank directors and supporters. The matter could have been settled amicably, he said, except for the "hardheadedness of C. J. Kelly . . . and to a lesser extent, of myself."

Less than a decade after his abrupt departure from Claytie's employ, Bill Haverlah was still ranching in South Texas in the early and mid-1970s and intermittently fending off Claytie's offers to return. "I was down there farming and ranching, and I was just happy as a lark," Haverlah said. That changed after the government wrecked his ranching business with a flurry of clever federal "programs." Attending Claytie's annual deer camp at the Matrix ranch south of Fort Stockton during that volatile period, he was a bit more receptive.

"Man, there's a big play going on down here in South Texas," he told Claytie. "I don't know whether you want in on it or not, but it's the old Austin Chalk play. It's been around for years, but it's not been very economic."

"Are the leases expensive?" wondered Claytie, who had long been intrigued by the Austin Chalk and had been quietly researching its potential.

"Oh, no, they're cheap."

Claytie, who had great respect for Haverlah as a landman despite his perceived annoyances, dearly wanted his friend to join him in another journey into the oil-patch unknown.

"Why don't you go back to work for me?"

"I'm not going back to work for a salary, Clayton," Haverlah said. "With you, I'm not gonna be a servant. I'll work for you, but it's gonna be on a commission basis, and I want an override on everything that I do."

"Aw," drawled Claytie, "you're tough."

"Clayton, there's no way I can work for you. You're too damn hardheaded. I'm hardheaded, too. I've had one round of that, and that's enough."

Sandy Jones quickly found working for Claytie similarly challenging. While on a plane trip with Sam Pfiester, Wayne Roye, and a couple of their coworkers in early 1975, Claytie learned during lunch that Modesta was pregnant. He hustled everyone back on the Sabre jet and instructed the pilot to return to Midland. He did not tell his travel companions why he was rushing home. "Everybody was quiet, thinking something bad had happened," Pfiester recalled, and Claytie said, "Naw, you all come over to the house tonight."

Pfiester was skeptical. "I've seen that trick before," he explained. "My dad, when he'd been drinking, he'd throw his hat at the door to kind of see if anybody shot at him. So when Claytie wanted us to come over, I figured we were his hat."

Meanwhile, Claytie contacted Sandy. "I want you to get eight dozen roses to the house, and I want to have a party tonight, and I want you to alert everybody, and I want you to tell them to be there at seven o'clock," Sandy quoted Claytie as saying excitedly. Why eight dozen? Nobody knows, not even Claytie, whose spirited and spontaneous lifestyle had already begun to mystify the multitudes. At his insistence, Sandy told no one the reason for the party. But that was not her biggest concern at the moment. "Oh my Lord," she thought, "it's the middle of the afternoon, and where am I going to find eight dozen roses?"

Somewhere—somehow—she did.

Among the first to arrive that night were Roye and Pfiester, who was destined to become exploration manager. They showed up together and immediately spotted the profusion of flowers. Instantly alarmed and suspicious, Roye turned to his cohort and issued that immortal exhortation: "Let's get out of here. . . . There's no telling what the little son of a bitch has done this time!"

Midlanders accustomed to seeing the maroon-and-white flag rippling insolently above Claytie's office building discovered something curious when they arrived downtown on an October morning in 1975. Attached to the flagpole and fluttering in the West Texas breeze was a pink baby blanket. It signaled no new effete war cry; instead, it heralded the birth of Claytie and Modesta's daughter, Chicora Modesta Williams, whom they called Chim.

Chim arrived on Claytie's birthday, October 8, and Sandy Jones was prepared. Inspired by an idea from Claytie, she and Roye and another of their colleagues acquired the huge pink blanket to fly above the Gulf Building.

"We had to alert everybody that Modesta's baby had arrived and that it was a girl," Sandy said.

Sandy couldn't count all the times she decided to quit during her nine years, but she would stay until the birth of her only child, Jill, in 1982. "It really was the best of times," despite — or maybe because of — all the craziness. "I would not hesitate to do it all again."

Sandy's pregnancy, in fact, would lend itself to one of Claytie's favorite stories. She was sitting in the office one day suffering obvious and great discomfort. "I just feel so bad," she moaned.

Claytie responded in white-hat fashion: "Well, why don't you take off this afternoon?"

Sandy bristled. "Don't tell me what to do!" she snapped.

It was an episode of perpetual grumpiness that led longtime colleague Bernie Scott to observe of Sandy and another expectant office mate, Lana Loyd: "The best two arguments for birth control, right there — Sandy and Lana."

Bernie figured in another of the early Claytie stories that became company lore. The boss admonished Bernie once for rejecting an offer to the Williams energy complex to join in the development of an oil well.

"Why'd you do that?" Claytie demanded.

"Because you told me to," Bernie said.

"You should've known better," grumped Claytie.

Aside from their periodic clashes, Claytie agreed that the nine years between Sandy's arrival and departure coincided with the best of times: "Those were the days—1972, 1973, to 1982—it was just straight up. Oil went from $2.50 to $40 and gas went from 50 cents to $6 or $8. It was amazing how much work we got done."

And besides his renowned ups and downs, his "Claytieisms" were becoming part of the company lexicon, such as:

"All I knew about banking was borrowing."

"Never let the tax tail wag the business dog."

"I believed strongly in the principle of OPM: Other People's Money."

A long-ago Associated Press story noted how Claytie was "as cunning as a coyote and often as wily," and how he "rose from a ten-thousand-dollar-a-year insurance peddler to oil multimillionaire in a roller coaster quarter century punctuated with good luck, bad luck, hard work, cold beer, and the competitive, indomitable spirit of a pit bulldog." He would in fact name one of his most difficult wells *El Chato,* Spanish for "bulldog."

As busy as he was in those early years of marriage, Claytie did find time one night to steal a car after a spat with Modesta. "I was still kind of a wild man in those days," he admitted. "I had a lot of energy and I drank a lot, and I drank too much that night. I was pretty miffed, and I walked out of a landman's meeting at the Midland Country Club and for some reason I got in the back of somebody's car [to lie down]. It was idiotic. Somebody could have shot me."

Conceding that "the Lord protects fools and drunks," Claytie awoke to discover that a late norther had blown in that spring night and he was "cold, miserable, starting to sober up," and asking himself, "What am I doing in this car?"

He tried to reenter the clubhouse but the doors were locked. He pounded on the doors but got no response. Modesta was long gone and only a handful of cars remained on the parking lot. Afoot, he started the long trek to town in the middle of the night when he was struck by a less than sober thought: "I wonder if somebody left their keys in their car."

Sure enough, somebody did.

"What's my choice?" he shrugged. "I can't sit there and freeze. So I got in that car—I stole that car—and I drove it to town. I parked in front of the Downtowner, which was the motel and bar of choice at the time and where we were staying."

Late the next morning, he showed up at the office, ran into his executive sidekick Bob Smith, and said, "Boy, you'll never believe what I did last night." When told about the stolen car, Smith burst out laughing. It seems that a close friend of Claytie's, Charlie Perry, a former SMU football player, was out at the club playing poker into the wee hours. After the game broke up, Perry discovered his car missing. "Smith," he said, "some son of a bitch stole my car from the country club." He called the police. Later that morning, an officer called Perry and said, "Well, Mr. Perry, are you sure what happened? Your car is in front of the Pub [at the Downtowner]. Don't you think you just left it there yourself?"

Claytie says every time he sees Charlie Perry now, Charlie says, "Where the hell are my car keys?"

It was fortuitous for Claytie that circumstances had led him to renew his banking relationship with longtime friend Buddy Butz. The son of a Pecos County banker, Butz had become president of First National Bank of Fort Worth, and he granted Claytie an oil loan to follow through on a new engineering report, setting up a revolving credit line of $3.5 million.

"Buddy was one of those rare bankers who wanted to help and nourish his customers, rather than mash on 'em like many bankers did," Claytie said. "With his help and guidance, my business grew from a loan capacity of the original $3.5 million to nearly $500 million by the fall of 1981."

Also with Butz's help, the Williams companies would grow from fifteen employees in 1972 to twelve hundred by 1981. While Butz never did anything contrary to the best interests of the bank, Claytie emphasized, "he was always supportive and encouraging and as my business grew; he took me to meet the chairmen of each of the new banks we brought into the line of credit."

The list of banks eventually included First National of Alpine, Republic of Dallas, First Guaranty of Mississippi, Capitol and First City National of Houston, Security Pacific, Wells Fargo and Union Bank of California, Continental Illinois of Chicago, Manufacturers Hanover of New York, First of Fort Worth, and the lead bank, Mercantile-M Bank of Dallas—where Butz moved to from the First of Fort Worth.

In a moment of reflection, Claytie once declared: "Karl, as he was known professionally, did more to nourish my business career than any other single person. . . . He was my best friend and confidante." Ironically, in 1987 Claytie and Butz had a falling out linked to the sale of Clajon, a pipeline deal mediated by one of Claytie's young executives. The disagreement mystified and upset Claytie and lingered, unresolved and unsettling, into the twenty-first century. "It was just a misunderstanding; that's all it was," Claytie said. Just as ironically, it was another Mercantile-M Bank executive who paid Claytie the ultimate compliment after a banking relationship dating to the late 1970s. Retired and living in a lake home outside Dallas, Dan Preston told a reporter that good bankers look for character in a borrower, the kind of person who honors the covenants of a loan in good times and bad—"and it was almost always tough times in the oil business."

Said Preston: "You try to avoid those who won't do that and cling to those who will, and Claytie Williams has consistently shown himself to have the highest character in both his professional and personal relationships."

Claytie prized his banking relationships. On the way to conclude a deal in Seattle once, he, Mel, and Paul realized they didn't have the money to complete the transaction. Paul said they called an Amarillo banker named Mike Mitchell from their limousine and said, "Mike, we need a three-million-dollar line of credit or we're going to have to call off the deal." Mike wanted the deal to happen, Paul added, "and we got the line of credit — in the car."

The deal was done with only minutes to spare, at a price unexpectedly favorable to Claytie.

"It was the wildest damn day of my life," said Mel.

Said Claytie: "Our banker made it happen."

"Don't mix alcohol with business, whether it's oil or cows."

With the dawn of the pivotal '70s, more of Claytie's ventures began turning profits, and his fledgling registered cattle enterprise was poised to become both a financial and social bonanza extending deep into the next decade. After making the down payment on the Alpine ranch in 1972, he told Ted Gray, the ranch tenant: "I'd like to meet all the area ranchers. Modesta and I want to be part of the ranching community." And they did so with typical Claytie gusto. Striving to be the best, eventually they would rank among the top commercial cattle operators in the United States with a one-time peak of twelve thousand mother cows.

His early ranching efforts concentrated on cows such as Herefords, but in 1975 he launched his registered purebred business, and his choice was Brangus, a cross of three-eighths Brahman and five-eighths Angus.

Claytie recalled from his A&M studies that the Brahman's superb qualities included heat tolerance, disease resistance, hardiness, ranging ability, and mothering abilities, though it was an animal with somewhat lower fertility and disposition and less marbling of the meat. "On the other hand, the Angus is more of a northern animal that is highly fertile, has the best marbling of the meat, and is becoming more popular in the South," explained Claytie.

Because a purebred operation requires good nutrition and good grass year-round, Claytie knew his Alpine ranch was not the ideal location for his new enterprise. While looking for a suitable place, his old friend Frank Velasco from the Fort Stockton Jaycee election days told him about a 320-acre irrigated farm for sale in Belding.

"I looked at it and bought it," Claytie said. "Frank already had a farm in the area and I got him to run my farm for me. That was 1974 or 1975 and he's been running my farms for me ever since."

Claytie also adopted the philosophy of an old rancher who once said he didn't want much land — just his own ranch and, of course, all the land that joined it. "One by one, we added farms from unsuccessful cotton farmers [including some from his dad's old ranch] until we had a total of almost six thousand acres of irrigated farmland with a total of thirty-two wells that would average almost two thousand gallons of water a minute. Over the years, we've farmed many crops, including forage crops, cotton, and alfalfa, but principally the operation is now totally devoted to farming high-quality alfalfa for dairy farmers and horse people."

Early in his Brangus enterprise, Claytie bought the cheapest animals, but he soon detoured sharply. "Modesta and I started buying the very best, and before long, we understood the game. Every time we'd attend a sale, we would buy the top female or the top bull. People would read about it and say, 'Well, gosh, that Williams guy's building a heck of a herd. He always pays the most money and buys the best.' We nearly always topped the sales. It was a little bit about the cattle business, lots about purebred breeding, more about salesmanship, and a whole lot more about *showmanship*."

In the mid-'70s, Claytie and Modesta attended a Brangus sale in Kerrville, studiously inspected the animals, selected the best of the herd, and bid on the ones they wanted. Afterward, they celebrated their purchases with several rounds of drinks. It was then that they spotted a "beautiful animal" entering the sales ring. "How did we overlook that?" Claytie exclaimed, hopping up and heading back into the sale area to resume bidding. Back at the ranch two weeks later, Claytie spotted a "little bitty animal" and wondered where the tiny heifer came from. "She's pretty," he said, "but she's like a dwarf." They checked the auction records and sure enough, that was the "whiskey-influenced" purchase.

Claytie giving instructions to ranch manager Guadalupe "Chappo" Ramirez

They kept that "Scotch Heifer" as a vivid reminder: "Don't mix alcohol with business, whether it's oil or cows."

After Claytie conducted his own first sale, he made another far-reaching decision: "If I'm gonna have people come from Houston or Dallas to Alpine," he said, "it's got to be an *event*. They're not gonna come just to buy cattle. So we made it a 'happening.'" It became *the* event in Brangus and a good excuse for a country bash—as if Claytie ever needed an excuse. By the late 1970s, the parties would take on a life of their own.

Claytie hired an excellent cowman, Gary Bruns, who grew up in a South Dakota Angus family, to oversee his cattle operations. "Gary was absolutely the top manager in the Brangus breed," he said. Bruns managed the registered cattle at the farm in Fort Stockton and later in Floresville, and the enterprise took off. "We always had the sales at Alpine because of the scenery and romance of the Davis Mountains, and the cattle country mystique."

Said Bruns: "I worked with him for seventeen years, and we had some great times."

Tom T. Hall and Danny Davis and the Nashville Brass headlined the early parties, which were cohosted by their ranching friends Ted and Addie Gray. Claytie described these as just "fun parties" and the guest list included mostly local ranch people, friends from Fort Stockton, and others in the oil and gas business.

But the serious partying was about to begin.

In 1978, three thousand people showed up for the first Brangus sale and postsale revelry at the Alpine ranch. Fifty-nine animals sold for nearly a quarter-million dollars, an average of $4,230 a head. The second sale a year later grossed $589,800, and the third produced $2 million-plus.

The parties cost a bundle, but the sales more than covered expenses. San Antonio auctioneer Bert Reyes told reporters the 1983 sale brought more money than any he had conducted in twenty-three years of auctioneering. (So intent was Claytie to sell his guests something—*anything*—at these spirited gatherings, he once parked a truck out by the side of the road to sell them hay.)

"Country-western singer Charley Pride and his band entertained during the postsale party before some five thousand people who attended the daylong, invitation-only affair," reported columnist Scott Campbell of the *San Angelo Standard-Times*. "Sheriff's deputies checked invitations along the caliche road to the Alpine ranch and young women, decked out in T-shirts and shorts, served drinks along the route and during the sale and party."

So consuming were the festivities that Claytie and Modesta prepared well for the onslaught: a long soak in their big bathtub the morning before the sale. "We'd just talk about the plans and events for the day and who would be coming," Modesta said. "Each of us had so many things that we had to do and take care of

Bull "650," prize sire of Claytie's Brangus herd, with Gary Bruns at far right

that our parting words to each other were always 'See you in the morning.'"

Said Claytie: "We'd sit in the tub, in the whirlpool, and we'd kind of get psyched up for the day. And it became somewhat of a ritual. Then she'd go her way and I'd go mine. I've always enjoyed her self-sufficiency, her independence."

Claytie pulled out all the stops, his flair for showmanship surfacing once again. Campbell reported how Claytie's fleet of six planes, flying in formation, made a swooping dive over the festivities while his maroon-and-white helicopter delivered guests nonstop between the Alpine airport and Happy Cove Ranch. "Gig 'em Aggies" stickers adorned gates and Aggie flags fluttered overhead.

"It was quite a day!" the columnist declared.

Best-selling author-historian James Michener attended the Brangus extravaganza twice, first with Claytie's childhood friend,

Austin socialite-philanthropist Jane Dunn Sibley. "He was enthralled," she said. "We were staying at our ranch east of Alpine and we took him into town and then out to the ranch for the cattle sale." When Jane wanted to leave for a rest break, Michener wouldn't budge. He got caught up in the party atmosphere, she said, "and he just would not leave that spectacle."

Jane said she and her husband had given Claytie a pregnant burro for a charitable fund-raising auction, and when she returned that afternoon most everyone was boozed up, and a man from Uvalde bought the obese ass for $5,000, $7,500, or $9,000, depending on who's telling the story. The man was accompanied by his wife when he went up to claim his prize, and the wife, with a nod to the burro, announced to one and all: "You know, that's not the only jackass here." Laughing, Jane recalled that "Jim Michener was totally immersed in the whole thing."

Determined to discover further evidence of the genuine Texas experience, Michener would make a third trip to far West Texas. For his book research, Michener wanted to tour Fort Davis, one of the Southwest's best surviving examples of an Indian Wars frontier outpost. So Claytie hosted the author on a sweeping visit via helicopter, instructing his pilot to land on the fort grounds set hard against the rugged beauty of the Davis Mountains. A state park ranger officiously confronted the visitors, warning he would issue a citation if they didn't leave immediately—and take their helicopter with them.

"Well, how much would a citation cost?" Michener recalled Claytie asking. Impressed by his host's rejoinder, Michener would delight in telling others he found Claytie's response "very Texan."

Claytie also introduced Michener to a blood-stained floor at the Brite Ranch, the result of a raid on Christmas Day 1917 by Mexican bandits who, as the story goes, hung the local postman from a rafter by his feet and slit his throat. Then, in a decidedly more palatable introduction, Claytie treated Michener to one of his favorite culinary pleasures: the cream gravy–smothered chicken fried steak so revered at Chicken Charlie's in Balmorhea. And, finally, in the pièce de résistance of Texas experience, Claytie commanded the pilot to land at the ranch of "Windmill Man" and party cohort David Ligon. Fortunately, one might argue, the course of Texas letters as well as the great author's decorous bearing escaped unsullied when the airborne visitors found no one home.

Claytie's fund-raising auctions became a fixture of the cattle sales. The proceeds were earmarked for the Chihuahuan Desert Research Institute, which is dedicated to the study of animals and plants of the Chihuahuan Desert of Southwest Texas and Mexico. He is a director and benefactor of the CDRI, and when pregnant white burros weren't available, Claytie auctioned off everything from ostriches and zebras to buffalo. One year he persuaded a festive buyer to shell out twenty-five thousand dollars for a plaque on a rock for the desert institute.

Because of his ancestors' Scottish blood on the Graham side, Claytie once hired a Scottish band, bagpipes and all, to perform at his sales parties. He showed up in Scottish garb, including a kilt, but decorated his uniform with maroon cowboy boots and a Mexican sombrero. "I was a cross-bred everything," he chortled. "A Scottish Mexican Aggie, or something."

If things got slow at the sales, he jumped in the ring himself. "People would start having fun, and fun was a big part of it," he said. Though such actions might have seemed yet another excuse for Claytie to revel among friends, longtime oil-field crony Stan Beard offers a more pragmatic and revealing perspective of his friend's mind for business. "At one of the Brangus sales when things were getting slow, Claytie jumped down in the sale pen and began pawing around in all that cow manure. It just totally woke everybody up and they started bidding again. Now the normal observer would say that Claytie had allowed himself to have a little nip and that he lost it and was just showing off. No! It was a calculated thing he was doing—it was a business move: if he would put himself in the position to do something [crazy] like that, it would be funny and also

Claytie and family lead the National Anthem at 1982 ranch party

would inspire everyone—wake them up—to start bidding again. And it did. . . . The point is, what you see is not always really exactly what's going on. There was some business calculation in there."

One time the bidding on a super prize animal had slowed after reaching maybe ninety thousand dollars. Claytie bounded into the ring and was doing his bull bit when a lady hollered, "I'll buy him!" Modesta hollered back, "You can have him!" After Claytie's bullish performance that day, the animal sold for nearly two hundred thousand dollars.

"That's when people had tax deductions," Claytie said. "They had money to spend, and they wanted to show it. One sale, I think it was in '83, there were ninety-one jet airplanes at the Alpine airport. And I thought, 'Well, these people are looking for a place to fly their jets and spend their money,' and I was just trying to help."

Beard believes there's more than meets the eye: "I consider Clayton to be a near genius in many areas of business, and that just

Claytie beating the drum and hamming it up at a cattle sale

doesn't always come across because he's so colorful and so self-effacing." Beard, who has worked and socialized with Claytie for more than four decades, says, "He's just willing to really appear foolish in order to accomplish what he wants. And not many guys in his category are willing to do that."

Beard describes Claytie—"He was a lease broker when I first met him"—as someone in whom he sees much to admire and appreciate, a substantive side to the man that, unfortunately, can elude

Claytie doing whatever it takes to make the sale

those who don't know him. Even while regaling one with stories of Claytie's engaging Brangus escapades, Beard cites Claytie's success as a chief executive: "He's created more millionaires than any single individual I personally know. It tells you a lot about a guy when people who have worked with him have become wealthy."

As Claytie's companies grew, the Brangus-sale guest list mushroomed to include people who probably wouldn't know a bull from a boar hog. But with entertainers such as George Strait, Merle Haggard, and Charley Pride, it mattered not. The postsale parties and dances extended into the wee hours. Modesta remembers, maybe a little wistfully, the ritual of flicking off the lights around 4 A.M., trudging up the hill to the ranch house, and collapsing into bed.

Claytie thinks the peak attendance of eight thousand occurred in 1984, the same year he staged a nationally televised Brangus heifer sale in the atrium at the new ClayDesta Plaza in Midland. With

Stan Beard with Claytie: old friends at Christmas

"tall, sexy, slinky" models standing by, each of the prize animals arrived at the auction block wearing a string of pearls around its neck. "We'd take the pearls off after each sale and put them on the next cow," Claytie said. "We didn't sell the pearls."

Although prices were high, Claytie had grown increasingly nervous about the direction the Brangus business was headed. In the spring of 1985, he sold off his older cows and in July he dispersed his entire herd. "I sold eleven hundred head at an average of fifty-five hundred dollars a head in the main dispersal, and a few months later the price collapsed. But I was already out of Brangus by then, thank the Lord. We sold $11 million worth of purebred cattle in a year's time."

Operations manager Bruns said if they had waited three months, they would have reaped less than a third of the proceeds. "The energy business went down and the cow business went down with it. Clayton pulled the trigger at just the right time. It was incredible."

Three years later, Claytie got back in the Brangus business with Bruns but to a less spectacular degree. Still, it was big news in 1995 when Claytie sold his operation to Eric and Carolyn White of New Braunfels, who bought the herd with Bruns as managing partner. At the time, Bruns was president of the International Brangus Breeders Association.

"Clayton and Modesta will be missed by all of us," Bruns told the *Brangus Journal* after the sale of Claytie's second herd. "Their love of cattle, their enthusiasm, and their desire to continually improve the industry has made a lasting impression on Brangus, and they are largely responsible for the popularity the breed has today."

Three

The Go-Go Years: Blowouts, Blowups, Big Riches, and a Half-Billion-Dollar Debt

Controlling a wild well, Giddings, 1981

"It's going to be the biggest change in our lives — ever!"

For Claytie and Modesta Williams, New Year's Eve 1975 would be an event like no other in a lifetime overflowing with elegant parties, global hunting trips, glorious celebrations, and too many peaks and valleys to count. When the earth shook in the wee hours of that December morning, it was not triggered by another of their amorous adventures, although Claytie contended later the 1975 experience was probably the next best thing. His Gataga #2 gas well in remote Loving County in far West Texas had just struck what would be a life-altering — and life-threatening — $40 million payday.

"It was a huge event, and it changed our lives forever," Claytie noted.

Just a short time earlier, Claytie's rig on the outskirts of Mentone, Tex., population sixty-nine, had broken through the eighteen-thousand-foot mark without a hint of success or even a whiff of gas. On the evening of December 30, Wayne Roye, Claytie's exploration manager, showed him samples retrieved from the down-hole shale formation. "It's tight," Claytie observed. "It's starting to look like we're going to get a dry hole."

Then he thought: "So here I am. I've put everything on the line, spent all this money. Damn!"

With disappointment consuming him like a bad hangover, Claytie retired to his nearby trailer. "I went to bed, sick at heart." A few hours later, in the early-morning darkness of December 31, the trauma of a recurring dream gripped Claytie: he was drilling a well

Gataga! First big gas flow and well test, January 1976

so costly—and apparently so stunningly noncommercial—that it could devastate him financially. Everything he'd worked for could be imperiled. "I'm lying in the driller's trailer house brooding, half-asleep, and thinking I've just drilled another damn dry hole."

At 5:15 A.M. the desert began to shake with a thunderous roar. The drill bit had struck a seventeen-foot cavern containing natural gas at 18,722 feet, and a full column of fluid followed by gas began moving up toward the wellhead under abnormal pressure. The force of the flow, known in oil-patch parlance as the "initial kick," shook the ground. A full-fledged blowout usually followed, though not always immediately.

Roye ran to Claytie's trailer.

"Get out!" he yelled. "We've got to run. She's gonna blow."

The immediate danger was an explosion and fire, with poisoning also possible, for the gas contained hydrogen sulfide. Even in small amounts, hydrogen sulfide can be lethal, killing a person in minutes. Claytie and Roye began running, until they realized they were headed downwind—the direction the wind would push any toxic fumes.

"That's when we figured out the trailer was upwind," Claytie recalled, "so we circled back to the trailer. We were in shock. It was frightening." The trailer sat fifty yards from the well.

Then, amid the chaos of the initial kick, Claytie said, "'What do we do now?'"

What followed would be a daylong convulsion of oil-field drama, little-town danger, and big-time dreams—a lifeline of dreams for Claytie and Modesta.

Gataga #2 did not enjoy an easy birth. Claytie had drilled a Gataga #1 nearby—a noncommercial well. Nonetheless, he was confident the Gataga field had a fifty-fifty chance to produce. These were good odds, especially considering any risk could be cushioned by Claytie's robust finances: oil and gas prices were heading up, and Clajon was producing a healthy cash flow. All he lacked was adequate acreage under Railroad Commission requirements to drill another well within the gas-bearing formation. He hired Austin attorney Frank Douglas to confront major oil companies opposing his acreage-pooling argument. Douglas maintained that Claytie's total adjoining acreage did in fact satisfy the regulatory agency's rules.

"We had a full-scale fight in front of the Railroad Commission and we won," Claytie said. "We won because of Frank's adroit abilities and because it was the little guy against the big guy, and generally the commission will tend to try to favor the little guy."

The well known as Gataga #2 commenced drilling, finally, in the winter of 1974–75.

Back in the trailer, Claytie did the only thing that seemed natural: he went to bed. "He went to sleep thinking he was broke," said John Kennedy, Claytie's drilling and operations manager. Kennedy, who joined Claytie's company in 1998, can re-create from various sources—including some who were on the scene—how the Gataga #2 story unfolded that morning of December 31, 1975.

"The events have been told by so many, for so long that they sometimes seem like folklore," he said. "When Claytie went back to sleep, he'd gone through a whole range of emotions: from thinking 'I'm broke,' to 'I'm dead,' to 'I'm OK,' to 'Oh crap, this is what happened last time—I'm broke.' Fear, panic, boredom, depression, all in a day's time. It's typical in the oil patch, and sounds like something a bipolar person would go through—90 percent boredom and 10 percent panic. Or depression."

All denial aside, if Claytie went to sleep thinking he'd entertained a carnival of emotions, he was naively mistaken. The sideshow was a kick, all right, but it was just a warm up.

Awakening an hour or two later, Claytie discovered the ground still shaking and thought, "Maybe I'm *not* broke." After gathering his thoughts, he realized he was upwind and a safe distance from the toxic fumes now racing through the wellhead at an estimated equivalent of 220 million cubic feet a day. He also realized he wasn't likely to die or go broke unless he did something profoundly stupid. Taking stock of his life, he came to an inescapable conclusion: his life had just changed. Forever. But before he could contemplate a new life and therein all its glories, he had to tend to business, immediately.

Claytie called Modesta, waking her.

"You've got to find all the gas masks in Midland," he said.

It took a few seconds for Modesta to collect her wits. "Now where does a little housewife go looking for gas masks?" It was still dark outside. "What's going on? What's happening?"

Claytie explained: "You don't understand what this means. This is huge, a 'holy mackerel' type deal. It is going to be a huge change in our lives."

While Claytie was talking, Modesta kept trying to untangle a jumble of emotions and was thinking, "Where do I go find gas masks?"

"You don't understand what this *really* means," Claytie repeated. "It's going to be the biggest change in our lives—ever!"

Before Modesta could leave the house to find a load of gas masks in the Midland darkness, Claytie called back. Forget the gas masks, he said. The well operators had masks for all.

But not for all sixty-nine folks in nearby Mentone, where the houses shook.

The danger persisted. A spark from the rig could start an inferno. The gas could settle in low areas where people lived, killing them in minutes. Claytie, his people, and the drilling crew reacted promptly. They started calling for help and advice. This was not your typical blowout.

When Gataga's drill bit hit the cavern—an extremely rare occurrence, Kennedy said—the well lost its high-density drilling mud, or drilling fluid, as it is also known. Drilling mud is a well lubricant used to stabilize a formation and prevent fluids or gas from entering the well bore and creating a flow, kick, or blow of gas or oil.

"In a blowout, the mud either goes away [in Gataga #2, into a cavern] or it blows and you lose it," Kennedy said. "It all depends on the pressure of the gas and weight of the mud. If you don't have enough mud, gas will start pushing out of the hole. Once it starts, there's no stopping it."

It was Roye who estimated the blowout flow at 220 million cubic feet of gas daily, which, said Claytie, "was a hell of a lot of actual flowing gas, the most I'd ever had. Nobody ever had that." More than once, Claytie wondered if all his gas, all his riches, all his dreams were going to expire in the desert air. It was not a hollow concern.

The blowout flow translated into a commercial value of $440,000 per day. "Because we were not in control of the gas when it was blowing out, we weren't selling it; we were wasting it," Claytie said. "We couldn't light the gas because we were fearful the fire might flash back and burn the rig and everything else."

Claytie credits Parker Drilling's top well man, Charlie Richardson, with bringing calm and organization to the scene. "Chaos reigns until you have a plan, until a leader brings direction," Claytie maintains.

Richardson's tactic to control the well involved continuously pumping salt water under pressure into the well to overcome and contain the gas pressure below. "His plan was exactly right," Kennedy said. "Pump as much water as possible as fast as you can."

Quickly the phone calls went out — to Halliburton, to water haulers, to other supporting services. Everyone on the scene took responsibility for a critical chore. The sense of urgency permeated the landscape as surely as hydrogen sulfide reeks of rotten eggs.

Claytie: "The well people were at the wellhead preparing and supervising the hookup of the piping for the trucks, so they could start pumping salt water down to kill the well."

By midmorning Claytie and Modesta, along with friends Gary and Susie Burnett, who arrived at the scene with their motor home, all got their emergency assignment: evacuate Mentone.

"It was scary and exciting," Claytie said.

Modesta and Claytie tracked down Punk Jones, the sheriff. "We could have a real tragedy if the wind changes and the gas settles in low pockets like Mentone," Claytie told him.

"With help from the sheriff, we started going from house to house and telling people the situation and asking them to leave. Public officials, including state troopers, blocked traffic."

They urged everyone to go to Pecos, Kermit, or Fort Stockton and assured them Claytie's company would pay for all meals, lodging, and other inconveniences. Some resisted, including a stubborn and crippled old man Claytie threatened to personally carry out of his house. "I'd like to see you try," the old fellow bellowed.

The sheriff had to get him out.

At another house, they found an old man rocking in his chair and proclaiming defiantly, "I ain't going anywhere. I been here a lot longer than you kids and I ain't leaving."

Then the old man's wife grabbed Modesta's hand and said pleadingly, "Come help me, Honey."

Modesta followed the woman to her closet, where, after grabbing her coat, she retrieved three or four silver spoons. *Her life's treasure,* Modesta thought. The woman had decided to evacuate, but ol' George wouldn't move, except to rock a little.

"Well, George, I'm going," his wife said finally.

The rocking slowed. "Well . . . I think I will too. But no whipper-snapper is going to tell me how to leave."

Claytie: "We evacuated the whole town—those who were at home—in half a day. Of course, that was only forty-five people."

He promised to reimburse everyone for their evacuation expenses, but one old codger refused to accept Claytie's money. "Son, you don't owe me a damn thing," he said. "It's the first time in years I've had Mama in a motel on New Year's Eve!"

For thirty days after the blowout, ten trucks remained on standby pumping salt water down the well around-the-clock to keep it under control. Ordinarily, a blowout is controlled by pumping water down the drill pipe and circulating it up the casing. But circulation would not work in this instance. "There was no bottom to the well," Claytie explained. "We had many of the trucks in the Permian Basin standing by and we hooked them up, one at a time, to the Halliburton pump truck and just kept pumping. We controlled it for thirty days by continuously having one truck replacing another as we continued to pump salt water down the hole to control the pressure. We knew if we ever stopped pumping, it was gonna blow again. It's the only well I've known of that happening."

When Gataga #2 was completed, it provided one more dramatic encore for Claytie: "It was a little bit of irony—all the blowing and flowing when we were drilling, then we get that under control, and then, when we tried to complete the well, it was dead!" The well appeared depleted, and all the trouble, all the expense, all the great expectations . . . they suddenly seemed all for naught.

"Oh no!" Claytie thought.

Explained Kennedy: "They had pumped in hundreds of thousands of barrels of salt water to control the well, and when they went to complete it, the gas couldn't push the salt water out of the hole."

After several days of trying to restart the gas flow, the production crew dropped what's known as soap sticks into the hole. According to Kennedy, "The soap sticks create tiny bubbles under great pressure that act like a bubble bath, and that helps the salt water start moving." As the gas-filled bubbles rise up the hole and the water pressure lessens, they get bigger and bigger and increasingly push the water ahead of them. "It's kind of like a locomotive," he said. "You get it moving, it keeps going, it's got momentum."

When finally in production, the well flowed at thirty million cubic feet daily—a $60,000 gross—enough that the first two months' production would cover the well's $3.2 million drilling and blowout expenses. For his interest in the well, Claytie received about $40 million of more than $60 million in gross revenues the well produced over its three-year commercial life.

Though acquisition of the Alpine ranch acted as the springboard to the lucrative registered cattle undertaking, and Clajon Gas would be his most prominent ongoing moneymaker, it was Gataga #2 in sparsely populated Loving County in West Texas that propelled Claytie into the energy spotlight.

"It produced my first television interview," he laughed, recalling a well-site session with Midland television anchorman Mike Barker. "I learned how to do sound bites."

Thirty years later, Claytie's memories of that day remain steadfastly relevant and fresh, for as he told a writer: "It was the biggest thing that had happened to us. It changed our lives. It was so exciting. It was like making love to Modesta."

With the benefit of hindsight, Claytie also would realize that while Gataga and its aftermath signaled the beginning of a new era in the Williams business cycle, it was the previous two decades that set the stage for the overwhelming saga that lay ahead. During the tumultuous years dating to the startup with Johnny May, Claytie,

Jack McCall, and partners had been involved in more than three thousand courthouse-recorded transactions in a four-county area of West Texas—Pecos, Reeves, Ward, and Loving.

"I started from very small deals up to very substantial deals that reflected the growth of our operations," he said. The staggering numbers—3,124 to be exact—also mirrored the "immense amount of work and deals and transactions that I made during that twenty-year span." Almost all involved some aspect of oil-field operations, including mineral, royalty, and working interest deals; oil, gas, and mineral leases; overriding royalties; pooling agreements; gas contracts; and even such necessary evils as bank extensions, mortgages, powers of attorney, and much more.

"And these things involved many oil and gas leases in my role as a broker or a principal and assigning overrides to people like Wayne Roye and Bill Haverlah and others who helped me go forward," Claytie said. More than a hundred right-of-way courthouse filings illustrated the pipeline construction so vital to the growth and scope of Clajon Gas Co.

In their sheer magnitude, the records offer an overview of a life lived on a fast, upwardly mobile track that embraced many phases of the oil business that outsiders could never comprehend.

"I was a busy little fart," jokes Claytie. "I marvel somewhat that I had the energy and the drive to work that hard every day."

While conceding that her husband spent those two decades working hard and playing hard and rarely neglecting his fishing and hunting activities, Modesta stressed that Claytie devoted weekends and a month each summer solely to daughters Kelvie and Allyson who lived in Austin with their mother, Betty.

That time frame, ending as it did after Gataga, was packed with what Claytie called a lot of work, a lot of fun, a lot of good people, and a lot of happy memories.

"But by and large, those first twenty years were extremely important," Claytie notes, "because many of the big things that came along later could not have happened without that consistent, steady progress and growth."

With a wan smile, he remembered that several years into the business, and two or three years into his marriage, he and Modesta would frequently make the return trips from Midland to Fort Stockton with a couple of six-packs and a dictaphone. "I'd dictate different ideas and different thoughts as we drove back, and then the next day I'd give them to Wynona to transcribe and type up. What was interesting then, I'd read them and say, 'Boy, that's smart; that's really smart.'

"And then toward the end of the dictation, I'd say, 'Well, what dumb son of a bitch could have had that idea? That's stupid as hell.'"

Among the new employees swept into the madness of the mid-'70s was Nancy Carpenter, another spunky young woman who joined Wynona Riggs in the Fort Stockton office. She had no official job title or job description until twenty years later when she received a degree recognizing her as Top Hand Emeritus in the Williams Institute of Hard Knocks. Nancy was cited for two decades of "map colorin', acre plattin', record keepin', lease filin', draft payin', check coverin', well spottin,' landman trackin', mail totin', landowner pacifyin', farm administratin', typewriter bangin', truck weighin', fish farmin', ten-key calculatin', fish fry organizin', hoer schedulin', employee managin', beer haulin', and Chic watchin'."

The document was signed by "Clayton W. Williams Jr., Dean of Bovine Waste."

More than thirty years after joining the company, Nancy still worked for Claytie in Fort Stockton and would produce her "degree" when asked her job title. "Ever get the feeling you're working in a madhouse?" she once was asked. "Every day," she smiled. Nancy explained that Claytie gave new titles in lieu of pay raises.

"Our job description was diversified."

"It's just the way things were," concurred Wynona, who spent much of her adult life in Claytie's tumultuous business empire before retiring in the mid-'90s. "We'd have VIPs come into town and we'd be out there washing the office windows."

Even while chiding Wynona for selective and often hilarious memory lapses—if not just colorful revisions—Claytie says she did a "bang-up job" running the Fort Stockton office and lease-records department, virtually alone for many years. "In all those years, she never missed a rental payment on any one of the millions and millions of dollars of oil and gas leases, and there were thousands of them. That's important, because if you're a day late, you lose the lease and your entire investment in it. This was a major job."

Wynona created Claytie's lease-records department. "Most people come into an existing department and learn the business," he said. "She started it from the ground floor with eventually twenty-five women who had no experience in the management of oil and gas rental payments."

As if running such a critical department wasn't enough responsibility, Wynona had four kids to care for, including stepson Mel, who would one day join the company and become Claytie's chief financial officer. "She'd pick the kids up at lunch and take them where they needed to go, and then get them to their after-school activities," Claytie said. "But she was always at the office taking care of business and all those leases—not one she ever dropped. If she was hard-nosed and grumpy you can understand why."

One day in the 1980s Mel approached Wynona and, as casually as possible, said, "Guess what I did today." From her childrearing experience, Wynona sensed something ominous. "I went to work for Claytie."

"Are you out of your mind?" Wynona screeched. "What were you thinking?"

Realizing he was thrilled, she sighed and said, "Don't come whining to me the first time he chews your butt out."

Except for sometimes finding money to pay bills, perhaps the toughest of his assistants' diversified duties was squeezing thousands of Claytie's guests at the annual Brangus parties into hundreds of hotel rooms in Alpine, Marfa, Fort Davis, Marathon, Fort Stockton, and anyplace else with a bed for rent. "There might be seven thousand people invited and five hundred hotel rooms," recalls Sandy Jones, "and he expected everybody to get one that wanted one, which was impossible. We had more fights over those parties. . . ."

Shaking her head in amazement, she recalled Claytie's infamous commandment: "Just make it happen," he would say, usually while bounding out the door.

Wynona maintains that among the most significant events of her career was Claytie's marriage to Modesta, whom she calls "my kind of girl—she did the stuff to him I'd love to have done."

Besides chipping his tooth once with a right cross, what might that be?

"Claytie came to work one morning, and he had scratches. We'd been together a long time, but there were still some places I didn't go. So I said, 'Everything OK?' 'Yep.' The phone rang and Modesta said, 'I didn't touch him. He got caught in the fan.' I said, 'Oooh.' Claytie said, 'Who was that?' I said, 'Oh, Wife was just calling to inquire about your health.' He said, 'That little brown-haired girl—she *could* have killed me!'

"I said, 'No, she *should* have killed you.'"

"Wife," she revealed, was his favorite nickname for Modesta, and at various times she was "Baby Bubbles," "Sweetheart," "Sugar," "Sweagger," and "Mother Morals." Later, she became "The Velvet Hammer."

Asked when it was that Claytie mellowed, Wynona just scoffed. "I have no idea. I never really saw that part of him."

A classic example of what she did see in Claytie—and how Wife/Baby Bubbles/Mother Morals handled him—played out one evening in the 1970s.

At the time, Claytie's fierce work schedule had curbed some of his nocturnal revelry, but not all. Perhaps the most notable episode was the "Chipped Tooth Caper" that unfolded in a Midland nightspot. Claytie, Bob Smith, Bill Haverlah, and the gang, all married guys, were "fraternizing"—Claytie's word—with several young women after work when to everyone's surprise Modesta walked in.

Claytie's version: "It's like all those deals; it started out pretty innocent. There was a bunch of my friends sitting around a table in a bar getting whiskeyed up. One of the guys was a geophysicist, who claimed to be a *palm reader,* and before long all these pretty girls started coming over to the table to have their palms read. Modesta hit the room like a shotgun blast and my guys scattered like a covey of quail, but I couldn't get away. I was caught red-handed. I didn't see her until she grabbed me and sank her fingernails into my shoulders like an eagle pouncing on its prey."

Modesta struck with such predatory enthusiasm that night she later was christened "Little Eagle."

Her version: "We were supposed to have gone to a movie that evening—I'd arranged a babysitter—and Claytie didn't show up and didn't call. Finally, I just went on to the movie." Later, with no word from Claytie, she figured he just might be at one of his favorite bars. "I walked in the front door of the Sans Souci and I saw Bob Smith standing there. When he saw me he turned ghostly white. Ha!—he couldn't say anything because he knew everybody was caught red-handed. I walked around the corner and saw Claytie. And he was 'fraternizing,' if that's the word." Claytie says he was probably helping the geophysicist read palms—or, possibly, giving a young lady a neck massage.

By all accounts, the couple made quite a scene exiting the bar, because a waitress followed them out to the parking lot and was looking on when Modesta unleashed a stinging right cross to Claytie's jaw. The waitress stuck her head back in the bar and screamed for help: "Some woman's beating up her husband out here!"

Already furious with Claytie and with fire in her eyes, Modesta turned to the waitress. "You just hush if you don't want some of this, too!"

"She chipped my tooth," Claytie grumped, unaware that he had dropped his car keys when she smacked him.

"He thought he was invisible," Modesta said, adding that she should have got him with a left cross as well. Instead, she drove off and left her wounded mate to fend for himself. A friend from Tenneco took him home with him for the night and brought him back the next morning to look for his car keys.

"I told him I needed to get there before all the Exxon people go to work because I didn't want their head landman, Jack Nauman, to [drive by and] see me lurking around the bar this early in the morning. I was trying to make a deal of some sort with him." So there was Claytie crawling around on hands and knees in a parking lot looking for his car keys when someone appeared at his side.

"Mornin', Claytie," said Jack the Landman.

Wynona's bite never matched the potency of her bark, and she couldn't totally camouflage her affection and respect for Claytie, despite relentless efforts. Once, after a long press interview sprinkled with tart one-liners aimed at her boss, she called Denise Kelly in the Midland office with a "reminder" for the person who interviewed her. She wanted Claytie's executive assistant or someone to pass along to the reporter one of Claytie's little-known and more admirable qualities that she had been remiss in mentioning.

"Wynona called to remind us that Claytie was very generous when people didn't know it, paying for the births and burials of Hispanic children and doing a lot of things he never got or sought credit for," Denise said. "It was a generosity of spirit Wynona just thought was the most noble of all."

That's not to say that Wynona wasn't sometimes appalled by that generosity, usually when Claytie instructed her to write checks for the babies of indigent Fort Stockton families—when funds did not exist to cover the checks.

"Go ahead and write the checks," he'd say. "The money will come from somewhere. It'll work out."

Claytie did not often publicly expose his compassionate side or the depths of his generosity, especially when assisting the less fortunate or comforting and caring for grieving friends and employees.

On November 30, 1974, the weekend after Thanksgiving, company accountant John Monroe was critically injured in an accident at one of the early deer camps. A Jeep driven by Wayne Roye overturned on a hillside, throwing Monroe and the four other passengers from the vehicle. It rolled over on Monroe, crushing his lungs.

His companions managed to upright the Jeep and raced back to the campsite, where Claytie and his hunting party had arrived only minutes earlier. "John was bleeding from the mouth and probably the lungs," Claytie said. They sped to the Fort Stockton hospital with Claytie cradling Monroe's head in his arms and encouraging him to hang on.

As they approached the hospital, John whispered, "Claytie, I can't hold on any longer. Please look after my girls." They raced him into the emergency room where medical personnel pronounced him dead. Still, Claytie tried to blow air into his lungs until convinced it was hopeless.

"John was a fine and conscientious young man and had a bright future with our company," Claytie said. "Telling his wife, Carolee, and his two daughters that he had just been killed at my camp was one of the hardest things I've ever had to do."

Carolee would later relate how Claytie brought his mother and her husband's best friend to tell her and the couple's young daughters of John's death. "He told me that John had died in his arms, and that my husband had asked him to take care of his girls." She said Claytie closed down deer camp for the rest of the season, flew most of his employees to Santa Anna in Central Texas for the funeral, paid for the service and burial, gave her checks from two of his companies at Christmas, and helped her collect insurance, workers' compensation, and later Social Security. "After things quieted down, Claytie personally took me to the ranch to show me the location of the accident. He took the better part of a day to help me grieve."

Because she suffered from a rare disease that impaired her ability to walk, write, and talk, Carolee said, Claytie sent her at his own expense to Baylor Hospital in Dallas. When she lost her teaching job because of her disabilities, he hired her. And when her daughter Stephanie was in college, she worked summers for Wynona.

"Claytie surely kept his word to my husband."

"Claytie outworked everybody—and outtraded everybody."

Two grumpy veterans of the oil industry had gotten to-gether again in late 1973—Claytie and Bill Haverlah—and the new oil-patch journey they charted would eventually propel them to ca-reer highs. Haverlah had quit the Williams companies in 1967 when the thrill of working for Claytie became more wearing than reward-ing and his liver cried uncle. Their personalities inherently blended like water and the oil they sought: Claytie, the bold, high-octane, risk-taker whose hard-drinking, brawling persona belied an oil-patch prescience and optimism reminiscent of legendary wildcat-ters; and Haverlah, the conservative, nervous, worrywart pessimist whose brilliance as a lease man and dealmaker was overshadowed only by his inability to keep pace with the frenetic work-and-play style of his boss. The chemistry of their reunion would prove, even-tually, both enduring and bountiful beyond belief.

"Haverlah was a great asset all the way," Claytie recalled. "I am extremely aggressive and optimistic; he is extremely conscientious, extremely conservative, extremely cautious. It was like that all the time. So we were a great team."

Thus, in late 1973, Claytie welcomed the opportunity while at deer camp with Haverlah to try to persuade him to rejoin him. Claytie had been researching the Austin Chalk play in South Texas, and he thought Haverlah the perfect one to pull together some lease acreage.

Haverlah did not exactly rush back into Claytie's corporate embrace. Neither would he come cheap. "I'll tell you what. I'm gonna wait until after the New Year, and then I'll go into buying leases for you."

Whatever misgivings Haverlah harbored about returning to the fold were likely dispelled by Claytie's generosity: a 1 percent override on production from the acreage he leased. That's how, from 1974 until 1976, Haverlah and his team of buyers wound up purchasing two hundred twenty thousand acres of leases in the so-called Austin Chalk Trend, a limestone formation in what's known as the East Texas Basin and the Gulf Coast. The formation extends from the San Antonio area across southeast Texas to Louisiana, Mississippi, and Florida and into the center of the Gulf of Mexico.

"Haverlah did a brilliant job buying those leases," Claytie said, evoking shades of their early Clajon days in West Texas. The leases were for ten years and provided for a one-eighth royalty and a one-dollar-per-acre annual rental. "I later gave varying percents of overrides to many of my top hands on all this acreage," Claytie said.

In those early days in Giddings, in the mid-'70s, Claytie and his gang drilled five wells, but they halted operations when four of them proved to be noncommercial. Fortunately for Claytie, oil and gas production in West Texas was at the time enjoying a surge, thanks to Gataga #2 and the ever-productive Rhoda Walker developments in Ward County. But Giddings was another matter.

"We went into a twilight zone from '77 to '79," Claytie said of his efforts in the Austin Chalk Field.

Giddings looked so bleak in that two-year span that in 1978 he tried to sell his acreage. Fate stepped in, again—fate, with about ten minutes or so to spare. In late 1978, with oil still languishing in the seven-dollar range, Claytie made an appointment with a Houston oil company in an attempt to unload his two hundred twenty thousand acres of leases.

"I was going to ask twenty dollars an acre," Claytie recalled, telling his story this way:

He is sitting in an anteroom of the office, waiting to see the vice president of the company about acquiring his acreage. The appointed time comes and goes. No meeting. Ten minutes pass. No meeting. Twenty minutes.

"He keeps me waiting thirty minutes, so I walked out, because I knew that anybody that makes me wait thirty minutes is already trading me out of ten dollars an acre."

Claytie would one day be grateful for the man's rudeness, because those two hundred twenty thousand acres would become the heart of the Giddings juggernaut.

"That is how fate works sometimes. Once again I was protected from my own ignorance by events. If he'd come out of his office, I'd probably have sold him rights to that acreage. At the most, I might have kept an override."

A short time later, in early 1979, the price of oil would rise nearly sixfold, to forty dollars a barrel, largely because of the revolution in Iran and its looming hostilities with neighboring Iraq, two countries whose oil reserves are among the world's largest. Further, the 1978 enactment by Congress of the Natural Gas Policy Act would soon sharply boost the price of newly produced gas.

These two developments could hardly be more combustible as they fueled a historic transformation of the Giddings play, and of those who came seeking its riches.

Just as the promise and pressure of Giddings dawned, Claytie suffered a loss both personal and professional—a disheartening split with geologist Wayne Roye, his business associate and drinking buddy during the crucial growing years of the 1970s. "Wayne was a tremendous asset and an important part of my business until I had to let him go in '78," Claytie said, explaining that Roye was more like a brother than an employee. But, Claytie said, Roye's drinking had become intolerable and was threatening to drag the whole company down. After fretting over the situation for months, Claytie turned for advice to old friend and mentor Bob Parker in Tulsa. "I walked in his office and I remember so clearly what he said: 'I know why you're here. You've got to fire Wayne Roye and you're not sure how to do it.' Bob told me the problem with some businesses is that as they grow, some people cannot keep growing with you. You have to accept the loss of those people and move on."

Roye did not go quietly, first hauling off the company's well logs and other data. He followed up with a series of harassing phone calls to the company employees, and Claytie began carrying a pistol. After Roye sent him a letter accusing him of cheating his partners, the two crossed paths — memorably — at a company meeting. "I knew he would be there," Claytie said. "I recall so well that in getting dressed that morning, I went to my drawer to put on shorts and there was a pair of yellow shorts and a pair of red shorts. I chose the red as an indication of my attitude that morning."

At the showdown later, Claytie, armed with his "boxing" shorts, strutted his 5 feet 8 inches straight up to Roye and popped him twice, knocking him into a wall. He slid down like the bad guy in a John Wayne barroom brawl.

"I've never regretted it," Claytie said. "I consoled myself by knowing that I was not dealing with Wayne Roye but with the disease of alcoholism."

The Giddings boom — so named for the town that was roughly the center of so much oil and gas activity — would burst across hundreds of square miles of south-central Texas landscape, frenetically so. By 1979, roads jammed with massive trucks hauling equipment and with pickups hauling tough men in hard hats, rig crews, roughnecks, and roustabouts — all looking for a place where they could sign on for work or find a beer or a bed to rest their heads. Suppliers and contractors, landmen and geologists and seismologists, mud men and pipe men and chemical men and specialists and technicians of all stripe and pedigree — they came and choked the roads and cafés and motels. Suddenly the somnolent little town of a few thousand, some fifty-five bucolic miles east of Austin, was quiet no more. The outsiders poured in, many from Houston, a hundred miles to the east, and the town could do little to prepare for or welcome the onslaught. Some three hundred oil-related companies would soon converge on the Giddings area to set up offices.

"You couldn't get a room anywhere," Claytie recalled.

They all came because of a dream, the next big play, this boom at Giddings, where oil was first discovered in 1960. What set Giddings apart was that it had also become a top producer of both casinghead gas and oil. Together, its oil and gas reserves constituted a major U.S. field. Included among those who joined the Giddings fray by the late 1970s were any number of dreamers, as undercapitalized as they were untutored in the ways and wiles of the oil patch. But their humbling lack of experience would be offset by some of the icons of the Texas oil scene — those whose reserves of wisdom were as deep and sustaining as the pools that lay thousands of feet below.

Claytie Williams, by boom-time Giddings '79, had earned his reputation the hard way, starting at the bottom and never giving up — his savvy sharpened and talents seasoned by the relentless, can-do Clajon work ethic that had stood him in grand stead. Thus, through grit and gumption, occasional fist and always fair play, he was, by 1979, well on his way to becoming an icon of the Texas oil patch.

In fact, it was right on the cusp of the Giddings madness that oil-patch colleagues recognized Claytie's extraordinary contributions to the industry and his exploratory drilling activities: they welcomed him into the All-American Wildcatters, an elite honorary fraternity of leading independents and presidents and board chairmen of the major oil companies. Admittance comes only after a majority vote of the membership. Initiated by legendary wildcatter Duke Rudman, the fraternity has as its motto, "Our word is our bond."

The '79 spike in oil prices started it all.

"The difference in economics between forty-dollar oil and seven-dollar oil was tremendous," Claytie said, "so the price opened the whole door to the Giddings oil play, which was the biggest boom in the United States."

It would be the biggest thing for Claytie and Clajon, for sure. Virtually overnight—it was over the next two years, in fact—"I went from $38 million in debt and thirty-eight employees to $500 million in debt and twelve hundred employees," Claytie said. From 1976 to 1982, Claytie would drill hundreds of wells in the Austin Chalk—most of those from 1979 to 1981, at an average cost of $650,000 a well—and lease more than four million acres nationwide. He opened exploration offices in Denver, Oklahoma City, and Houston and expanded those in Fort Stockton, Midland, San Antonio, and Jackson, Miss. Because of Giddings production, Clajon would become the largest individually owned gas company in Texas by 1982 with deliveries up to 250 million cubic feet a day. "Our natural gas liquid extraction plants ranked fifth in the United States. Our oil production averaged about ten thousand barrels daily, and Clajon's liquid products totaled more than twenty thousand barrels daily."

According to the Texas Railroad Commission, the Williams Company ranked as the twenty-second largest producer of Texas oil in the first quarter of that year—ahead of such well-known companies as Champlin, Tenneco, Superior, and Sohio. It was the sixty-first largest producer of gas.

"One of the most important people in the development of both Clajon Gas and the Giddings operation was Clarence 'Quatie' Wolfshohl," Claytie stressed. "He managed a very complicated system as we built it, and to this day he remains a trusted and forward-looking employee and manager."

When Claytie and his talented band of oil-and-gas sleuths descended on Giddings en masse in 1979, they confronted challenges of almost biblical proportions. Not the least: where would they work, and where would employees live? Unlike other operators, Claytie held off on drilling until he could situate his employees. In a rush construction job, Claytie built a ten-thousand-square-foot office complex in east Giddings that included an equipment and pipe yard, workshop, and helicopter pad—all operational by Thanksgiving 1979. For employees' living quarters he rounded up eighty-five trailers and moved them to the rear of the complex's forty-two-acre site, a challenging task handled by Claytie's cousin, Robert Graham.

"We built a trailer-house town and called it Williamsville," Claytie said. "It's still called that today."

Besides securing the capital investment for building an office complex and housing, Claytie outlined for the local Giddings *Times & News* further challenges to finding success in the Giddings field: the erratic peculiarities of extracting oil and gas from the Austin Chalk, the cost of acquiring pipeline right of way and construction, and the durability of the field, where production could be expected to deplete by 40 to 50 percent a year.

With his office and employee housing in place, Claytie now entered the Giddings game the only way he knew how—boldly. "I stayed with my M.O.," he said. Flush with bank credit that rose proportionally with the value of his oil and gas reserves, he would accelerate his drilling program, lay more than nine hundred miles of pipeline, and construct two gas-processing plants, the sites determined by the location of the purchaser's pipelines.

"We had a deal going," explained Claytie. "We always built pipelines to gather our own gas while competing to buy other producers' gas. All we had to determine was if we were going to sell to Valero or Lone Star or somebody else."

Because of prior business dealings, Valero quickly emerged as the logical buyer of Clajon's gas. Valero was the new name of a gas company previously known as LoVaca, to which Claytie had sold gas from his West Texas production. LoVaca had recently become embroiled in lawsuits and regulatory problems, and because of its shaky financial history had no risk money or credit to build gathering lines.

Clajon and San Antonio–based Valero/LoVaca seemed a natural fit: utility-type supplier Valero had the markets but no gas of its own; Clajon had no markets but plenty of gas to sell.

The only thing left was the deal.

"Valero was represented by a very smart and hard-nosed trader, Dan Eldridge," Claytie said. "He recognized that small volumes of gas were scattered over hundreds of square miles and that we had a very large financial risk in gathering, processing, and delivering this gas to Valero, and that Valero had no risk."

The problem: reaching an acceptable price.

The traders, Claytie and Eldridge, engaged in several contentious meetings.

"We knew where we needed to go," recalled Eldridge, "it was just a matter of how we got there."

Eldridge made a "final" offer; Claytie rejected it.

Claytie: "The deal was dead."

Eldridge: "Clayton was pulling for more and more money, and we had people in the middle saying that there wasn't any gas there, that there would never be any gas there. So how do you pay a guy for building a big system up front, and still not overpay if he's right and Valero's wrong? That was the dilemma in my mind."

Claytie: "Dan went back to management, pushed them to increase their price more, and barely got them to. He came back to me and I accepted it. We had a deal! Good trading!"

The fee to gather line gas from multiple wells: $1.28 per million cubic feet, said Bob Lyon, then the Clajon president who handled the contract for Claytie. The Valero contract would more than validate Claytie's gamble in the Giddings field, bringing Clajon millions in revenues . . . until one day, unexpectedly, the payments stopped.

In the early days of the Giddings boom, Claytie and Clajon got an unexpected boost from the Texas Railroad Commission. The reason? Oil companies were all flaring their gas, a time-honored practice across oil-patch Texas.

"You could fly from Austin to Houston at night and it was almost daylight because all the wells being drilled were flaring, or burning, their gas," Claytie recalled. Given the shortage of gas and oil at the time, a public outcry commenced, prompting the Railroad Commission to issue a no-flare order: companies couldn't flare their gas for more than ninety days after completion of a well.

"That order actually helped us because after ninety days a producer couldn't produce his oil well until somebody ran a pipeline to it. With the no-flare order, it became imperative for us to gather the casinghead gas as quickly and as efficiently as possible. Unlike the engineering-oriented companies, we were entrepreneurial-oriented and our competitors wouldn't lay to a well or a field unless it was tested and they knew it was good. We took the attitude that we're gonna lay the line because we had the geology—we were confident that certain areas would produce. We laid pipelines to many locations before the wells were drilled."

Clajon was the fourth pipeline company to get into the Giddings action, competing against bigger, more established companies such as Perry Gas Systems, Mitchell Energy, and Phillips Petroleum.

"We eventually gathered and processed 60 percent of the gas, and more oil and gas than all of them combined," Claytie said. "So our aggressive attitude combined with our geological knowledge made us a helluva competitor." Or, as fellow oilman Charlie Perry was fond of saying: "Claytie outworked everybody—and outtraded everybody."

Clajon came about its aggressive attitude quite naturally, thanks to its master. Sometimes that aggressiveness turned inward. One day while flying over a pipeline under construction, Claytie noticed his crew was standing around, not working at all. Though Claytie was convinced otherwise, the right-of-way permit had not been granted.

Within minutes, Claytie called managers together for what one describes as a "thirty-minute ass-chewing I'll never forget." Sufficiently chastised, the manager charged with securing the permit did in fact obtain one immediately, two people were fired, and the pipe crew got back to work.

A bouquet of flowers and a bottle of Chivas Scotch would soon appear on the offending manager's desk, a Claytie reminder that "it's only business, nothing personal."

Claytie, say his colleagues, never lost his personal touch with employees, as demonstrated one day in Giddings after nearly two weeks of rain. His crew was building a major pipeline and once again it began to pour. The men were miserable, worn out, and ready to quit. Charlie Moody called Claytie to the field and suggested he come spend some time with the pipeline crew. Claytie did, joining the workers in the trench for two days, helping where he could and providing encouragement.

"With the boss on the ground, we got it going," recalled Claytie. "It's like I say, the best fertilizer is the footprints of the owner. It was a real good lesson in leadership. If the boss or a platoon leader is suffering with the men, then they will stay and do their job. Sometimes, without leadership, they won't."

As in any boom area, expenses escalated, from the cost of pipe and supplies to contracting services and people. Nothing was now more difficult than finding experienced oil-field hands, especially for a company of thirty-eight people that would expand to a thousand-plus within a year or so. "We hired some nonprofessionals, including three A&M engineering graduates," Claytie said. "They may have had a degree, but they had no actual experience. That's what the boom did. You took what you could. We hired college graduates and found some old hands. Eventually, Dave Greenlee took over managing the Giddings office and hired some professionals."

When the oil business really got to booming, you couldn't hire anybody to do anything, Bill Haverlah recalled. "It was horrible. The roughnecks and stuff, I mean they were druggies and jailbirds out of prison."

A drilling superintendent became a particularly menacing presence. "I had to fire him because he was intimidating all of my people," Claytie said. "I slept with a knife by my bed that night in my trailer in Williamsville."

Among the professionals that otherwise impressed Haverlah were the seismologists who determined well locations. "They were using some kind of science," he said. "I don't know if it was voodoo or not, but they were pretty successful. We weren't drilling any dry holes."

At one point, the company drilled more than forty consecutive commercial wells and, working around a shortage of drilling rigs and a myriad of other obstacles, eventually got production up to fifteen thousand barrels a day. "We kept on going and at one point we had nineteen drilling rigs running out there," Haverlah said. Later, they would also be successful when switching from vertical to horizontal drilling.

Said Claytie: "Besides Haverlah and Quatie Wolfshohl, we had a helluva team of men and women working their asses off in Giddings. That was the key, and without Travis Lynch and his team of gas buyers, none of this would have been possible.

"You had to have a team of men out dealing with the producers to acquire their gas. Travis had to sell himself, he had to sell Clajon, he had to sell different producers that Clajon was the right company to deal with. He had to convince them that we ran an honest meter and that we'd pick up their gas quickly so they wouldn't have their well shut in because of the no-flare order.

"I used to say about Travis and Aubrey Price, my longtime pilot: 'Don't tell Travis or Aubrey to go kill somebody and then change your mind the next day . . . because that somebody will already be dead.' Those two had a 'we-can-do-it, we-will-get-it-done' attitude, and they did. They hustled so much that we bought nearly all the gas. The workers in the field and the gas buyers up front formed a solid team and kicked ass."

It took everyone working together to make a huge accomplishment like this come to pass, he said, citing the philosophy of the late Green Bay Packers coach Vince Lombardi: "The difference between mediocrity and greatness is the feeling these guys have for one another."

The teamwork in Giddings underscored that philosophy, he said. "In 1982, we had the second largest natural gas liquid plant in Texas and the fifth largest in the United States, and these people were major factors in the success of the system. We also had gross combined revenue that ranked twenty-first when compared to the top one hundred publicly traded companies headquartered in Houston that year. How did we do it? We did it by making good, smart deals and contracts, with hard work, good service, and aggressive buying and pipeline construction."

Inspired by the heady boom days of financial blessing, Claytie generously shared his good fortune. Before the '70s ended, he contributed a substantial overriding royalty of production in the

Giddings/Austin Chalk play to Texas A&M, the Trinity School in Midland, and the Chihuahuan Desert Research Institute.

"The Giddings oil boom was wild," Claytie said. "Our operations were scattered over an area one hundred miles in length and ten to thirty miles wide, all along gravelly county roads. There were a great many wrecks and a great deal of oil-field theft."

Claytie once had a drilling engineer who "would order mud out to the well, bill the company, then sell the same mud to me two or three more times. That was rampant in the oil field."

Haverlah complained that thieves were stealing as much as the company was selling, but Claytie said it never got quite that bad. "But," he conceded, "we had to have our own police force in the Giddings Field to keep them from stealing the oil."

To prevent the oil-field banditry, Claytie took a novel but shaky step in 1980 with the formation of a new company. After the Giddings Oilfield Association was first created to assist with security, Claytie formed Clayco, an oil-field trucking company to collect, purchase, and resell his Giddings oil. Clayco never met expectations and was plagued by accidents, in part because qualified drivers were nonexistent, and the combination of inexperienced drivers traveling narrow, gravel country roads with sharp curves created a deadly mix. Trucks, top-heavy with oil, frequently overturned, killing several drivers. Claytie found out later that as many as nine of the drivers he hired in his efforts to curb the oil-field theft were themselves ex-convicts.

By early 1981, the *Oil & Gas Journal* reported, the Giddings Field was producing nearly 90,000 barrels of oil and 245.4 million cubic feet of gas a day from 1,072 wells. An oil and gas expert called Giddings the "largest developing field in the United States." Claytie indicated it was somewhat of a mixed bag, "a huge, wonderful field with lots of benefits . . . and lots of problems."

That summer, while sheep hunting in Canada, climbing mountains, riding horses, and sleeping on the ground every night, Claytie did some soul-searching. He was not satisfied—at all—with how his business was performing.

He considered his financial plight: everybody wanted raises, pipe prices were skyrocketing, interest had risen to 21.5 percent; the price of everything was going up, up, up. . . .

"I realized I'd lost control and outside forces were running my businesses—not me. In that quiet and reflective time I decided I should sell some of my oil production and some leases and get my finances back in order."

Regaining control would be neither easy nor fast.

Giddings took a toll on Claytie's family life, though it was not without its lighter moments. "I came home on Saturday night, stayed Sunday, and left Monday as a rule. We were living in an apartment, and Modesta was raising the kids and overseeing the building of our new house in Midland. I had put together five million acres in a two- to three-year period. We were just busier than hell and I was just never home."

Modesta has her own perspective of that time.

"It took me two years to build the house," she said. "That was when I put up three pictures on the wall. One of them was the builder, one of them was the painter, and one of them was Claytie.

"I'd say, 'Kids, which one of these is your daddy?' They picked the builder."

"Never happened," Claytie says, though not convincingly.

In 1982, with the boom turning to bust and his company vastly overextended, Claytie was forced to sell Clayco, his trucking company.

"So much for my idea of preventing theft," he said.

About the time of the Clayco venture, Claytie had amassed an oil, gas, and ranching empire with more than a billion dollars in revenues, according to the *Dallas Morning News*. Now, as the oil industry teetered on the edge of a historic tumble, he was looking at hundreds of millions of dollars in debts to a syndicate of banks.

Retreat? Yes and no.

During what he called "The Wreck" of the '80s, he would upgrade and then cash in his registered cattle operation, sell off his Giddings oil production, diversify into banking and real estate, launch new academic and philanthropic adventures in Aggieland, break ground and build a Midland office park, create a telecommunications company, challenge an industrial giant in a historic legislative battle, sell his phone and gas companies, and wiggle honorably and miraculously, and sometimes reluctantly, out from under debts that crushed countless numbers of his wildcatting colleagues.

And then the saga of Clayton W. Williams Jr. would get *really* interesting.

As the oil boom of the '70s had gained momentum, Claytie's activities as an independent wildcatter, innovative rancher, registered cattle breeder, real estate developer, fledgling banker, and Aggie philanthropist sparked a flurry of media scrutiny. It was difficult to pick up a business magazine, oil journal, or ranching publication without some mention of Claytie's deeds and occasional misdeeds. Texas newspapers published lengthy feature stories on the "colorful Aggie millionaire," usually favorable but always peppered with the assorted zingers known affectionately as Claytieisms.

The Mentone oil well blowout and evacuation captured newspaper headlines and captivated television newscasts, and the subsequent Gataga drilling reports appeared in oil and gas journals for years. The August 1976 cover story in *Drill Bit Magazine* focused on the Delaware Basin, and one of the leading oil specialists in the country, John Pitts, wrote: "The biggest game in the Delaware Basin is the deep gas play. The biggest name in the game is Clayton Williams."

Another writer, Sam Pendergrast, quoted Claytie in an October 1976 story in the *Midland Reporter-Telegram* as saying: "Everybody knows I'm an Aggie when they see my class ring . . . while I'm picking my nose."

A business magazine quoted an unidentified oilman as calling Claytie the "biggest sonuvabitch" in Midland. "But," the energy executive added, "the guy's brilliant."

In December 1977, *The Cattleman* magazine published photographs of Claytie's Brangus cows and calves grazing on lush grasslands, and the headline on the story blared: "Clayton Williams Is Making More Grass and Using It Better." Author Paul Horn led off his story this way: "They call this the changeless country, a land that has its own hard-and-fast rules about cattle ranching so you are forced to operate pretty much like your grandfather did before you. It's the vast, rugged, stoic Big Bend of Texas, a fine country to raise cattle in if you are conservative, cautious, and patient.

"Apparently Clayton Williams read a different rule book, heard a different drummer, or dreamed of some changes he could make in this changeless country."

Horn went on to say that Claytie saw beyond the jungle of catclaw and grazed-out gullies and recognized unique water and grass management possibilities on his ranch north of Alpine. With the tangle of brush replaced by verdant grasslands, the old formula of running eight to ten cows to the section is no longer operable. "He has increased his carrying capacity with careful water management and rotational grazing of up to twenty-five cows per section," Horn wrote, concluding: "They still call this changeless country but after you spend a day with Clayton Williams you get a different meaning for the word. Clayton didn't move any mountains or bring in the ocean but he performed enough minor miracles with grass and water and fencing to qualify as the No. 1 'changer' in the Big Bend."

Between print and broadcast interviews, Claytie found time in 1977 to create two companies, Century Pipe & Supply and Maverick Mud, that validated again his risk-versus-reward entrepreneurial style. Century was headed by Carles Gibson and Maverick by Dick Oldham, both friends he'd met in Fort Stockton. The aptly named Maverick was born in a postmidnight cocktail session at Claytie's home after a black-tie party.

"I think there might have been a little bit of wine there that night," Oldham said.

"We didn't drink wine then," Claytie reminded him.

"Hell, no," Oldham suddenly remembered. "It was Crown Royal [whiskey]."

Oldham, who was working for another mud company at the time, quit his job the next morning to start Maverick, a sales and service company that supplied the chemically enhanced clay-and-water drilling lubricant called mud.

"Claytie contacted someone that morning and told him to put one hundred and fifty thousand dollars in the bank for Oldham to start this company," he remembered. "Hell," Oldham recalled saying, "I will never need that much money."

That was in 1977, he said. "In 1981, we had revenues of over $12 million [and a net profit of $3 million-plus] with no debt. We never borrowed any money until later on." Sounding slightly skeptical, Claytie quipped: "I don't think I ever had anything to do with a company that didn't borrow money."

Said Oldham: "Those five years with Maverick were some of the happiest times of my oil-field career. The problem was, we were in business for ten years. But the first five were wonderful." A victim of The Wreck of '82, Maverick's revenues dropped from $12 million in 1981 to $7.5 million the next year, and in due course a cash cow became a cashless coyote.

"We sold our assets to one of the major oil companies in '87 and retired our debt to the bank," Oldham said. "And we should have done it a year or two earlier."

Like Maverick, Century Pipe and Supply traced its beginnings to a 1977 cocktail session, this one at Claytie's office in the Gulf Building.

"I was working for Grant Oil Company," Carles Gibson said, "and I'd go by in the afternoon and have a drink with Claytie and Wayne Roye and Jim Shepherd." One day they were discussing Claytie's drilling program and the difficulties of obtaining the tubular goods, the oil well casing, for deep wells.

"Let's just start a pipe company," Claytie suggested.

Eventually, it became a fifty-fifty arrangement between Claytie on the one hand and Gibson and his partner, Frank Pannell, on the other. Like Maverick Mud, the pipe supply company netted a high of more than $3 million the year before the crash in 1982. And while Maverick once turned down an $8 million buyout offer, Century spurned a $30 million offer. And not unlike the mud venture, Century flourished throughout the boom, then stumbled onto the sales block in the bust. An Abilene firm bought Century for a song in the mid-'80s when a lot of oil companies and banks went broke.

"First National of Midland did go broke in '84," Claytie said. "That bank had a policy that any officer could loan money, but it took two people to turn down an oil loan. That was absolutely crazy. The whole industry was caught up in that, and there were a lot of bankruptcies. The Federal Deposit Insurance Corporation had an entire building here in Midland to take care of all the bankruptcies."

During the early success of Maverick and Century, Claytie's romance with the media flourished. Even the area weekly papers would get all atwitter over his non-oil-patch endeavors such as his ability to produce tons of hay in a Davis Mountain area never known for such agri-magic. "West Texas Ranch Yields Two Tons of Hay Per Acre," announced one. Said another: "Area Rancher Cultivates Native Grasses; Bales Two Tons of Hay."

Meanwhile, Claytie and Modesta's annual Brangus cattle sales commanded bigger headlines and longer stories as the proceeds escalated into the millions and the sounds of the country's biggest C&W stars and bands echoed through the mountains and valleys surrounding Happy Cove Ranch. Over the years, the headliners included George Strait, Merle Haggard, Charley Pride, Johnny Paycheck, Janie Frick, Tom T. Hall, and Danny Davis and the Nashville Brass.

The activity in the Giddings Field generated dozens of stories, many reporting on the overriding mineral interest on eighty-six thousand acres he gave A&M in 1979. "It has the potential for being

THE FORT STOCKTON

Sunday, February 25, 1979

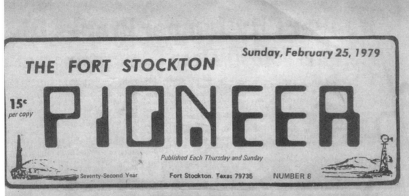

PIONEER

15¢ per copy

Published Each Thursday and Sunday

Seventy-Second Year   Fort Stockton, Texas 79735   NUMBER 8

'Claytie' Gives Aggies Big Royalty Gift; Could Be 'Largest Gift Ever' To Texas A&M

Clayton W. "Claytie" Williams Jr., a Fort Stockton native and independent oilman who flies an oversized Texas A&M flag over his Midland office building, has given his alma mater an overriding royalty interest in approximately 6,000 acres with a current market value of $.37 million.

The acreage is located in various parts of the Brazos, Burleson and Robertson counties in Central Texas, on the ringe of one of the state's newest oil fields.

Drilling is expected to being in the near future and royalties could be almost 10 times the market value, university officials note.

The income will fund the Clayton W. Williams Jr. Endowment in the Texas A&M University Development Foundation, and the income from the endowment will benefit various academic and student programs.

"This has the potential or being the largest gift ever made to Texas A&M University," President Jarvis E. Miller said. "We re particularly pleased hat Mr. Williams has designated the income to be distributed broadly to include academic programs, athletics and student aid."

Robert M. Rutledge III, the university's development director, said the income will be divided, providing 50 percent to he Center for Education and Research in Free Enterprise, 15 percent unrestricted to the foundation, 10 percent for National Collegiate Athletic Association-

grams, 10 percent to benefit women students, 5 percent for the Texas Aggie Band, 5 percent for general student financial

aid, and 5 percent to The Texas A&M University System Press, a scholarly publishing house.

Williams, a 1954

graduate of Texas A&M with a degree in animal husbandry, is the son of an Aggie, Clayton W.

(See WILLIAMS, Page 5)

GIFT TO TEXAS A&M...Clayton W. Williams Jr., right, gives Texas A&M President Jarvis E. Miller the Aggie "gig 'em" sign after handing over an overriding interest valued at $2.7 million to the university. Williams, a native of Fort Stockton now living in Midland, is a 1954 Texas A&M graduate. He is an independent oil and gas businessman. The leases Williams gave to A&M are in three Central the biggest gift ever made to Texas A&M University," then-president Jarvis Miller told the *Dallas Times Herald*. "And most pleasing is the fact that Mr. Williams has designated the income to be distributed broadly to include academic programs, athletics, and student aid."

Published estimates suggested the Giddings gift could eventually bring the university $10 million.

"I give my gifts not with the feeling of obligation, but with love and a little ego," said Claytie, who made a number of contributions to the university over the years. "A&M has done a lot more for me than I have for A&M."

Such largesse no doubt contributed to his selection in 1981 as a recipient of the Distinguished Alumnus Award, one of A&M's most coveted honors and the springboard to more media attention.

In 1980, Claytie had formed Wil Gas Company of Midland, a processor of natural gas liquids, and a year later it was generating major news with plant openings near College Station. The larger of the two processing plants was a $24 million facility at LaGrange with a design capacity to process two hundred million cubic feet of gas per day. Perhaps because the location was closer to the Gulf Coast than the Big Bend, the dedication ceremonies featured not barbecued goat but a Louisiana shrimp and crawfish boil followed by a party and dance. Among those attending were two hundred company employees, a number rapidly expanding in the Williams empire.

A smiling, rumpled cowboy wearing a mud-splattered Stetson and clutching a branding iron adorned the cover of the August 1981 issue of *Texas Business*. A provocative teaser wondered: "The Next Billion-Dollar Aggie?" A prelude to the story by Carrie Moline Steenson set the tone for an exceptional article: "Controversial oilman/rancher Clayton Williams Jr. has risen quietly from a $10,000-a-year insurance peddler to near-billionaire in only 15 years. Along the way, he has made both archenemies and a circle of friends who would practically kill for him. Yet few would dispute that Williams is one of the most ingenious, colorful, ruggedly individualistic entrepreneurs that Texas has ever produced."

Steenson acknowledged that the sweaty, rugged, mud-spattered guy she watched castrating and branding bull calves while shouting out orders in Spanish to his Mexican ranch hands did not fit her image of a budding billionaire.

"Nevertheless, as rich and powerful as he is, Williams still generally is considered an outsider to much of Midland's landed gentry who regard him as eccentric and crude," she wrote. "For instance, he flies an oversize Texas A&M flag atop a downtown Midland building, paints all six of his aircraft maroon and white, has a swimming pool in the shape of an Aggie boot, and loves to stand on bar tables while imbibing and sing Mexican songs."

Claytie's circle of friends and admirers, she asserted, viewed him as an honest version of the *Dallas* TV villain J.R. Ewing with the character's shrewd business instincts, persuasive charm, and penchant for using power. Claytie detested the Ewing image, but told her, "I am a warrior. I don't mind having enemies. I just like to know who they are so we can get the fight going."

He said he was nowhere near becoming a billionaire because of his heavy debt load, but he told Steenson he was working on it. To that end, he said he spent much time in his six planes hopping from one business venture to another.

"I'm on the move a lot," he said, "and every once in a while I get tired. I wish I had twice the time because I love my family, I love to hunt and fish, I love my business, I love to work cows, and I love my friends whom I don't see much anymore 'cause I'm so damn busy."

Letting his mind race back once over that remarkable period, Claytie said: "During the boom years beginning in 1979, my personal and physical and family life were stretched extremely thin. Rather than the regular exercise routine I'd developed to stay in shape to hunt sheep, I was spending two or three days in Giddings, one in San Antonio with Bill Haverlah, and tripping around to Houston, to Jackson, Miss., to Oklahoma City, to Denver, and back to Fort Stockton. That's when pilot Aubrey Price and the jet came in handy, because I don't see how I could have done it otherwise."

Still, he seized every opportunity to slip away to the Alpine ranch to exercise, rest, enjoy his family, and simply get a respite from an unrelenting workplace and an ever-increasing media spotlight.

"Summers at the Alpine ranch when the children were young would restore me for the trials and tribulations of the coming week," he said. "These were good rainfall years, the cattle prices were good, and there were always enough projects to keep me busy. . . . I was also fortunate to have good health, a supportive wife, and many good employees to make it through this extremely busy period."

"Along with the ranch came my ranch foreman, Guadalupe 'Chappo' Ramirez and, later, his son James. Chappo has always been there through thick and thin, a man of complete integrity. His wife, Josie, looks after our payroll there, and they are among my dearest and closest friends. His son James is following right along in his footsteps. What a pleasure it has been to me to go to the ranch, work on projects, work cattle, and always have these two solid men there to help me every step of the way. Chappo is as much of a workaholic as I and he was by my side through many, many ranch projects."

Almost a year to the day from publication of the *Texas Business* profile that speculated about a billionaire Aggie, *Forbes* magazine issued its latest compilation of the four hundred richest Americans. Sixty-seven Texans made the so-called Forbes Four Hundred List, eight of them from Midland—and each of the eight was credited with major resources and income in oil.

At age fifty, with a fortune estimated by Forbes at $100 million, Claytie was among them. "I just barely made the cut. But I made it."

The West Texas multimillionaire probably was an early entry on the *Forbes* evaluation list, but he surely caught the magazine's attention in April 1982. That's when publications such as *The Wall Street Journal* and the *Houston Chronicle* reported the sale of 152 of his oil and gas wells in the Austin Chalk for $110.5 million to Denver-based Petro-Lewis Corporation.

Most of the wells were in Burleson County and had proven reserves estimated at five million barrels of oil and seventeen billion cubic feet of gas.

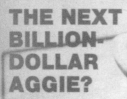

AUGUST 1981

Texas ✪ Business

$1.95

THE NEXT BILLION-DOLLAR AGGIE?

The 50 top-paid execs in Texas

Business' best friends and toughest foes in the legislature

...on Williams Jr.,
Midland oilman

Author Clayton W. Williams Sr. signing one of his books at Fort Stockton

"It's the biggest sale I ever made," Claytie told the *Chronicle,* "and it's the first time in seven or eight years I've sold anything."

The sale was made to pay off debt on bank loans and because of a slowdown of oil-field activity in the Giddings area. He still owned seventy producing wells in the Austin Chalk and had five hundred and fifty thousand acres of nonproducing oil leases across Texas and the United States.

"Within forty-five days after the close of the sale, the price of oil dropped from forty-two dollars to twenty-eight dollars," Claytie said. "The mistake was not selling the gas properties as well."

The announcement of the sale came from College Station, where Claytie and his family were attending a reception at the Aggieland Inn for his eighty-seven-year-old father. Texas A&M University Press had just published Clayton Sr.'s last book, *Texas' Last Frontier: Fort Stockton and the Trans-Pecos, 1861–1895.*

Claytie was still a bit huffy over the response to his previous announcement that he planned to "auction off" the 152 wells along with half his nonproducing properties. He had angrily canceled that sale after the word *auction* apparently caused word to spread that he was encountering financial difficulties.

"I've had people call me up and say, 'I hear you're broke.' Well, I'm a long way from being broke."

In fact, just a few weeks before the sale to Petro-Lewis, he told a reporter the rumors of his financial plight were greatly exaggerated. It was during a wildcatters reception at the Midland Petroleum Club honoring him and his company management, and Claytie was in no mood to mince words.

"Hell," he grinned, "I'm one of the most solvent sons of bitches around."

As if to underscore his contention, the Forbes Four Hundred struck again, naming him for the second straight year as one of the nation's wealthiest — this time with a net worth of $200 million-plus.

Said *Forbes* in its published capsule:

Clayton Wheat Williams Jr.
Oil. Midland, Tex. Married, 5 children. Quit as $10,000-a-year insurance salesman 1957 with $2,000 savings to begin career as oilman. Struggled through 1960s, then successive major finds (Austin Chalk, Edwards Trend). Now $1.2 billion revenues including six ranches, 300,000 acres. . . . Most flamboyant Midlander; building immense office plaza north end of town. Reports of financial disaster greatly exaggerated. With $220 million bank debt, net worth exceeds $200 million. "I'm not a billionaire yet, but it's nice to have a goal."

" I gave Modesta an unlimited budget to decorate this building, and she overspent it 43 percent."

12

With oil hovering around forty dollars a barrel in early 1981, Claytie formed ClayDesta Corporation, a Midland-based commercial real estate development and property management firm. The centerpiece of this enterprise would be development of a glittering $42 million, 183-acre office park north of downtown christened ClayDesta Plaza. And while he never missed a chance to tell folks that all he knew about banking was borrowing, he also formally entered the financial wars as founder of ClayDesta National Bank. Both the bank and Claytie's company offices were located in the plaza, which also would house the offices of most of his Midland employees when it opened in late 1983.

Claytie selected friend and confidante Bob Smith as executive vice president of the corporation, but his business cards reflected the special camaraderie that existed between the two diehard Aggies: they identified Smith as "Executive Sidekick" rather than executive VP.

"I guess I'm the guy who puts out the fires," Smith told a business writer shortly after his appointment. "Whenever there's a problem, it seems like I'm the one trying to fix it." In his early Midland days, in 1967, Claytie rented a room and desk from Smith in his offices. After Claytie purchased the Gulf Building in 1973, he rented office space to Smith and hired him in 1975. "Working here is an adventure," Smith confided to a writer. "You never know what kind of project you'll be undertaking or where you'll be going next. There always seems to be a challenge ahead."

ClayDesta groundbreaking, 1982

Claytie chose David Jones, executive vice president and head of lending for the American Bank of Waco, as president of ClayDesta National. And he installed Modesta as one of six directors. When people lavished praise on the showplace complex and what he called his "forty-dollar-oil office," Claytie would just smile and announce that Modesta was the spirit and force behind the eclectic and exotic monument to West Texas oil. "I gave Modesta an 'unlimited' budget to decorate this building," he would say solemnly, "and she overspent it 43 percent."

For Modesta, the project was almost like birthing, welcoming a new baby, and it did become a family affair.

"I loved putting my heart and soul and my time into planning it with the architects, the decorators, the building contractors, and the landscapers. It took all my time, but I could bring my kids down here with me, and that was wonderful."

Claytie's dad was confined to a wheelchair and battling cancer but that didn't keep him away. "We brought him in here to see what was happening, and he thought it was fabulous," Modesta said. "He was so proud of Claytie and enjoyed his success in building this huge building. So did his mother and my folks, of course."

The heartbeat of the complex was the breathtaking atrium, which featured fountains and plants and took on a special holiday glow at Christmas when decorated with hundreds of red poinsettias. Though it changed seasonally and sometimes dramatically, this is how Sandy Sheehy, in her book *Texas Big Rich,* described the edifice:

> In true Texas tradition, it boasted the vastest atrium and the tallest houseplants in the United States. Under a skylight composed of dozens of glass pyramids, speckled brown ducks splashed in an artificial stream fed by its own waterfall and waddled beneath towering rubber plants, thirty-foot ficus trees, Brobdingnagian philodendrons, and three-story Norfolk pines. At the center was a fountain spurting fifty feet into the air. In an arid, pancake-flat city where contact with nature

often meant enduring dust storms and dodging tumbleweeds, the atrium acted like a magnet. People strolled down the flagstone paths and ate their lunches on its wooden park benches. But pleasant as it was, this indoor oasis seemed otherworldly, as if it were plunked down on some distant planet to remind deracinated interstellar colonists what Earth was like.

Claytie's private office was only minimally less striking than the atrium, although not a single "Brobdingnagian philodendron" or a "deracinated interstellar colonist" could be found. Instead, wild-game trophies and photos, plaques and awards, Aggie memorabilia, and framed news and magazine articles decorated the walls.

"You know," Modesta said, "when we put it in, we really changed the complexion of Midland. The city was all downtown, the big buildings, everything. ClayDesta started a new area and a new era. It was Claytie's dream to have the independent oilmen out here north of town and the majors downtown where they had always been." The complex, coupled with a new loop around Midland, helped divert traffic from downtown and changed the whole dynamic of Midland.

Modesta and Claytie loved to host parties and other charitable and social events because they wanted their plaza to serve not only as the center for independent oilmen of the area but also as an entertaining place for the people of Midland.

"Claytie's such fun, and when there was something going on in the atrium, he would go down and participate whether he was invited or not," Modesta reported. "I've had to pull him out of a couple of weddings when he wasn't supposed to be there. But you know Claytie. . . . When we finished the building, we had a huge party. We wanted everybody to come and enjoy, and they did. It truly was a showplace. People would bring their friends and say, 'You've got to see this. There's not anything like it in West Texas.' Some outsiders thought we were just a little dumpy town out here, and they'd come out here and see this and . . . well, we were very prideful, I'll have to say."

ClayDesta atrium

Relishing the memories of the style shows, the weddings, and the various galas, Modesta continued: "It was beautiful, and it lent itself to creativity and imagination for people to do things. . . . It makes a happy place when you see people walking around and looking at the flowers and going up and down the escalator and the glass elevators."

Although no one could predict it at the time, ClayDesta Plaza would become in the tumultuous years ahead a reflection—if not a symbol—of the shifting fortunes of Claytie, his empire, his city, and a huge chunk of West Texas.

In December 1981, roughly the tenth anniversary of his clash over Wynona Riggs' desk, Sam Pfiester resigned to launch his own oil-patch career. "Have we had enough of each other?" he asked Claytie that day, joking that they mutually agreed such was the case. More than twenty years later Sam would look back on his departure and woefully recall that he bailed out at the absolute peak of the oil boom.

"What unplugged the whole damn industry was that I quit and went out on my own," he laughed. Until he met Claytie, he said, he didn't really know what wildcatting meant. "The truth is, you have a hell of a lot more failures than successes. That is the nature of the beast. Hell, Williams throws the dice with his own money. And anybody in the oil business knows that is the last thing you want to do. Yet he will pick himself up and dust off his britches and go on. He's a complex and extraordinary guy. All of us who have been around him for thirty or forty years love him, though there are complexities there that I don't understand. But damn, what a guy!"

Meanwhile, at the height of the media frenzy in April 1982, the hometown *Reporter-Telegram* kicked off a weekly feature about Midland oil and business leaders called "Focus," and naturally it chose Claytie for its inaugural profile.

He admitted to being flattered by the relentless media attention of the last two or three years. "I think because I'm kind of a character, because I'm outspoken, I've had more attention than I'm due. There are a lot of other people I think they should be talking to. I do think this: a person who has benefited by the freedom we have has a duty, frankly, to stand up and say his piece."

As the interview continued, Claytie started laughing and joking and confessed that he thought about entering politics once, but soon abandoned that idea. He told how he'd run unsuccessfully for the student council in high school and for president of the Fort Stockton Jaycees.

"I'm not a politician," he said, "I'm too blunt." One day he could look back on that statement and say, "How prophetic."

Given all his media attention, it was not shocking that Claytie wound up one weekend sipping cocktails with the likes of former Pres. Jimmy Carter, actor John Travolta, oil baron T. Boone Pickens, and broadcasting executive Ted Turner.

The occasion was the 1984 annual Golden Plate awards and banquet in Minneapolis, and this old small-town West Texas boy was one of the fifty honorees. The American Academy of Achievement created the awards in 1961 to honor extraordinary and inspiring "exemplars of excellence" in special fields of endeavor, according to the *Reporter-Telegram*. Previous winners included such luminaries as western movie star Gene Autry, bandleader Lawrence Welk, Dallas Cowboys coach Tom Landry, and Gen. Omar Bradley. The academy had just recently expanded the acknowledgments to include three hundred honor students from the fifty states, and the Golden Plate recipients shared their success stories and secrets with them. Claytie received a standing ovation after addressing the youngsters.

"It was an outstanding experience interacting with the top students and the top achievers in the country," Claytie told the *Reporter-Telegram*.

He did not tell the newspaper about the reception where Travolta, the star of such box-office hits as *Saturday Night Fever* and *The General's Daughter,* began flirting with Modesta. "I was over visiting with some people and I look around and see that John Travolta was really working on Modesta. I thought I better get my little ass over there and reclaim my territory."

Modesta couldn't resist tossing a little fuel on the fire. "He was a doll, and pretty cute," she said teasingly, "but Claytie didn't let me hang around and talk to him too long."

In September 1985, an energetic and totally unsuspecting young brunette applied for a job with the Williams companies. She had never heard of Clayton Williams Jr., but she loved ClayDesta Plaza and the "soothing and calm influence of the atrium with the fountain, waterfalls, and wood ducks playfully swimming in the water installations."

Denise Garrett's first thought: "What a beautiful and calm environment to come to work in."

That delusion soon imploded, but in the beginning it was almost calm and peaceful, because she was hired as an assistant to attorneys Paul Latham and Jim Hunnicutt. She did not meet the boss until a month later, on Claytie's fifty-fourth birthday. She introduced herself and told him she enjoyed working for his company. Scurrying around in his customary dither, dealing with half a dozen projects at once, Claytie's first words to Denise: "Welcome aboard; we're busy." His first request: Would she work the upcoming Thanksgiving weekend for triple time?

"Yes," she said, being single, needing the money, and wanting to establish herself as a team player. The following January she moved from the legal department to the War Room, working as Modesta's assistant and eventually as a coassistant to Claytie with Julie Faubel, a former staff writer at the Midland *Reporter-Telegram*. Perhaps unwittingly, Denise, whose father had been an oilman, would take to her new job like ducks to the atrium pond, quickly absorbing industry detail and nuance. And perhaps more important, the Texas Tech graduate who studied music and marched in the Red Raider band displayed a gift for pleasing the maestro whose baton never rests.

"It was the perfect setup," Denise said, being "behind the wall" in Modesta's office but still exposed to "the middle of the hubbub" that was Claytie's central command. The timing, however, was terrible.

"If you like working for a nonprofit organization," Claytie told her, "you'll love it here."

One lesson she quickly learned: even in the most turbulent times, it helped in the oil business to keep a sense of humor.

At the time, oil prices were dropping precipitously, and during her second week on the job, a migraine headache sent Claytie to the hospital for several days. Executive Sidekick Bob Smith visited him one day, announcing that he had good news and bad news. The bad news was that oil prices had dropped a dollar a day for ten consecutive days and was down to ten dollars a barrel. "The good news?" Claytie asked darkly. "Just ten days left to go," Smith replied.

Claytie's hospital stint was followed by a period of across-the-board pay cuts and other painful cost-cutting moves.

Although those first few years were "really tough," Denise said it was educational and invigorating and that Claytie somehow made it fun learning firsthand "how to be a survivor."

In May 1988, Julie Faubel's husband was transferred to Scotland, and when she resigned, Claytie asked Denise to be his executive assistant. She was thrilled, and remained so through the ups and downs of the next two decades when she increasingly became a highly respected "go-to" player on Claytie's administrative team.

"Whew! What a fun ride it's been!" she said, reflecting on those highs and lows with Claytie, her marriage to Richard Kelly in 1989, and the birth of twins Clayton and Garrett in 2003. She called her twenty years as Claytie's Jackie-of-all-trades "an eye-opening life experience that no university could ever offer."

Said she: "The skills I've learned from watching and listening to him are varied and numerous and fascinating."

Accustomed to the prickly tongue of Wynona Riggs and the feisty give-and-take of Sandy Jones, Claytie found Denise Kelly a new experience. "She's like my grandmother Mernie," he joked. "I can do no wrong."

13

Claytie's innovative entrepreneurial activities spawned a truly Byzantine venture in the early 1980s that opened with a bang, bang, bang and ended with a thud and a subplot that rivaled anything dreamed up by a morose Hollywood scriptwriter.

It began innocently enough, as spelled out by Claytie and a professional hunter named Gordon Cundill in November 1982. They sat down that day with the *Reporter-Telegram* to discuss Hunter's Africa, a safari company they would operate in Botswana, Zambia, and Tanzania. Cundill described the joint venture as "essentially a high-cost, low-volume business" whereby the company would lease from the government a forty-five-thousand-square-mile area for the exclusive use of its clients. Hunters would pay roughly twenty thousand dollars for a twenty-one-day safari and could take exotic game ranging from elephants to crocodiles.

Were it not for the serious money involved, the project would generate lively fodder for a bad TV sitcom. The undertaking was beset by problems early on, Claytie said. "No sooner were we in operation in Tanzania than the government arrested three of our hunters, contending that we were in the process of starting a Portuguese revolution to retake the neighboring country of Mozambique."

The arrests would plunge Paul Latham, then company counsel and now its chief operating officer, into an extended campaign to free the men and get them safely out of the country.

With oil back home declining from forty dollars to twenty-eight dollars a barrel, Claytie was distracted by the struggles in the energy arena and dispatched other trouble-shooting executives to help cope with the African mess. But they discovered much of the damage already done. The company was headed for ruin, despite Claytie's investment of $6 million. He would recover only $75,000 from a related lawsuit before selling Hunter's Africa to the McFarland Group of Botswana for $500,000 — plus one free hunt.

Years later, Claytie came to better understand what happened in Africa and why, and the lesson it taught him. "The basic concept was sound and solid," he said. "We had a very large portion of the finest hunting areas in Botswana, Zambia, and later Tanzania. We could've easily conducted forty safaris a year in Botswana alone. The country was stable, the concessions legal and secure. I put the capital in to develop the area, build the roads, improve the camps, and furnish good-quality vehicles for the hunters. So we had the raw material and the concessions and the capital to run the property. We simply needed better management, oversight, and accounting procedures."

Few debacles tested Claytie's celebrated sense of humor as this one had. But the humor survived, if not the safari company.

"I often said I got a 10 percent return on my investment in Africa and people would say, 'Oh?' I told them 'Yes, I got 10 cents back for every dollar I put in Hunter's Africa.'"

The misadventure was almost as ironic as it was expensive. Although he owned the coveted hunting site for five years, Claytie was too busy wrestling The Wreck back home to enjoy it.

"Modesta and I never set foot on it."

Then there was also the chilling and long-running sidelight to the African saga that Paul Latham called "the scariest and one of the most rewarding experiences of my life."

The Hunter's Africa subplot began for Paul on an August morning in 1984 when Claytie marched unannounced into his Midland office and reported that a man named Adelino Pires, his son, and a nephew had just been arrested and imprisoned in Tanzania for unknown reasons. "I'm thinking, who the hell is Adelino Pires?" Paul remembers. "I had no idea who these people were and why Claytie was looking at me so intently." Then Claytie smiled and said, "They're our professional hunters. Get them out! We've got to stand by our people."

Thus began a bewildering ordeal for Paul and Claytie's chief of security, John Omohundro. Some six months later they would complete the risky, delicate, and frustrating rescue mission. But not before one harrowing African episode after another, beginning with their arrival in the Tanzanian capital of Dar es Salaam. "Our passports were temporarily confiscated; we were strip searched and then escorted by police to our hotel," Paul said. Police stonewalled them, and the United States ambassador offered no help, just a warning: "If you're arrested, we would not be able to see you for three to six months. Good luck."

They did learn that the Tanzanian government suspected the imprisoned hunters were CIA agents and that the safari hunting camps were staging areas for invading mercenaries aiding a Portuguese resistance group dedicated to retaking Mozambique. As improbable as that was, Paul and his team also got word that the prisoners had been moved to Mozambique and that security officers there were torturing the three men in an attempt to obtain confessions.

After hiring a lawyer whose information was "worthless," Paul and John found an English-educated attorney and sent him into the fray. He returned two days later with a succinct message: "Leave your things; state security is coming to arrest you." Paul said they avoided arrest by minutes, escaping on an Air France jet to Paris, then flying home to the United States. Returning later to Tanzania to meet with their lawyer and officials, they were followed constantly by state police and discovered that listening devices had been planted in their hotel rooms.

"Incredibly, we were told to leave the country or face imprisonment as conspirators," Paul said. The craziness continued unabated through weeks of on-again, off-again negotiations until finally the trio was moved back to Tanzania. After extensive questioning and abuse by Tanzanian authorities, they were freed and permitted to leave the country on a commercial flight to Switzerland.

"Adelino Pires and the boys had survived a terrible ordeal with dignity and bravery," Paul said. "They had been questioned and tortured daily for almost six months. Adelino told me that death at one point was an attractive proposition." The company was finally able to recover its equipment and move it to Kenya, ending the Tanzanian debacle.

But the bottom line, as Claytie commanded: "We got 'em out."

"I have never witnessed a warmer rapport between speaker and crowd."

14

In March 1984, two prominent members of the Association of Former Students of Texas A&M University appeared in Claytie's office on a stealth mission of sorts. It was a stealth visit only in that Claytie was not informed of the purpose. One of the callers was Randy Matson, a world-class shot-putter and Olympic gold medalist of the 1960s and executive director of the association. The other was Jack Fritts, president of the association. They came seeking a $2.5 million financial commitment for a proposed multimillion-dollar alumni building. If their quarry was responsive, it would be named the Clayton Williams Jr. Alumni Center.

It would not be a hard sell, the first clue being when tears flooded Claytie's eyes. "He was so overwhelmed and honored that he cried on the spot," laughed Davis Ford, Claytie's Aggie friend from Austin and now a board member of Williams Energy. "When he had to write a multimillion-dollar check later, with oil prices plummeting, Claytie cried even harder!"

Oil had sunk from forty dollars to ten dollars a barrel, but Ford, an environmental engineer, tells an insightful story about Claytie when it came time for the final $1.7 million payment: "When I became president of the Association of Former Students, the building was still under construction and Claytie still owed the bulk of the money on his pledge. Two members of our board of directors at the time, one an oil and gas executive and the other a banking executive, told me that with the tumbling oil prices there was no way Claytie could meet his commitment. Our annual board meeting was held in Colorado Springs at the Broadmoor Hotel. Billy Clayton, the former Texas House Speaker, and I, along with Claytie, flew to the meeting."

Picking up the story, Claytie said the two skeptical board members were waiting for him to fall on his face when he couldn't make the payment. "It was envy and jealousy on the two men's part because the building was going to bear my name," he contended.

When it came time to make the presentation, the tone had been set.

"Billy Clayton established the sad mood for the occasion in his introduction, and I stood before the group with the biggest hangdog look you could imagine," Claytie recounted. "At my side, covered in plain wrapping paper, was a six-foot-long display board that Billy had indicated was an extended timetable for meeting my financial commitment."

Ford said Claytie, looking contrite and dejected, stood behind the display board and advised the directors that because of the oil and gas downturn and other negative factors he would not meet the original payment schedule. With the two cynical board members sporting "I told you so" expressions on their faces, Claytie unwrapped the board. A shocked silence seized the gathering, particularly the two doubters.

"I'm going to pay the son of a bitch off right now!" Claytie blurted. What everyone had thought was a revised timetable for payment was instead a six-foot check for $1.7 million.

Recalling how a standing ovation shattered the gloom of the occasion, Ford saw what he interpreted as a "satisfied smile" on Claytie's face. However, a grinning Claytie revealed later that "what I was really thinking was how I'd like to tell the two doubters to take that six-foot check and stick it up their cynical asses."

After Claytie's tearful commitment and Davis Ford's election as president of the association, Ford had made a point to get to know the Aggie benefactor better. Accompanied by Randy Matson, Ford soon visited Claytie in Midland and was shown around his memorabilia-filled office.

"I paid particular attention to the area dedicated to his late father, Clayton Williams Sr.," Ford said later, at the May 1985 groundbreaking of the alumni center. "He, too, had been a wildcatter, a rancher, a public servant, and a West Texas historian. An electrical engineer in the A&M class of 1915, [the elder Williams] truly made a mark in the history of the Fort Stockton and West Texas area."

Ford also noted that as Claytie viewed a photo and spoke of his father, his eyes teared and his voice began to break.

"I thought it was appropriate to include this feeling in my introduction," Ford explained, "and commented that the legacy that Claytie had received from his father was now being translated to hundreds of thousands of Aggies through the Williams name that would adorn this great building for decades to come."

Besides Claytie and Ford, the official party for the groundbreaking ceremony that spring morning in 1985 included Frank Vandiver, president of A&M; David Eller, chairman of the board of regents; Arthur Hanson, chancellor of the A&M System; H. B. "Bartel" Zachry, CEO of the Zachry Company and a member of Claytie's class of '54; Robert Smith, class of '61 and chairman of the A&M Development Foundation Trustees; and Randy Matson.

With the news media in place and the television cameras recording the ceremony, Ford said he felt the occasion appropriate for a quote from Winston Churchill: "In every man's life there comes a time when he is figuratively tapped on the shoulder to do a very special thing — unique to him and suited to his talents. What a tragedy if that time finds him unprepared or unqualified to perform that task."

"Well," Ford continued, "Claytie Williams had been tapped on the shoulder by the Association of Former Students to do a very special thing, and because of his father's legacy, his own talents and tenacity, and his ability to produce in our free-enterprise system, he was both prepared and qualified to take his place in A&M's history."

When Claytie rose to speak, he introduced his family, which included Modesta and his mother, Chic, and told the assemblage, "My dad is here in spirit." He got as far as the significance of the event and his love for A&M before emotion overcame him. He finally

Claytie and Modesta, center, *presenting final check for the A&M Alumni Center with,* left to right, *Randy Matson, Mike Baggett, Davis Ford, and Billy Clayton*

gave up, uttering a desperate "Gig 'em!" and sat down to a booming ovation.

"I have never witnessed a warmer rapport between speaker and crowd," Ford said.

Few realized at the payoff that Claytie wanted desperately to borrow the money to make the final alumni-center payment, but he was so overextended that the banks refused his requests. "If the banks would've let me pay the last $1.7 million of what I owed to A&M, I could have worked through [the oil and gas downturn]," he said. But it was not to be. Actually, it was a combination of negative factors that converged in the early and mid-1980s to create the quandary that forced him to sell the cash cow of the Williams conglomerate, Clajon Gas—the deepest regret of his business career.

The sale price was more than $225 million, including notes and other financial considerations, allowing Claytie to reduce considerable debt and calm nervous bankers. As difficult as the sale was for Claytie, the transaction did provide a few Claytie-like moments.

The scene: Midland, Claytie's office in ClayDesta Plaza; spring, 1987. The prospective buyer was former Treasury Secretary William Simon's old law firm, which specialized in handling leveraged buyouts. Paul Latham, then Claytie's chief counsel, remembers a room full of high-powered lawyers, six of them, sitting in a row on a green couch — "like birds." A covey of Claytie's secretaries worked nearby, "and the lawyers were hustling them like buzzards," Paul recalls. Claytie and the lead negotiator, Manford Stein, who had been a protégé of William Simon, sat apart at a round table, dealing, arguing, getting frustrated. Paul joined them at the table: "I was there to take notes; I wasn't supposed to say anything."

Negotiations hardened. Claytie couldn't get the last $10 million he wanted.

"That's all I'm going to do," Stein asserted, indicating the $220 million range was his top offer. "We don't have a deal!"

It was as if Claytie didn't hear him. He laughed at Stein's rejection. Then he bolted out of his chair and turned a somersault — right in the middle of his office in front of some of New York's most prestigious lawyers. Paul looked at the birdlike lawyers roosting on the green couch, their attention suddenly diverted from Claytie's fetching secretaries. "The lawyers were stunned."

So, apparently, was Manford Stein. "OK," he said, "you can have the ten million bucks."

As unnerving as the stunt might have been to those uninitiated in oil-patch wheeling and dealing, the $10 million floor flip could hardly have surprised those who knew Claytie. "It was impulse," Claytie said. Well, maybe, impulse like a fox. "It was sort of like jumping in the ring at the Brangus sale, trying to get the people to raise the price."

For all the levity the floor flip created, what was to come two months later — the closing on June 3, 1987, in New York — would become known as "the funeral." On what seemed like the hottest day of the summer, Claytie, Modesta, and the Clajon entourage gathered in a huge room where it took more than three hours just to sign the closing documents. Witnesses say Claytie and Modesta were close to tears the entire time, and surely shed a few quietly, privately. Afterward the new owners of Clajon hosted a champagne dinner at one of the toniest restaurants in town. Claytie and the gang toasted a sip or two, then fled for the airport and the company jet for the long, sad flight home.

"I still miss my gas company," Claytie would say nearly twenty years later, long after Clajon became a billion-dollar public entity under new ownership. "That was a great company, by far my best. I started it from scratch and it was a wonderful bunch of people. Clajon's really what kept me from going under in the bust."

Part of Claytie's cash-flow problem was the millions dedicated to his growing portfolio of investments, most notably a digital communications company, but the situation was compounded by diminishing oil and gas prices and failure of a major gas buyer to honor a contract.

"I'd sold most of my oil properties in 1982 and I wasn't in trouble in the oil bust of the '80s until the gas prices dropped in '86 and '87," he said. "I was selling all my gas to Valero of San Antonio, which is now a major refining company. When the price dropped, they quit paying me. Bill Greehey of Valero [board chairman and former chief executive officer] and I are friends to this day, but he was fighting for his life and I was fighting for mine."

Much has been written about the oil booms and busts of the late '70s and '80s, but few recall or realize the intrigue behind the rise and fall of energy prices that shook much of the world—especially Texas. As Claytie says, most people know that the "oil boom" of 1979–1981 was caused by the interruption of oil supplies resulting from the Iran-Iraq war, which sent the price to forty dollars a barrel. Many also know that the market fizzled when Saudi Arabia increased its oil production substantially by 1986, when prices plunged to ten dollars a barrel.

"A third factor—and maybe the most important—the Reagan administration used its power and influence to persuade the Saudis to increase their output and thereby lower prices," Claytie says, explaining that Ronald Reagan had a more sweeping reason than economics for wanting the price of oil to fall. "The objective was to deprive the Soviet Union of liquidity and cash flow, destroy their solvency, and win the cold war. It succeeded. It took down the energy industry and damn near got me along with it!"

But the story behind the collapse of the gas industry may be more compelling.

"Few people know," Claytie said, "that the boom in natural gas prices in the late '70s and the bust that brought my empire crumbling down was caused not by market forces but by government interference."

The intervention was known prosaically as the Natural Gas Policy Act, the NGPA, which went into force December 1, 1978. "I didn't realize until years later how important that government act was—along with the price of oil—in causing The Wreck."

Prior to the NGPA, Claytie explained, virtually no natural gas was sold into interstate commerce, or between the states, because government regulations kept prices critically and artificially low.

"Thus, all newly drilled Texas natural gas was produced, sold, processed, and consumed within the state of Texas. This situation created a multifaceted boom within Texas and similarly in other gas-producing states like Louisiana. Substantial industry developed in Texas to utilize all the available gas. This in turn deprived industrial states in the north and east of natural gas for their industrial needs. They were not happy," said Claytie, grandly understating the political and emotional friction caused by the issue. "Bumper stickers such as 'Let the Bastards Freeze in the Dark!' did not help. In fact, they cost Texas dearly."

Responding to complaints from the northeastern states to correct the problem and the disparity in prices, Congress passed the NGPA in 1978. "This act mandated substantial and automatic price increases on gas sold at the wellhead so that interstate gas companies could compete for Texas gas," Claytie explained. "This law and industry's aggressive action, coupled with the Iran-Iraq war, brought about the biggest boom in the history of our oil and gas industry."

But by 1986, he said, the federally mandated gas prices had risen far above what the market would bear. Industry began cutting back on energy purchases, particularly natural gas. "We had priced ourselves out of the market complying with Congress's act," Claytie said.

Chaos ensued, resulting in the bust of 1986, a replay of the 1982 collapse, and undermining Claytie's financial foundation.

"Valero, my customer, assigned my contracts to a subcompany, Reata, which lowered the price it paid me in violation of the contract terms between us," Claytie said. The failure of Valero to honor its contract, coupled with the cash demands at the time of his communications company and the huge commitment to Texas A&M, forced Claytie to sell Clajon Gas.

"Between the oil-price drops and the natural gas chaos, gas pipeline companies and producers went broke across the nation," he said. Indeed, the energy industry had taken a horrendous hit. "In the oil industry we went from 5,000 active rigs to 550. I was just a little leaf on a tidal wave."

Claytie clung to Clajon as long as he could, but the bankers were howling like wolves and the potential "shame" of not meeting his Aggie commitment was too much to contemplate. "So it was just a collapse across the board, and I had to sell the company if I was going to meet that commitment. Our entire industry shrank proportionately. I survived. I didn't go broke, but I sure as hell went bent."

Complicating matters, Texas took a triple whammy: banks and real estate headed south along with oil. "This financial hurricane spread from energy producers to real estate and across the entire Texas economy," Claytie recalled. "We lost most of the major banks to bankruptcy and takeovers."

Of the economic tripod that historically sustained the Texas economy—oil, banking, and real estate—Claytie would in time be convinced that one of the three stood stronger and more responsibly than the others: oil.

"So many people in Texas thought the whole wreck was the oil business. In hindsight, we have learned that the biggest losses were in speculative real estate and real estate land loans, and they were loaning on assets. Today you can't borrow money on soft assets. You've got to have something real, not stock and not land that's overvalued."

To this day, says Claytie, bankers contend oil loans are bad. To the contrary, he says, "I've seen a figure suggesting that 88 or 89 percent of all oil loans paid off. . . . The Wreck was not oil."

Instead, he maintains, The Wreck was caused by (1) the unrealistic low price triggered by the oil glut, (2) the political backlash of the "freezing bastards" bumper sticker, and (3) the collapse of the real estate market. "Of course," he admits, "the bad banking loans just gutted our entire Texas banking economy."

Claytie acknowledged that even from his perspective at the time—as both a bank director and an oilman who survived the economic calamity—he didn't see the importance of the Natural Gas Act as his oil and gas business deteriorated. "Because I was so deep in trouble," he said, "I couldn't be that reflective. I was just trying not to drown."

One of the gut-wrenching aspects of the fight for survival was the layoffs. Dick Oldham of Midland, the longtime friend who headed Maverick Mud, remembered seeing Claytie standing alone beneath a tree outside his office and weeping quietly. He was distraught about letting many of his employees go. Even more vividly, Modesta recalled her husband coming home one day, falling across the bed, and bursting into tears. "Really crying," she said, quoting Claytie as saying, "I can't stand to hurt people. It is not their fault that they are getting fired; it is my fault that I have to let them go. I haven't done a good job."

It was a scene she would not easily forget.

"I remember the kids coming in, and they couldn't understand why Dad was crying. It was hard to explain to them."

In explaining his philosophy about such unpleasantness, Claytie cited the Giddings experience with Bill Haverlah: "When Bill and I started staffing up our Giddings properties, experienced hands were simply not available in the boom times of 1979. So we hired many bright young people, men and women, from A&M and other area schools and particularly from the South Texas area where we were active and had gained some measure of respect. I knew in a layoff, it was important the person be told that it was not his or her fault so they could go forward without a sense of failure—and with severance pay and benefits."

In the initial layoff, he said, "I told them all that at once. I later realized that termination should be a two-day process. In the future, I would tell them one day they were laid off and ask them to come back the next day after they'd had time to digest the news. Then I would tell them what a good job they'd done, give them severance pay, benefits, and so forth. Since they'd had time to get over the shock, they were better able to listen to me as I tried to counsel them."

Beginning in 1982 and lasting throughout the decade, Clayton suffered numerous layoffs and pay cuts, blaming himself or his upper management for not doing a better job of planning. "Unhappily, I became an expert at layoffs, beginning in '82 but actually extending until '98." He consoled himself with the knowledge that many of those young men and women left better trained and better prepared to investigate, evaluate, and play the oil business.

For all the grim economic news of the mid-1980s and 1990s, one enterprise among Claytie's holdings remained a shining beacon of success—the Williams Ranch Co. operations.

With ten ranches under fence—eight in Texas, two in Wyoming—the properties totaled 349,550 acres. The largest jewel in the ranching crown was the historic Sullivan Ranch north of Medicine Bow, Wyo., which boasted a spread of 250,000 acres and an aggressive, comprehensive program initiated by Claytie to develop its natural resources. Claytie was most pleased that Martin Sullivan, grandson of the founder, chose to stay on as foreman and partner when he bought the ranch in 1981.

"It is a great place where you can fish on any one of more than thirty ponds and a few streams in the morning, have a nice lunch and hamburger cookout, or come back to the lodge, take a nap, and watch the prairie dogs in the evening," Claytie said. "Some of our friends like to climb with Modesta and me to the top of the mountain in the morning, which we do to keep up our exercise. It is a grand place."

A guest took a short drive around the ranch one day and spotted mule deer, elk, antelope, prairie dogs, prize cattle, hawks, pelicans, and eagles. "I doubled the elk herd at the ranch and substantially increased the game population," Claytie said.

By the mid-'80s Claytie was riding high with his ever-growing and prosperous ranch properties. In 1984, for example, the Williams ranching and agricultural interests shipped seventeen thousand yearlings, including ten thousand from the Sullivan Ranch, to nine feedlots in Colorado, Kansas, and Nebraska. Another Wyoming spread, the thirty-five-thousand-acre Cronberg Ranch, shipped two thousand yearlings.

Back home, most of the interest focused on the forty-two-section Happy Cove Ranch, which was the scene annually of Claytie's exuberant and flashy Williams Brangus and Production Sale and Ranch Party. In the mid-1980s the Happy Cove Ranch ran twelve hundred commercial Brangus and two thousand yearlings; its budding farming operations produced eleven hundred tons of hay, largely through resourceful land use and development.

Other ranches in West Texas and across the state were enjoying a similarly bountiful time with cattle and farming operations. But no spread generated as much attention as the Sullivan Ranch, the ninety-six-year-old family operation that Claytie bought in '81. The Sullivan, Claytie decided, would be a sporting showcase and a prime example of how to husband the land and its resources: thus, he began an extensive program of water and land enhancements.

"Claytie has chosen to increase the value and productivity of the ranch by constructing reservoirs on live streams capable of producing excellent trophy and pleasure fishing," reported the December 1984 Williams Companies newsletter. In the works: forty new dams, of which thirty-two would hold water and be stocked with a variety of trout, including rainbow, brook, cutthroat, and golden. Trash fish were removed from existing streams, and barriers were con-

structed to prevent their return. Four dams underwent major reno-
vations, and seventeen new ones would be completed by early 1985,
with another ten scheduled to be ready later that year. Claytie hired
an expert to conduct extensive water-chemistry testing and to evaluate aquatic life on the ranch. Ever mindful of the financial stress
of the early 1980s, Claytie made ranch improvements with his own
workers and equipment.

"I moved a crew to Wyoming with bulldozers, dump trucks, and
a road grader. We brought our cook and our chuck wagon, and our
men camped out and lived where the work was because it would
have been totally prohibitive if they had to drive back and forth to
town every day. So we built the ponds very cost effectively."

Billy Weiser moved from Giddings to oversee the first crew,
which included Claytie's bulldozer driver for more than thirty years,
Domingo Dominguez; then later came longtime Claytie buddy
Charlie Moody of Fort Stockton to take over the crew for the final
construction. "They stayed from June through almost October and
did a helluva lot of work," Claytie said.

The Sullivan Ranch holds fond memories for Claytie. "The size of
the ranch was immense, even by Texas standards. We had one pasture of over one hundred square miles. I recall Clayton Wade and
Jeff and Adam Pollard were out horse-backing in this pasture from
before dawn until after dark. When they came in, they couldn't eat;
they just fell into bed."

On one outing with Martin Sullivan, "we helped move twenty-
eight hundred head of yearling steers some several miles," Claytie
recalled. "It was the largest group of cattle together I'd ever seen."

He remembers, too, the thrill of hunting afforded by the ranch,
where "Wyoming antelope are as wild as ours in West Texas are
tame." Once he dropped an antelope running away from him—"one
of the longest shots I ever made," measured at 603 paces by hunting companion Steve Steinle, whom he had hired to run the hunting
and fishing operations.

All across Claytie's ranching and farming empire, especially
at his prized Wyoming ranch, the mid-'80s reflected a flush and

promising time, an aberration considering the economic wreck that besieged the oil patch, banking, and real estate in Texas.

Looking back on those traumatic times of the oil-patch '80s, Claytie, as always, could force a smile or dismiss his despondency with a joke or humorous anecdote. "What's the difference between a pigeon and an independent oilman?" he'd ask. The punch line: "A pigeon can still make a deposit on a Mercedes."

But there came a time in the summer of 1986 that Claytie's personal and professional life hurtled totally out of control, a time when he became so overcome with despair that he turned for help to a source some would find surprising. Everything was out of whack—the oil and gas industry, the real estate market, cattle prices. He'd ruptured a disc branding a calf and the injury was more than just painful. Worst of all, his elder son Clayton Wade had gotten hooked on drugs. Claytie and Modesta were flying almost weekly to Dallas to support Clayton Wade in his drug-rehab program. "That took a major part of our time over an eighteen-month period," Claytie said.

When reliving the experience of that hot summer morning on a jogging trail at Happy Cove Ranch, Claytie spoke of his religious grounding and where it led that day. "I was raised a Christian, by my mother particularly, and by my dad to a lesser extent," he said. "I believed in God, but I don't think you really come to terms until you're flat on your back. That's when you know you need help. . . . Suddenly, there on the mountain trail, I was just overwhelmed. My boy's on drugs, my back is giving me trouble, and I'm asking myself if I'm going broke. I didn't know if I was going to make it."

Dropping to his knees in a pasture, he said, "Lord, you take it. I can't handle it. It's too big for me. And Lord, if it's your will, you take over and I will just keep working. My job is to keep working and wherever you take me, that's where I will go."

Things began to improve.

"It's been better since then," he said. "I've been able to do my job as best I can and go forward. I did turn it over to the Lord, but every once in a while I tend to try to take it back. I am not a perfect Christian by any means, but I am better than I was. I am who I am, and I'm comfortable with that. I couldn't have gotten any lower than I was at the time. I'm going broke, I'm going to be a cripple, and my boy's a drug addict."

With no place else to turn, he turned to God.

"And it worked. Thank you, Lord."

"If anybody perceives you to be slick or dishonest or crooked, they're not gonna mess with you."

15

In one of several related news stories in the late 1980s, a writer described Claytie as a West Texas farm boy, cowhand, insurance salesman, real estate investor, energy developer, communications pioneer, and cattle breeder. But the reporter went on to reveal that Claytie was wrapping up what he considered the most satisfying and rewarding endeavor.

No, he was not forgoing beer drinking or mariachi singing or whacking some loud-mouthed lounge lizard. He was hanging up his robes as an academic celebrity.

Claytie was reluctantly concluding a multiyear stint as a coprofessor of a course in entrepreneurship at Texas A&M with an equally gregarious soul mate, Dr. Ella Van Fleet, an award-winning visiting management authority and lecturer—and talented songwriter.

"These two professionals combined theory and reality so we are exposed to a large array of ideas to stimulate our thinking," volunteered one student. "They both provide a tremendous inspiration."

Gushed another: "It has stressed the importance of combining common sense, business opportunities, and dreams. Probably the most significant lesson I have learned is not to be afraid to fail."

Officially entitled Management 489: Special Studies in Entrepreneurship, the course was also known by other names, such as "How to Make a Million Dollars," or simply "Claytie's Class."

Claytie christened it "Bullshit 101" until a student one day raised his hand and said: "Mr. Williams, we want to change the name of your course. Your bullshit is so advanced we want to call it Bull-shit 489."

And Bullshit 489 it became — at least in some circles.

As Claytie loved to tell students and curious reporters: "Ella teaches theory, and I come in and shoot the bull."

Stacking the deck from the start, Ella invited Aggie coach Jackie Sherrill to attend the inaugural class, and Sherrill showed up with a football that had been signed for Claytie by all his players.

"Claytie was a babbling idiot he was so nervous," Ella said. "He didn't just bring Modesta with him; he brought the whole damn company . . . and half the town. I was chiding him later and he said, 'Well, I brought all these people along in case I couldn't think of any-thing to say.' I thought, 'Are you kidding?' You know, Claytie *never* runs out of anything to say."

The dynamic duo hit it off at once, probably because Ella could be just as unpredictable and cantankerous as Claytie, and intro-duced him to his first students in a manner only someone like Clay-tie could appreciate.

"When I first invited Mr. Williams," she told the class, "I thought he was an unemployed teacher because people kept saying he was a man with no class. . . ."

Before he recovered from that zinger, she struck again: "When he was born, his parents looked for a loophole in the birth certif-icate — but the state said they had to keep him. They didn't know whether to get a crib or a cage."

And this: "For years, he was an unknown failure. Then he be-came a known failure. . . . But to him, business was always looking up. Always does when you're flat on your back."

As a young Aggie, he was a miracle worker, she deadpanned. "His aptitude test showed he should be a mattress tester . . . but he man-aged to graduate."

Her sharp wit and sly smile camouflaged a string of debilitat-ing health problems, which rather than dwelling on, she joked about.

"I have survived a liver transplant and a few other retrofittings of tubes and pipes from an unidentified twenty-seven-year-old male in California—so, unlike Claytie, I am significantly younger than I was when he and I were teaching the classes," she was still wise-cracking years later.

Claytie called her "tough, a great lady and a great teacher."

Theirs was both an enduring friendship and an educational experiment that teamed the university instructor with this successful entrepreneur. The course and the concept behind it were designed by Van Fleet in 1982. The popular postclass beer and "Deathburger" assemblies that came later, at a campus fast-food joint called the Chicken Oil, were Claytie's idea.

Among its many innovations, Ella said, the course was intended to "bridge the gap between the classroom and the world of free enterprise . . . and to emphasize the need for balancing a purely analytical approach with a strong value system, a people orientation, and an unwavering sense of integrity, ethics, and character."

The premise also was to develop "a better appreciation of free enterprise, the basis of America's strong entrepreneurial drive."

Despite the running jokes about bull manure, Ella said, Claytie often did just the opposite: "He said he was always bullshitting, but he just cut through a lot of it."

The class quickly became the most popular in the College of Business Administration, then was selected as the "Best Class" in the annual "Best & Worst of Aggieland" competition.

"It's been such a popular course that we've had to limit enrollment," department head Dr. Michael Hitt said in 1986 after Bullshit 489, also known as MGMT 489, was named the most innovative business class by the Southern Business Administration Association. "We try not to turn too many students away, but have had to do so because we simply didn't have the capacity to handle them," Hitt said. "The students love the course. . . ."

The Texas and national news media loved writing about it, showcasing articles in such publications as the *Houston Post, Austin*

Professor Williams teaching an entrepreneurship course at Texas A&M

American-Statesman, Dallas Times Herald, Bryan-College Station Eagle, Private Clubs magazine, and even the Associated Press.

Elizabeth Bennett, writing in the now-defunct *Houston Post,* sat in one evening with a class and then joined the "C&E Show" (Claytie and Ella) at the Chicken Oil, the popular beer and burger joint. The Houston reporter told how Claytie flew in from Midland on his private maroon-and-white jet twice a month during the spring semester to join Ella for their Bullshit 489 night course and how afterward he treated the students to brew and "Deathburgers," so named for Chicken Oil hamburgers spiked with fiery jalapeño peppers.

"His candid, down-to-earth advice about the business world — both in class and during the free-wheeling drinking sessions that follow — is giving forty-eight lucky Aggies a rare exposure to the real world beyond the classroom," she wrote. ". . . The straight-talking Aggie is sharing philosophies he developed during more than a quarter century of trial and error—philosophies often at odds with the conventional wisdom about 'Making it Big.'"

Stressing that Claytie was never reluctant to discuss his entrepreneurial failures as well as his successes, Bennett quoted him as saying: "I teach a lot from my errors and my mistakes—and Lord knows I've made plenty of 'em. I formed a lot of companies that were failures in the early days, and I learned from those failures. So I use them and I laugh at myself and say 'don't do that.' It gets me interacting with the kids—they laugh at me and I laugh at them—and I get involved with them."

She also pointed out some of the themes he touched on in his lectures—philosophies that would continue to come into play along the rocky road he would travel over the next quarter century:

- The key to success is integrity. "If anybody perceives you to be slick or dishonest or crooked, they're not gonna mess with you."
- There's nothing wrong with making mistakes. Running a business is a series of making mistakes and correcting them, "and I like my employees to feel like they can make a mistake without getting mashed."
- There's nothing wrong with the man at the top frequently changing his mind and issuing conflicting orders. "It's ego that keeps someone from admitting a mistake and backing up and starting again."

During the 1987–88 academic year, Ella won a Leavey Award, presented annually by the Freedoms Foundation of Valley Forge for excellence in private enterprise education. She accepted the award in Austin on a particularly memorable day: Only hours earlier, "My big, ugly back brace had been removed. Following back surgery, I wore that brace from November 1986 until the day before the presentation in May 1987, and I was still having trouble walking and sitting."

The Leavey award came just after the Seventy-First Texas Legislature honored her with a resolution for her "many contributions to the College of Business Administration at Texas A&M."

Ella often was the singular recipient of the national awards and recognition, but she always credited Claytie. "Although I was the recipient," she said, "Claytie was what made it possible, so we both were proud of all the honors. We made a pretty good team." Similarly, when Claytie received state and local awards, he was equally quick to share the accolades.

"More seriously, I thought that two of Claytie's larger contributions to the class were his emphasis on integrity and his willingness to admit errors," Ella said. "Students seemed most surprised at the mistakes he had made—and that he had been able to survive them only because he had the capital on hand to bail himself out. Another point is that Claytie was a *huge* role model to the students. He and his background made them believe in themselves—that they, too, could be successful if they worked hard, remained honest, learned from their mistakes."

As the "C&E Show" neared the end of its six-year run, Ella wrote Claytie a letter thanking him: "Your innate ability to inspire the students makes teaching so much more effective and enjoyable. I think that most of the students know how fortunate they are to have had this opportunity to cross paths with you."

Revealing again their warm and often lighthearted relationship, she added: "Since you have unquestionably demonstrated your ability, it seems appropriate finally to issue you an official license to practice your trade. Accordingly, I trust that you will find the enclosed 'License to B——S——' of great value to you in continuing to do what you do best."

The enclosed License to Bullshit resembled a standard driver's license complete with a photograph of Claytie in cowboy hat, and proclaimed: "This is to certify that the person named and described on the reverse side has been licensed to exaggerate, fabricate, distort, or just plain lie."

It was authorized and stamped by Dr. Fulla Krapp, Commissioner of Fabrication.

Claytie had met his match. And he loved it!

After leaving A&M, Ella relocated with her husband in Scottsdale, Ariz., where she confronted her ongoing health problems with quiet courage and a sprightly sense of humor. Though no longer teaching, she continued writing songs and in 2005 produced a classic album containing such lively tunes as "I Don't Like Sushi" and "I'm Takin' Off—and I Don't Mean My Clothes."

Claytie and fellow Aggie Davis Ford share a favorite story about their part-time teaching experiences. Ford taught an engineering course as an adjunct professor at the University of Texas during Claytie's teaching tenure at College Station.

"Claytie," Ford asked, "how much does A&M pay you for teaching that bullshit?"

"Oh," he shrugged, "they pay me about a thousand bucks per month for six credit hours."

"Hell, Claytie, I just make eight hundred bucks a month for teaching twelve hours of complex engineering at UT. . . . That's not fair!"

With a lopsided grin, Claytie retorted: "Just goes to show you, Davis, that bullshit taught at A&M is worth 2.5 times more than complex engineering at Texas!"

"He is the sun and we are all the little planets that rotate around him."

What do you say when you're about to marry a guy's beautiful young daughter, and your future father-in-law tells you he likes to hunt, fish, work, and have sex, and then asks: "What about you?" How does a young man respond when the father of his new fiancée asks irritably, "Why don't I just take you outside and whip your ass?" What does a daughter expecting her first child any moment tell her father when he checks his calendar to attend the delivery and says: "Friday would be a good day for me"?

Nobody ever suggested it would be easy being a wife, an offspring, or an in-law of Clayton W. Williams Jr., father of five, grandfather of six, and master of almost all with whom he comes in contact. Not easy, but always eventful.

The operative word is *fun,* according to daughters Kelvie, Allyson, and Chim, and sons Clayton Wade and Jeff.

"Fun, crazy, wild, and loving," says Kelvie, the first of two daughters by Claytie's early marriage to his high school sweetheart, Betty Meriwether. "All the kids in Fort Stockton loved him because he'd get down and wrestle with you and chase you. Everybody called him Uncle Claytie."

Says her more rebellious sister Allyson, the second born: "He is so much fun, and he does everything at such a fast pace, fast forward . . . and he's just bigger than life—although life does intervene every once in a while."

Clayton Wade, whom Claytie and Modesta adopted as an infant in 1970, talks forthrightly of his family entanglements during his youthful fling with drugs, but says: "We had a lot of fun. He'd teach me how to do stuff, work cattle and build water troughs and whatnot. He taught me how to hunt, mostly rabbit and quail . . . and that's one of the great things we've always done together."

Describing his dad as "amazing," Jeff, also adopted as an infant, in 1973, says he was mightily impressed when Claytie built a major irrigated farm complex piece by piece from portions of the family's old Fort Stockton ranch. That's where Jeff now lives and works.

Adds Chim, youngest of the Williams brood and born on her dad's forty-fourth birthday in 1975: "I say 'thanks' every night in my prayers that I was born into this family. We have so much fun. We love to shock each other and it all comes straight from the head honcho. . . . We get tickled at him all the time."

Really, how do you describe a vitamin-popping dad who once swallowed his hearing aid with a pocket full of pills; a hunter who waded into an icy lake in his boxer shorts to retrieve a dead duck; and a taskmaster whose nephews Scott and Clay Pollard, after a summer working the fence line at Happy Cove Ranch with Hispanic laborers, christened him "Tío Terrible"—pronounced *ter-REE-blay*.

In Spanish, it means Uncle Terrible.

Claytie has never been reluctant to impose his work ethic on anyone, family or otherwise. Kelvie relishes relating the time Claytie glanced out the window of his ClayDesta office and spotted a worker leaning on his shovel. He soon concluded that the worker was goofing off and sent an aide scurrying downstairs to fire him. Returning shortly, the aide reported, "You can't fire him, Mr. Williams."

"And why the hell not?"

"Because he doesn't work for you; he works for the telephone company."

Greg Welborn remembers well his first meeting with his father-in-law-to-be. He and Chim joined Claytie and Modesta at the

Alpine ranch, and Greg and Claytie drove down to Fort Stockton together to go fishing. "We were fishing in this little bitty boat," Greg recalled, "and I asked him what he liked to do for fun. He said, 'Well, I like to hunt, fish, work, and have sex. What about you?'

"I said, 'Oh, uh, I like to hunt and fish.'"

But after his previous introduction to Modesta, Greg should have realized he was not joining an ordinary family. She was seated at a table with a friend at an outdoor restaurant when Chim brought him in to meet her mom, who had acquired some costume false teeth and glasses that made her eyes look as big and fetching as the bottom of a Coke bottle.

"Mom," said Chim, "I'd like for you to meet Greg."

When she turned and smiled at him, he was too stunned to speak. "Poor guy," Modesta said later. "I don't think he's forgiven me yet. He was expecting this sweet, nice little mom, you know, and I did that to him. He was at a loss for words."

The Welborn introductions were mild when compared to Jerry Groner's early experiences with Claytie. When Jerry and Allyson got engaged, Allyson phoned her dad from College Station. It was after midnight, and there was this partial exchange:

"Hi, Daddy, I'm getting married."

"What?"

"Jerry and I are getting married."

"Oh God, Allyson! Are you pregnant?"

"Noooooo!"

When Claytie next arrived in College Station to teach his biweekly B.S. 489 course, Allyson guided him to a bar and pointed Jerry out to him.

"Oh, he has shifty eyes," Claytie said, further endearing himself.

It got worse. When Jerry and Allyson appeared in Midland for a party shortly after their engagement, Allyson needed a coat and borrowed one from Modesta. When she gave her daughter a fancy fur to wear, Jerry "hit the ceiling," in Allyson's words. "I'm never going to be able to afford you and all these fancy coats," she quoted him as saying. After the party, she said, Claytie got to fretting about

Claytie with sons Jeff, left, *and Clayton Wade*

the coat incident, and told Jerry, "You know, my daughter can wear whatever coat she wants."

Presumably displeased with Jerry's attitude, Claytie inquired of his future son-in-law: "Why don't I just take you outside and whip your ass?"

Modesta laughingly and steadfastly insists that Claytie's relationship with his sons-in-law mellowed over the years, and both say it never really was all that rocky to begin with. And Claytie warned them early on of the pitfalls of having a father-in-law like him. Interestingly, both later worked for Claytie, although Jerry, a topflight lawyer and land man, left the company in 2006 to branch out on his own. Greg, with a degree in Natural Resources from A&M, worked in Dallas as an arborist and started his own tree care company in Austin before joining Williams Energy in 2003. Kelvie's ex-husband, Memphis pediatric neurosurgeon Mike Muhlbauer, was one of the few in-laws or outlaws who never worked for Claytie.

However, Mike lured his father-in-law to Memphis once for medical tests at a renowned neurosurgery clinic, an episode no one will ever forget. Claytie, who had suffered a mild stroke in Texas, underwent a series of tests at the Memphis clinic. Afterward, still groggy from the anesthesia, he was rolled out in the hallway on a gurney. "Daddy was just lying there in la-la land," Kelvie recalls gleefully, "and suddenly started singing 'Old Dogs and Children and Watermelon Wine,' that Tom T. Hall song. He sings it from the first to the last, in perfect pitch, never missing a word. He had an audience of nurses standing around looking at him and laughing and saying, 'Isn't that cute?'

"Just before the performance ends, an old guy rolls up in a wheelchair and sits there eyeing the scene curiously, if not suspiciously. He finally nods at Claytie and says to the nurses, 'I'm not gonna come out sounding like that, am I?'"

Hunting with Claytie is an adventure, and not only because he is a persistent and demanding instructor — "Keep both eyes open when sighting through the scope. . . . Squeeze, don't jerk, the trigger." The exciting part is riding with him in a Jeep.

"He is going to take you places in that Jeep you never thought possible and scare the hell out of you along the way," warns Jerry, whose favorite Claytie stories include the "Cactus Caper." He and Allyson were newly married when Claytie took him hunting at Happy Cove for his first mule deer.

It was a good news/bad news deal, Jerry joked, recalling that he got a three-hundred-pounder, but not before the eight-point animal had run down the mountainside into a deep draw. Claytie was at least mildly exasperated that they would have to drag the animal back up the mountain, "and he keeps running me through the cactus." Near the top and winded, Jerry paused to remove some of the painful cactus needles — "I have prickly pears sticking out of my scalp" — and Claytic says, "Come on, let's get this son of a bitch to the top." When Jerry points to the cactus, Claytie impatiently declares, "Come on, damn it, let's go. We're almost there."

"But Clayton . . . ," Jerry moans.

"I don't give a damn, let's go," says Claytie, and proceeds to run his new son-in-law through still *another* cactus.

Humorously relating this story, Jerry said he wasn't certain that Claytie intentionally ran him through the cactus patches. "He might have," he smiled, "because we had to go to the bottom of the mountain to get that damn deer."

Claytie confesses nothing, but says: "It's hard work hauling a deer up a mountainside."

Even nephews Clay and Scott Pollard could not escape Claytie's work ethic. As schoolboys, they helped their uncle build a fence one summer on the "back side" of Happy Cove Ranch — mountainous, rocky terrain that had never been fenced. "Get your bedrolls, your toothbrush, and your gloves," Clay remembers him saying before dropping them off on a Sunday evening where they set up camp with a fencing crew of Mexican nationals. "I'll be back next Saturday night to get you."

Clay recalled that everything about that job was intimidating. Like a mule, you had to carry all your supplies—barbed wire, crowbars, water, food—across tough land that had no trails. For much of the hole-digging the boys had to haul an air compressor and jackhammer. "The chain on that thing weighed about eighty-five pounds," Clay said. "One day I'm carrying it and I slip on the rocks and fall on my back and that chain crushes the air out of my chest. Here I am—about a 135-pounder—I just wanted to go home. I'm not trying to impress anybody. Scott, now he was older, about seventeen and weighed about 170, played football. He wanted to impress all those men." Work was seven to seven—twelve nonstop hours except for a thirty-minute lunch break.

Finally, Saturday evening came. "We were way down in the flats digging, and I look up and see Claytie standing at the top of the hill and I think, 'Oh, God, he's come to get us!'"

Clay said he ran up the hill, yelling, "Hey, Uncle Claytie, how you doing?"

Claytie thundered, "Get back down there with those men. I didn't tell you to stop working!"

Said Clay: "So I tucked my tail between my legs and walked back down to the bottom of that mountain until he said it was OK to come up. Oh man, I got to learn everything the hard way."

Almost everyone who ever met Clayton Williams Jr. has a Claytie story, but Kelvie has a slew of them. He told her when she was expecting her first child, Michael Clayton, he wanted to be with her in Memphis when the baby was born. But as they spoke on the phone that day, the baby already was past due.

"Well Daddy, I don't know when I'm gonna have the baby," she told him.

Consulting his calendar, he said, *"Friday is a good day for me."*

And sure enough, she laughed, she went into labor on that Friday, and Claytie flew to Tennessee, bringing Modesta and most of the family with him.

"That was when he had the plane, and everybody flew up, and everybody was there when the baby was born," Kelvie said. Shaking her head at Claytie's "Friday is a good day for me" comment, she added: "Doesn't that sound just like him?"

Kelvie recounted how many mornings he routinely carried his vitamins around in his robe with "a wad of thirty, fifty, or a hundred pills in the pocket." At least once he removed a hearing aid while talking on the phone and stuffed it in the pill pocket.

"Well, you can imagine," she said. "He almost always swallows the pills in a big clump, and this was one of those times." And, yes, he swallowed the hearing aid.

After returning from a trip to Hawaii, Claytie handed his assistant Denise his hearing aid and asked her to see about getting it repaired. She glanced in horror at the grotesquely mangled device and asked what happened. He sidled off without responding but wandered back by her desk later. "If you must know," he mumbled grumpily, "I thought it was a brazil nut and chomped on it."

Claytie's disaffection for dogs was a long-running joke, an exaggerated one actually, but he blamed the aversion on the renegade canines that attacked the sheep and goats he raised as a youngster in Fort Stockton. Celebrating a gas well once on party boats at Amistad Lake, he decided a dog named Wallace "needed to tinkle," so he tossed him overboard into the lake. In no time, Claytie realized that was a mistake. "Wallace is just treading water," he said aloud. "The damn dog is going to drown!"

Eyes sparkling at the memory, Kelvie said: "Daddy had to jump in and save him."

Although never cheap, Claytie could be frightfully frugal, especially in his leisurely pursuits.

"They had a deal for senior citizens at the movies that if you saved your popcorn bucket, you could get free refills," Kelvie said. "So he drives around forever with a smooshed popcorn bucket in his car so he won't have to pay for popcorn at the movies."

Another time, Kelvie said, she and her dad were hunting at an icy pond when Claytie shot a duck that then fell into the water. She watched in silent astonishment as he calmly removed his pants,

Son-in-law Jerry Groner, left, and nephew Clay Pollard working with cattle on the Alpine Ranch

waded into the freezing water in his boxer shorts, and retrieved the bird.

"Let's don't waste meat," he said haughtily, ignoring his bird dogs snuggled warmly and dryly in the back of the vehicle. "None of those dogs was ever worth killin'," he groused.

Sighed Kelvie: "He was not about to leave one duck in that pond."

There were lots of good times hunting and fishing, especially deep-sea fishing, she said, although both tended to get seasick. "He would eat crackers and drink beer; that was his medicine to keep from getting sick. Beer and crackers. That didn't work too well for a ten-year-old girl, but it was good for him."

On her first dove hunt, at age seven, Kelvie knocked down two birds with one shot, which thrilled Claytie to no end. "That's why I love to go hunting with him, because he gets so excited," she said. "I got my first deer when I was twelve. I made one shot across the way and got it, and he was so pleased with me and so happy."

Kelvie and Allyson shared youthful mortification over Claytie's propensity to sing with the mariachi bands, whenever and wherever the opportunity arose, especially when they vacationed in Mexico.

"I would think, 'Ahhhh, how can you do that?'" Kelvie remembered. "I wanted to just crawl under the table. As a teenager, that was terrible."

Said Allyson: "When I was little I was totally embarrassed, but then when I got to the drinking age, I decided his singing with the mariachis was kind of fun. It was cool!"

The two older daughters also shared with Modesta a disdain for some of the ranch chores Claytie introduced them to, most definitely during roundup activities. "Nobody wanted to work with him, because he would get mad at you and yell and everything," Kelvie said. "He has unreadable hand signals and he changes them all the time." Once, during her early college days, she was at the ranch during roundup when Claytie became totally "unspooled" and shouted: "Kelvie, I'm going to send the wets [illegal immigrants] to college instead of you!"

Claytie, Modesta, and most of the family were with Allyson and Jerry when Joshua, their first of two sons, was born in 1987, but a company tragedy prevented his being there when second son Jered arrived on February 16, 1990. "I'm sorry I am not going to be there for you, and I promise I will make it up to you," she remembered him saying. About two weeks later he did, descending on the Groners' home in Dallas with a flock of media folks at his heels. The next day, a photograph of Jered, cradled in his grandfather's arms, appeared on the front page of USA Today.

"That was neat," said Allyson.

Claytie was also present when Clayton Wade and Kristy's son Aubry was born on March 28, 2005. But he appeared preoccupied in the waiting area, noticeable only when someone realized he was studiously reading a book upside down.

In July 2005, Claytie was keeping close tabs on the imminent arrival of Chim and Greg's baby, which had the audacity to choose his birthing day while Claytie was in Pittsburgh trying to close a bond-sale deal. When word reached Claytie that Chim was on the way to the hospital, Claytie hurriedly closed the deal and headed for Midland on a jet charted for just such an exigency. Celebrating on the way home—both the deal done and the grandson pending—he acknowledged "being a little nipped when I got off the plane." Landing at 7:10 P.M., he lead-footed it to the hospital, a roughly twenty-minute drive.

Modesta: "Greg is extremely emotional and pretty straight-laced, and I'm rubbing his shoulders when Claytie walks in."

Claytie hands Greg his drink: "Here, you hold this while I go talk to my daughter," Claytie says.

Modesta shakes her head when telling the story. "Greg's wife's having a baby, and he's holding a drink for Claytie!"

A few moments after Claytie's arrival, Hyson Welborn was born at 7:48 P.M. on July 14, 2005.

After the birth, Claytie did what he always does. "When I have an achievement, I like to celebrate, so what am I gonna do?" Claytie, who had "snuck a few nips in" while at the hospital, donned a scrub cap and smock, gathered friends, family, and willing passersby, and headed for a bar creatively called "The Bar," where, because it was late, he didn't recognize anyone. So he did just what came natural: he bought drinks all around.

One bar habitué reacted to Claytie's generosity with an observation no doubt as sincere as it was grateful: "Some idiot came in here wearing a medical doctor's scrub cap and wanting to buy drinks for the house, so we took him up on it."

A reporter asked Modesta once if Claytie, with all his fatherly love and compassion, was a "diaper dad." Modesta was aghast at the question. "Oh, no. Oh, no, no, no," she said, harking back to a time when Clayton Wade was a baby and Claytie took him out to the Coyanosa Field.

Claytie with grandsons Joshua and Jered Groner and Michael Clayton Muhlbauer

"Claytie drove back thirty miles because he didn't want to change a dirty diaper. That poor kid. I'm sure Claytie rolled down the windows and everything else."

As it turned out, little Clayton inherited his father's proclivity for horse trading. Don Edwards, a friend of rancher Ted Gray's, drove out to the Alpine ranch one day in his pickup, and up rides ten-year-old Clayton Wade on his horse. After chit-chat, Edwards asked playfully if the youngster would like to make a trade for his horse. In an instant, young Clayton was out of the saddle and handing the reins to his newly acquired friend.

"Yes, sir," he said. "I'd like to trade this horse for your truck."

However innocently, even Claytie's minor adventures often morph into major sagas with lingering story lines. In 1973, he and Modesta were hunting on Gataga Mountain in British Columbia, totally inaccessible by radio or phone contact, when Wynona Riggs received a phone call in the Fort Stockton office.

"Is Mr. Williams there?" the caller asked.

"No, he isn't," replied Wynona. "Can I take a message? I am unable to reach him now."

"Would you tell him his baby has been born?"

"Oh, damn!" she exclaimed, concerned at once about what might happen when adoptive parents were unable to pick up their baby, in this case son Jeff. She finally located the outfitter who arranged the hunting trip. The next day, he sent word back that the message had been delivered. The Western Union telegram had been placed in an envelope, stuck in a plastic bag, weighted down with rocks, flown over Gataga Mountain in a small plane, and dropped into the campsite.

Claytie and Modesta headed home as quickly as possible and their pilot friend Bill Hargus, nicknamed "The Stork," flew them down to San Antonio to pick up the baby. That's why Jeff's full name is Jefferson Wheat Gataga Williams. That's also how the Gataga #2 well that blew out near Mentone in 1975 got its name.

For all the familial ups and down and overall wackiness, nothing better illustrates the depth of devotion that bonds this family than a poignant exchange of letters between Chim and Modesta on the youngest daughter's wedding day in 2003.

As Jeff marveled that day about how his mom and dad were "more in love now than the day they first married," Modesta was quietly composing a letter that echoed the special intimacy and affection historically shared by the Williams clan for one another.

Addressed "To My Dear Chimaloo," Modesta wrote:

> *"Sweet Love Child," this is what you've been to us all your life. The thrill we had when we were told that you "were on your way" was the best adrenaline rush that could be.*

You have been so cute, so precious, so loving, so rotten spoiled, so teenager, so lost, and now look at who you have become. You are a fine, courteous, loving, caring, generous friend and daughter. We both lost a few battles but we have won the war.

I choked on tears, but sweet, happy tears, as I carried your wedding dress from your room in Midland to take to the ranch in Alpine for your wedding and marriage to Greg. The symbolism of carrying the dress from your room where you were a little girl to the place where you are to become the bride and wife of a fine young man was a time and feeling of sweet emotion that I will never forget.

We willingly and lovingly give up our little girl to become a wife and a future mother, but we will never surrender our closeness and friendship with you that we've always had. How fortunate to have been blessed with love and devotion in a family. We can and do let others into our lives but still retain the close relationship between us.

We will always be here for you no matter what. You have matured beautifully and will make a wonderful partner for Greg. Both of you are very fortunate to have each other. You are good for one another.

Hold tightly to each other but never smother the love that you have.

My wish for you on your wedding day is for health, wealth, and happiness and the time to enjoy it.

May God bless you and Greg and the marriage that you are going into.

Unknown to her mom, Chim was also composing a letter that day, addressed to her parents. In its own youthful perspective, it was every bit as beautiful:

I have looked forward to this day since I was a little girl. You both have worked hard to instill in me values of diligence, strength, laughter, courage, and humility. The person that is standing here today is a product of your love for one another. You both have raised me under the light that your love for one another has produced, and because of that I have blossomed into a successful woman that will continue to carry that light into my own marriage. The two of you have made it through hard times and showed me that if you cling to one another through the driving rain you can make it through to brighter and better days. I will take that lesson, among many others, with me into my marriage.

So, here I stand about to make the one promise under God to the man I love and will love for the rest of my life, and I look back over my shoulder, to the two of you and say, "Thank you, you have made me into the person I've always wanted to be, and I love you both more than you ever imagine."

Wish me luck!

It was signed, *"Chimaloo."*

"Now, before you get mad and before these guys pull their guns and shoot me, let me tell you why we're going to do it this way."

17

As Professor Clayton Williams Jr. traversed the financial hills and hollows of the 1980s, he joked often about his entrepreneurial diversity, and the pitfalls therein. "I'm in oil and gas, real estate, banking, and cattle—everything that's losing money," he told *D Magazine* with a bit of lighthearted candor. In 1984, acting not so much on a whim but a sense of necessary adventure, he took an uncharacteristic plunge into high technology. The idea sprung from an unexpected problem that developed at his fledging Midland office complex, ClayDesta Plaza. A major company postponed its move into the plaza because of a months-long delay in obtaining phone service. Concerned with the threat of losing such occupants, Claytie installed a shared-tenant service for the entire complex, which allowed the major tenants to move in and occupy the space—and start paying rent. Seized by innate curiosity and what he described later as a mental lapse, he then began exploring the foreign world of telecommunications and the opportunities of the new digital technologies.

"We just kind of eased into it," he told the *Reporter-Telegram*.

The newspaper reported how, with a $45 million investment, Claytie formed a new company, ClayDesta Communications, and placed one of his brightest young executives, Randy Kidwell, in charge. The company built the first all-digital system to connect several West Texas cities to Dallas. Eventually, a digital microwave network extended from Amarillo to Lubbock, Midland, Big Spring, San Angelo, Abilene, and Dallas–Fort Worth. And a digital fiber optics network stretched from Dallas–Fort Worth through Waco, Austin, San Antonio, and Houston.

Supplementing its communications network with a long-distance pricing schedule, ClayDesta first targeted residential customers and then zeroed in on the business market, "a profitable battle ground for most long-distance companies"—not the least of which was mighty AT&T.

"We are what the free-enterprise system is about," Claytie told the *Reporter-Telegram*. "We are the competition. We brought the customer a better product at a better price. We are a growth company. I think the main thrust of our company will be better and cheaper. . . . I think the posture of this company for some time will be 5 percent growth a month, rather than 'hallelujah, go, go.' Where that leads us, I don't know.

"This was shades of my Clajon start-up: a better product, at a better price, and with a smile."

Where it led was down a serpentine road to a David-versus-Goliath battle, a war that spilled over into the Texas legislature, scrambled up the Capitol steps via horseback, and then propelled Claytie into the statewide political arena.

For ClayDesta Communications to survive, the company needed to position itself against not only AT&T but the likes of Southwestern Bell and MCI. To gain name recognition and attract customers, the company needed a quality television advertising campaign. ClayDesta gambled with a small start-up Midland company called Admarc.

"It was a big deal for us, a very big deal," said Admarc executive Joe Milam. "We were pitching this thing literally for our own survival."

Admarc adopted Claytie's mantra, the hallmark of his Clajon-Coyanosa success: deliver a better product at a better price. Produced around a Pony Express theme, the commercials were simultaneously "high-tech and high-touch" and featured Claytie galloping across the mountains and pastures of his Alpine ranch and pitching the merits of ClayDesta as an anonymous spokesperson on camera.

"We never identified him as the owner of the company," Milam said. "We never identified him as anything. It's just that when Claytie is being Claytie, he has a look in his eye, a demeanor on camera, an honesty that people immediately like."

But before a word was spoken on camera, Milam faced a crisis in a cow pasture that threatened to scuttle the campaign before it took off. Milam's director had fallen ill, and a Hollywood director was recruited at the last second. His name was Scott Redman, who happened to be in Dallas when contacted. Redman agreed to fly out for the first shoot at Happy Cove Ranch.

This is Milam's abbreviated but otherwise unabridged account of that cow pasture saga:

"I'm already down there at the ranch trying to explain to Clayton what we're going to do and that we have a director coming in. Our people were picking him up at the airport in Midland and bringing him out. I'd never met Scott Redman, but I'm scared to death that Clayton won't like him. There are people standing around Clayton out in the middle of the pasture wearing sidearms, and I'm envisioning myself as coyote food. After about four hours, Scott Redman arrives at the set. And Rebecca Harrison, who was our art director, gets out of the vehicle, and her face is as white as a sheet of paper. And she comes walking over to me with eyes as big as a cow's, and I know that Rebecca is scared. She says, 'I don't know if this is going to work or not. You need to come talk to Scott.'

"So I walk over to meet Scott. He has on black parachute pants, high-top tennis shoes, and a black, short-sleeved T-shirt with 'Los Lobos' on the front of it. His sunglasses have yellow frames, and he is Jewish and from Brooklyn and currently living in Sherman Oaks in California. My life passes in front of my face . . .

"I take him over to introduce him to Clayton, and Clayton begins to tell Scott how we're going to do this commercial. He's not malicious or mean-spirited, he's just telling this New York Jew—smoking Camel cigarettes with no filters and his high-top tennis shoes on and slightly taller than Claytie—he's just telling Scott how he's going to do his job.

"And Scott says, 'Mr. Williams — I'm going to call you Claytie — let me tell you how you are going to do this commercial because on this set, you're not in charge, I'm in charge. And this is the way you're going to do it. Now, before you get mad and before these guys pull their guns and shoot me, let me tell you why we're going to do it this way. I'm going to commit to you; I'm going to work as hard as you do to make you look on camera like you want to look on camera, and I'm going to make you sound like you want to sound on camera. And when these commercials are finished, you're going to be proud of your appearance rather than embarrassed at your appearance. Now, you pause for a moment, and let's think about this and let's see if you can live with those rules: Me in charge, not you. Me working as hard as you're going to work to make you look like you want to look. If you can accept that, we'll go forward from here. If not, let me know. I'll go back to Midland, get on the airplane, and fly back home.'

"Claytie and Scott are nose to nose. Time is frozen. The tension is so much that the cattle are walking away. All of Claytie's entourage have never, ever in their lives heard anyone speak to Clayton like that — with respect, but also very demonstrably. I'm thinking that people are unbuckling their thumb straps on their sidearms, and Rebecca and I are expecting to be coyote food because nobody would ever find us out where we are. And Clayton's there in his cowboy hat, looking very tense, and all of a sudden he looks directly in Scott Redman's face, and Scott Redman looks in his face . . . and Claytie says, 'I like you. Let's do this.'

"I have never seen anybody work as hard as they did. Scott was there every day when Claytie got to the set and he was there when Claytie left the set. They worked so hard together. The West Texas cowboy and the New York Jew developed a chemistry that was staggering to watch. They were elevating each other to a level of performance way beyond their honest-to-goodness capabilities.

"Claytie's performance and the commercials were spectacular. We were accomplishing something on this set that was truly remarkable; we were getting the real, honest, atomic-level Clayton Williams on camera. At one point, after the first take that he really nailed, as soon as Scott yelled 'Cut' and turned around with this huge smile on his face, the crew spontaneously broke into applause. And this was a feature film crew, basically the one that did the movie *JFK*.

"We all knew at that precise moment that we had something magnificent going here; something magic was happening."

Claytie's gamble appeared to have hit the jackpot.

Joe Milam's recollections of the Redman-Williams Follies also provided a couple of black magic incidents during the filming process. In one commercial, a complicated maneuver called for Claytie to chase a heifer and a calf into a dry creek bed, approach a certain mark, rein up his horse, jump off, walk to another mark, and deliver his lines to the camera.

"So we're doing it, doing it, doing it, and the cow will go wrong or the calf will go wrong or the horse won't stop where he's supposed to stop or Claytie doesn't have the right look, the right feel," Milam said. "Finally the cow is perfect, the calf is perfect, the horse lands on the his mark perfectly. Claytie comes off his horse before the horse is fully stopped and the reins drop perfectly. Clayton hits his mark perfectly, he looks into the camera, and he says, "I forgot my damn lines!"

Claytie wasn't above a little intentional levity, as when he sat atop his horse extolling the virtues of ClayDesta, stressing on camera his company's ability to make good on its promises. "If you don't believe it," he announced boldly, "you can kiss my damn ass!"

"By the start of the legislative session in January 1987, I had not yet sold Clajon," Claytie recalled, "but ClayDesta Communications was the focus of my energy. There was a bill introduced to deregulate AT&T, which was a lot bigger outfit then than later. And we were fearful that if they deregulated, they'd cut prices, crush us . . . and it would be the end of us."

Brokenhearted over the possible sale of Clajon Gas and other pieces of his empire to reduce bank debt, Claytie was probably spoiling for a fight.

And AT&T would get it.

Scott Redman directing Claytie in a 1984 commercial

"I didn't have a heck of a lot else to do, so I went down to Austin and spent most of the session lobbying three or four days a week. Billy Clayton, the former Texas House Speaker and my Aggie buddy, was my mentor, and we worked mostly with the liberal Democrats. They were for regulation and the Republicans were against it. So right off the bat, I was on the opposite side of my political colleagues."

Besides the awkward allegiances, Claytie found lobbying to be tough work.

"You meet some legislators for breakfast, some for lunch, some on the House and Senate floor, some for drinks, and some at the Broken Spoke. They *made* me go dancing out there at that joint," he said.

And while his country charm and natural persuasiveness were major assets, Claytie discovered that David was no match for this Goliath.

"We fought and we lobbied and we argued our case, but we were not winning our war against deregulation," he said. "We're not getting anywhere. We're losing. AT&T is a pretty big guy. We had a floor fight in the House, and everybody thought that was fun. But no; we're losing. We're just bullshitting because nobody's listening to our side."

But then a friendly television newsman gave Claytie an idea he thought might appeal to his showmanship—the showmanship he'd demonstrated in offbeat and attention-grabbing appearances before the Texas Railroad Commission on behalf of the struggling oil industry. (Former Texas House Speaker Gib Lewis remembers most vividly the presentation when Claytie arrived at the commission hearing on a gurney, swathed in bandages from head to toe, and proclaiming that "this is the condition the Texas oil and gas business is in.")

"I tell you what you do," Claytie recalled his TV friend saying. "You go out and get your cowboys, load up your horses, ride up the Capitol steps, jump off your horse, and hold a press conference. I'll have the cameras waiting."

"Well, I wouldn't do that," Claytie said, about a split second before a big smile crossed his face and he reconsidered. "Yeah, I would."

So he did, drawing Modesta into the mix to give the scheme a touch of class.

An Associated Press story the next day, May 9, 1987, appeared in the *Dallas Morning News* beside a photo of a grinning, flag-waving Claytie in cowboy gear and surrounded by his "posse" of ranch cowboys on the Capitol steps, where he was "mounting" a protest.

"Texas oilman and cowboy Clayton Williams galloped up to the Capitol steps Friday to warn the Legislature that passing a bill to deregulate AT&T would be a 'bum steer,'" the story said, quoting a stinging declaration from a state legislator: "Only a fool would deregulate a monopoly, and that's what Texas would look like if this bill passes deregulating AT&T."

Asked if he thought the Senate-passed bill could be amended in the House, Claytie replied: "I'd just as soon it walked off somewhere and died."

Riding horseback to the press conference on the steps of the Texas Capitol, Claytie leads the fight against deregulating AT&T

The bill in fact did die in conference committee, and some on both sides of the regulatory issue attributed its demise to the splashy news conference on the Capitol steps.

. "It ain't over 'til it's over," bubbled Billy Clayton, copping a line from some ancient philosopher, maybe Yogi Berra.

Cynics might argue that it was all for naught, because pressure was mounting on a cash-strapped Claytie to sell the communications company. "As the price of oil and gas declined, so did the fortunes of ClayDesta Communications," said his friend and fellow Aggie, Davis Ford, explaining that Claytie was growing his phone company in part with an infusion of cash from his oil and gas properties. Claytie knew a sale could result in a relatively small loss, but there was an escape route available. Subordinated debentures, commonly called unsecured corporate bonds, had been used to raise funds to assist in the initial financing, and Davis Ford had helped sell the speculative "junk bonds" to Austin friends. If forced to sell ClayDesta, financial advisers were suggesting he take the unsecured debentures "off the books" in order to get a higher price for the company, Ford said.

"No way," Ford remembered Claytie saying. "A debt is a debt and if I sell the company I will do what is necessary to make sure the investors get their money back, dollar for dollar." Claytie was not legally required to act in such a manner; it was just the mark of the man, Ford stressed. "It underscored the honesty of Clayton Williams."

Joe Milam for one saw a cruel irony in the prospects of a sale because, he said, ClayDesta Communications was a rapidly growing company and anything but a failure. "People had started flocking to the service," he asserted. "From the top of Texas to the tip of Texas, from Amarillo to Beaumont. The service was that good."

But when the price of oil fell to ten dollars a barrel, Claytie could no longer fund the company, and a sale appeared imminent. "I'd had so much stress and duress for so long, and now we had a good offer and a good price, so I said, 'Let's do it.'"

How beaten down was he? "I was so beaten down I considered going into politics."

With or without Claytie at the helm, his Admarc commercials had taken on a life of their own, garnering several industry honors, foremost among them an award from the New York International Videotape and Film Festival and a much-coveted Clio, which annually recognizes advertising's most creative efforts worldwide.

Claytie's betting on the little hometown media company and Joe Milam made him look savvy indeed. And then came the call to Milam from some advertising people in New York.

"Who is this actor?" they wondered. "We want to hire him."

When Claytie heard about the call, he wisecracked: "Find out what they pay. I may need a job."

Four

Campaign dinner, 1990, with Sen. Phil Gramm, Pres. George H. W. Bush, First Lady Barbara Bush, and Gov. Bill Clements

"Maybe this is the time to give back."

18

With the sale of ClayDesta Communications in the works, and with the final semester of teaching with Ella Van Fleet at A&M at hand, Claytie and Modesta invited a couple of employees to their Midland home to exchange gifts on Christmas Eve 1988. "It was a very relaxed setting . . . and we were in a little bit of a coasting mode, not sure what we'd be involved in at the first of the new year," recounted Denise Garrett, soon to become Denise Kelly. Brenda Chambers, Modesta's assistant, joined the small gathering sipping wine and swapping gifts around the Christmas tree in the trophy room. Claytie wandered off to field a phone call, and when he returned Denise noticed that he seemed preoccupied.

"I just got the darnedest phone call," he announced. "Some folks at the Republican Party leadership in Texas want me to run for governor!"

Although few beyond the inner circle knew it, that was not his first political overture—just the most significant.

"The first person to ask me to run for governor was Jim Ross," Claytie recalled. "He and his wife, Billie, were Republican activists and came to a party my sister Janet had given for David Ligon." The suggestion came after Claytie and his guitar-pickin' cohort had rendered a "beautiful" version of their Spanish favorite, "Juan Charresquedo."

"Well, Claytie," Ross said, "you've done everything else; you should run for governor."

Billy Clayton had watched Claytie's deft handling of the legislative skirmish with AT&T and had grown increasingly impressed with his political and communication skills. The former Texas House Speaker sensed that Claytie had enjoyed the lobbying effort on behalf of his communications company as well as the reputation for honesty and openness he'd acquired in Austin political circles. The Speaker raised the issue of such a race several times, and one day he said, "Claytie, now's the time to make your move."

Claytie appeared uncertain.

"You'd make one helluva governor," the Speaker pressed. "You tell it like it is, you're honest, and everybody knows your record. I think we can win this thing."

Although swayed by Billy, Claytie kept telling his friend, "Let me think about it."

Another who suggested a gubernatorial bid was Robert Anderson, the Arco Oil Company pioneer who had witnessed some of Claytie's classic performances on behalf of the oil industry at Texas Railroad Commission meetings. After one of Claytie's most outlandish routines—this one in Lubbock—Anderson walked up and said, "Claytie, you're something else. You ought to run for governor." A former Midland mayor, Ernest Angelo, likewise urged Claytie to enter the race.

Such was the background on Christmas Eve when Claytie told his guests about the phone call from the Republican Party. "I'm really flattered because they said they're asking me to run for one reason: they think I can win." Once she realized he was serious, Denise said, "Wow! What a great governor he would be." She felt confident, she said, because of his "business skills, his people skills, his focus, his determination, his intensity, and his compassion." If anyone should know his credentials, Denise would, for she had helped him fight and survive the oil and real estate crashes and the legislative war with AT&T.

"You know," Claytie said, "I'm thinking about doing it. I'm thinking that life has been so good to me, and with the sale of ClayDesta

Communications, maybe this is the time to give back. Or to at least make a run at it."

When Denise left the house that evening, she did not know whether he would run, but "just because of the twinkle in his eye," she thought he would.

Claytie and Modesta left for a hunting excursion to Pakistan the day after Christmas, and they extended their trip to discuss the topic in relative isolation. Upon their return, Denise realized at once that not only was Claytie still considering the race, but he was talking quietly about it with trusted associates.

"He's going to run!" she told herself.

In early February 1989, the Associated Press thrust Claytie back into the media spotlight, even generating an eight-column headline in the *Los Angeles Times*.

"While many prominent Texas businesspeople are short on cash and long on debt," the AP said, "entrepreneur Clayton W. Williams Jr. says he's debt free for the first time in ten years and may even run for governor."

The story reported that Claytie had agreed to merge his long-distance company with fifty-five thousand customers into Atlanta-based Advanced Telecommunications Corp. in a deal that would pay him $33 million in cash and $10 million in stock. Claytie, who says today it was less a merger than an outright sale, told the AP: "I've battled back like a lot of people in Texas and emerged with a good financial statement. It's not as good as it once was, but it's better than a lot of people."

The AP story reported the move would erase the remainder of what once totaled almost a half-billion dollars in debt spread among more than twenty Williams companies. It cited what Claytie had labeled "The Wreck"—the economic catastrophe of the 1980s that crippled the state—and said: "The dizzying collapse of the Southwest oil and real estate empires in recent years has produced a list of prominent victims that reads like a Who's Who of Texas tycoons." Among the victims were former Gov. John Connally and

Brownwood entrepreneur Herman Bennett, countless banks and real estate operators, and numerous oil companies. The account in the *Times* acknowledged that Claytie avoided the fate of many "because keeping ahead of the economic tide was one of his specialties—even his bank, ClayDesta National, is making money in a state where troubled banks have become a fact of daily life." (From 1980 through 1994, 599 banks failed in Texas, including nine of the ten largest banking organizations. The $60.2 billion in failed assets represented nearly 44 percent of the state's total banking assets, according to a study done in 2000 by Michael E. Williams, Ph.D., and Michael W. Brandl, Ph.D., of the University of Texas at Austin. In many ways, they wrote, the banking calamity was "worse than the banking crisis of the Great Depression of the 1930s.")

His formula for escaping fatal harm by The Wreck: cut your losses, and if it doesn't work, unload it.

"We worked like hell going up, and then when The Wreck came, we worked like hell going down to keep from going broke while everything fell apart," Claytie said. He told the AP the depressed real estate market and further cutbacks in the energy sector had converted him to a bargain hunter. "The oil business is still sick, which means there could be opportunities, because of The Wreck, for a small, efficient operator."

Calling him "ever cheerful," the AP described Claytie as optimistic about discovering hidden profit in unfamiliar businesses: "It's like being an old hunting dog looking for birds. If you get out there and get to hunting you'll find some birds, but you've got to get out there first."

Meanwhile, Denise's instincts proved to be well-founded: this old dog had set his sights on the Texas governorship.

Though politically inexperienced, Claytie had been a lifelong supporter of Republican issues and candidates, both financially and as a behind-the-scenes advocate. He was a recipient of Ronald Reagan's Presidential Achievement Award and a charter member of the Associated Republicans of Texas. He was a member of Gov. Bill Clements's Business Development and Jobs Creation Task Force as well as a member of the Governor's Blue Ribbon Committee on Petroleum and Natural Gas, part of the Texas Energy and Natural Resources Council. He was even a past member of the Republican Eagles, a support group for the Republican National Committee.

With close friends such as Billy Clayton, Gov. Bill Clements, and the politically savvy Davis Ford, Claytie was also privy to sound advice crucial for such a race. But in those early, hectic days, nobody was more important than LaVerne Foster of Midland and Republican volunteers, virtually all women.

"They were a huge help," said Brenda Chambers, who had earned her stripes as Modesta's assistant during the ClayDesta Communications adventure. It was Brenda who once described Claytie as "a teddy bear with an attitude." With the madness shifting to the political arena, both Brenda and Denise were suddenly under siege. "Along with our increased workload came increased phone calls," Brenda said. "Most people wanted to be Clayton's best friend, but the random hate calls kept us on our toes."

Added Denise: "I can only say that LaVerne Foster looked like the Lone Ranger and the cavalry all rolled into one. She really helped get the ship righted when we were about to be submerged in a sea of unknown waters." All who've worked for Claytie can expand on his notorious inclination to casually assign employees difficult if not impossible tasks. "The difficult we do right away," said Denise. "The impossible takes a little longer."

As former assistants Wynona Riggs, Nancy Carpenter, Sandy Jones, and Julie Faubel could attest, working around Claytie normally could be physically, mentally, and sometimes emotionally challenging—and these were far from normal times. It was Nancy who insisted that a portrait of a tough old buzzard hanging in the Fort Stockton office captured the Claytie work persona. "Patience, my ass," said the inscription. "I'm gonna kill somebody."

Brenda, recalling those preelection days and nights, said: "In general, it was a roller-coaster ride . . . with more than its share of ups and downs." Denise remembers the difficulties of keeping up with Claytie's dictation, scheduling, and phone calls—and the cry of exasperation that burst from Modesta's office one day. It was Brenda, transcribing a dictation tape in which Claytie announced that such-and-such letter "goes out to *all* the Chambers of Commerce in Texas" and followed with another letter that "goes to all the Aggies in Texas."

Brenda and Denise prided themselves on their joint efficiency, but this was a staggering demand. "I know I turned pale," Brenda said. "I think I considered throwing myself off the third-floor balcony." Denise said it was more than symbolic that Claytie kept a mock hand grenade on his desk bearing a sign: "Complaint Department — take a number." The lone number was attached to the pin of the bogus grenade.

That's when LaVerne Foster and the GOP women rode to the rescue, endearing themselves forever to a couple of executive assistants hunkered down, Denise said, like comrades in a foxhole.

Meanwhile, the fledgling Williams troops lured Austin political guru Buddy Barfield away from Texas Railroad Commissioner Kent Hance, the early frontrunner in the 1990 governor's race. Barfield would assemble and manage Claytie's team. It was Billy Clayton who orchestrated the hiring of Barfield as well as a bright and charismatic U.S. Customs narcotics investigator named Todd Smith, who came aboard as a regional field director. Smith, only twenty-eight years old, would soon become Claytie's traveling companion, handling the "field" media covering the daily campaign. His recollections would provide a hilariously intimate and insightful account of what went on behind the scenes. He recalled that his mother watched TV coverage of campaign activities and often chastised him: "Now, Todd, you've got to be more careful not to let your emotions show, because when Clayton says something, your mouth drops."

After Barfield enlisted several campaign advisers, Claytie summoned the group to Midland for a roundtable session that exposed the Williams political style. Among the advisers were New York consultants Dick Dresner and Jay Townsend, and Joe Milam of the award-winning Midland advertising firm Admarc.

The meeting was scheduled for Claytie's eclectic office in Clay-Desta Plaza, but a rare snowfall prompted a change. "Let's just have everybody meet at my house instead of at the office," he instructed Denise. "I'll have our housekeeper Maria fix a nice lunch and we'll just meet around the fireplace in the trophy room and it'll be cozy and everybody will be relaxed."

Few of the Austin politicos and none of the New Yorkers really knew Claytie when they gathered that day around the fireplace to swap opinions. When they finally broke for lunch, everyone was hungry.

"I had Maria fix my favorite lunch," Claytie announced.

One of the New Yorkers, visions of prime rib and thick T-bones no doubt dancing in his head, asked, "What are we having?"

"Frito Pie," replied Claytie. "It's my mom's favorite, too."

"Frito Pie?" said the incredulous New Yorker.

"You bet, and I'll show you how you fix it," said Claytie, spreading layers of Fritos, sliced onions, cheese, diced tomatoes, chopped green onions, and heaven knows what else atop a bowl of home-made chili. Denise thought the Yankee visitor was going to faint.

Thus, on a snowy winter day punctuated with Frito Pie, the Clayton Williams political roundtable concept was born beside a fireplace surrounded by trophy animals from Alaska, Africa, Afghanistan, and other points afar.

What some would proclaim the most bizarre governor's race in Texas history was on.

On June 21, 1989, after an introduction by State Rep. Tom Craddick of Midland, Claytie formally announced his candidacy at an Austin news conference. He then invaded Houston and Dallas before flying to Midland for a giant kickoff rally in the ClayDesta atrium. With a band blaring, a buffet offering sustenance, and the Midland High School cheerleaders prancing and dancing, he launched a long-shot campaign for the GOP nomination that many professional politicians predicted was doomed.

"From day one, Clayton wasn't given much of a chance," recalled Barfield, explaining that the West Texas cowboy-oilman hardly fit the image of a Republican politician. If anyone had examined the dynamics and demographics to conduct the standard preelection polls, "he never would have gotten in," his campaign manager admitted. Barfield pointed to the strengths of the other Republican candidates: former Secretary of State Jack Rains held a huge Houston base; Texas Railroad Commissioner Kent Hance of Lubbock was "everybody's favorite candidate from the Republican establishment"; and attorney Tom Luce entered the race a bit later but did so with solid political credentials as the Dallas establishment candidate.

"So when you looked at it," said Barfield, "you had a Dallas candidate, a Houston candidate, and a seasoned politician in Kent Hance who had been around the track several times and had most of the structure of the party on his side. . . . This was an uphill battle that Clayton could never win."

So why did Barfield jump Hance's political ship to join such a shaky quest? Personality, for starters. "You just meet him and there's a glow and a gleam that I've never seen in any other type of candidate," said Barfield. "You can't meet Clayton Williams and not just fall in love with him. You could sit there and ask him, 'Why are you getting into this?' Without rehearsal or any other type of process, he'd say: 'I'm gonna get in, I'm gonna win, and I'm gonna win the war on drugs.'" As many knew, the drug war was personal: Claytie's elder son, Clayton Wade, had gotten messed up with drugs in his early teens, and the family's attempts at rehabilitation had been long, intense, expensive, and not always successful. Barfield asked Claytie once if, given his choice, would he choose winning the governor's mansion or winning the war on drugs.

"I'll take winning the war on drugs and go home."

Accompanying Claytie on one of his first campaign events, Barfield discovered the magnitude of his challenge; the occasion was a Republican leadership meeting in Houston. Expecting the traditional eight- to ten-minute speech with a couple of minutes of answering questions, Barfield watched in horror as Claytie spoke for what seemed like two hours. "He walked around the crowd—and I think this was some of the more blue-blooded of Houston—and told 'em, 'We're gonna get this state off the welfare tit,' all sorts of things like that. People were falling out of their chairs."

While entertaining to some, word spread that the West Texan was not only a political novice, but also a crude one: he could be dismissed as a candidate, he couldn't win, and his opponents had nothing to worry about. If anything, Barfield asserted, people began to underestimate Claytie even more. Though a political novice, he was hardly an unknown after his widespread media coverage throughout the 1980s. The Associated Press proclaimed of Claytie: "An optimist by nature and a gambler by choice, he is at once charming, crude, bold, brash, serious, flip, salty, and rarely immune to a good time."

"Just wait and see," Claytie responded to the skeptics, repeatedly declaring his war on crime and drugs and vowing famously to introduce youthful narcotics offenders "to the joys of bustin' rocks."

The Williams campaign team devised an innovative plan to boost its politically unknown underdog from last to second in the 1990 GOP primary—winning outright appeared impossible—then uncork its best shot in a runoff, most likely against establishment favorite Kent Hance. After Claytie committed millions of dollars to the campaign, his team earmarked a substantial chunk of it for an early, unconventional TV blitz. The scheme was to introduce the candidate's "drugs and crime" issue to the voters during a traditional lull in the campaign, thus providing a base to build on for the final weeks of the primary. Austin's political pros scoffed at the irregular strategy, Buddy Barfield remembered.

"But we went up on TV for a two-week run of the bio and came in right behind that with the famous 'Bustin' Rocks' ad. Besides his hard line on drugs and crime, his ads stressed his business background and his experience in—and support of—education. He proposed financing his war on drugs and crime by cutting state operational spending as opposed to raising taxes. And with his proven leadership and 'can do' spirit, he vowed to 'make Texas great again.'"

It worked better than anyone dared hope. A poll after the TV push indicated the time was right for an outsider and that Clayton's personality, as Barfield put it, "hit a home run" with voters. As if to underscore that assessment, Claytie began a campaign speech one day by saying, "Look, I'm not a lawyer and I'm not a politician, and I'm running for governor." A guy stood up and started to walk out. "Sir, where are you going?" Claytie asked. "You told me all I need to know," the man said. "I'm gonna vote for you."

If his personality was a home run, his celebrated rock-busting ad was a grand slam. As Joe Milam tells it, he and Claytie were on a flight to Amarillo when the subject of kids and drugs came up. "I've been thinking about what I want to do," he recalled Claytie saying. "I want to establish some boot camps for some young first-time offenders because, frankly, a lot of these young men have grown up in troubled homes, in circumstances where they didn't have a role model or an authority figure, and they just haven't learned discipline. They're not bad kids; they just need a chance."

A military-style boot camp, he said, would provide youngsters who deserved a second chance the opportunity to learn discipline, to learn to rely upon one another, to believe in themselves, and thus to achieve and succeed.

"What I want to do is introduce these young people to the joys of bustin' rocks."

Milam said when he heard that line he apparently "lit up like a Christmas tree" because Claytie smiled and said, "Oh, you like that?"

"Man, I do," Milam said.

Milam crafted the commercials using college students from the Sul Ross rodeo team and cowboys from Claytie's Alpine ranch, and he emphasized Claytie's rock-bustin' words, which became the touchstone of the Williams campaign.

"He said it exactly like he said it on the jet," Milam said—"with a little gleam in his eye and that little twinkle in his smile, where you know he's playing with you, but you know he's serious, and you know that he's the kind of guy that if anybody on the planet can pull it off, he can. It's that same little grin, that same little look in his smile that people recognize for reality—a look that you don't see in political guys."

NBC-TV picked up the spot and ran it on the *Nightly News*. "The impressive thing was, they ran it respectfully, because this oil millionaire from Texas may actually have a valuable idea," Milam said. "It would, in fact, in the right circumstances and if properly done, engender life-changing attitudes in the young people that are involved in the boot camp. And some of the leading criminal experts in the country said, 'Yeah, this concept has some legs.'"

The commercial transformed the primary election, Milam said, and surely prompted Tom Luce's exasperated comment to a reporter late in the campaign. He claimed darkly that Claytie's thrust was "all gimmicks" and that the multitude of problems facing Texans "can't be solved with thirty-second commercials."

Further, Luce said, "I don't think we can ride horseback into the space age."

"Depends on the horse," Claytie quipped.

According to the Associated Press, the fireworks formally opened with the New Year: "The official political season started Tuesday with a fury as two Republican gubernatorial hopefuls exchanged heated jabs. . . ." A five-column *Houston Post* headline announced that "Williams, Hance Campaigns Begin New Year with Salvos," and Mary Lenz began her story thusly: "Workers in two Republican gubernatorial campaigns kicked off the New Year Tuesday by accusing their rival candidates of snooping, drinking, fistfighting, slinging sleaze, and misleading the public."

A news release from Claytie's camp disclosed that "someone" paid a high-ranking member of the National Republican Congressional Committee to conduct a covert investigation of its candidate. An indignant Carole Keeton Rylander, cochair of the Williams statewide campaign with Roy Barrera of San Antonio and Eddie and Fran Chiles of Fort Worth, told an Austin news conference the

LONESOME GOV

STARRING
Clayton W. Williams, Jr.

"clandestine operation" was conducted by the NRCC's director of strategy and research, Gary Maloney.

"We know that Mr. Maloney contacted the ex-wife of one of Williams's high-ranking executives in the middle of the night, did not identify who he worked for, and proceeded to ask several inappropriate questions about Clayton Williams," Rylander said, reading from a letter of protest sent to NRCC chairman Lee Atwater and cochair Ed Rollins. "I cannot understand how an NRCC employee — especially one as high up the ladder as Mr. Maloney — could get involved in conducting this kind of negative research on a fellow Republican."

The questions, Rylander said, included queries about "whether Clayton drinks, if he used foul language . . . and how he conducts his personal life and business affairs."

The *Post* wasted no time identifying Kent Hance as the mysterious "someone," and spokesperson Mark Sanders acknowledged that the campaign had paid Maloney five thousand dollars to inspect Claytie's business activities. Maloney said he was acting as an independent consultant and not working for the NRCC when he conducted his Midland research. While denying that the Hance campaign was interested in Claytie's drinking habits or personal affairs, Sanders contended that Maloney's research proved that Claytie misled the public in his TV ads when he claimed he had created one hundred thousand Texas jobs.

Bill Kenyon, Claytie's press secretary, said his boss never stated that he employed one hundred thousand people, but that his twenty-six companies had created that many jobs. "I think," said Kenyon, "this is the opening round for a whole bucket of sleaze coming out of the [Hance] campaign."

Regardless of slung sleaze, clandestine investigations, fistfights at the Midland Country Club, and just the normal political skullduggery, Claytie emerged from nowhere to suddenly discover himself running slightly ahead of Hance, and with momentum riding shotgun aboard his bandwagon. In a novel move, Claytie and Modesta recruited teenage daughter Chim to join them on a motor home campaign trip into East Texas. Chim in turn invited Davis and Gwen Ford's daughter Katy to accompany them on the search for Piney Woods votes. Based on all reports, the girls attracted substantially more boyfriends than votes for Claytie.

But the momentum continued to grow, and about a month before the March 13 primary *The Wall Street Journal* caught up with Claytie at a College Station fish fry serenading six hundred supporters with his "reedy" rendition of "Cigarettes and Whiskey and Wild, Wild Women." He told hundreds of cheering Aggies: "There's never been a governor from Texas A&M. But there's *gonna* be a governor from Texas A&M."

The *Journal* noted that Hance was the closest pursuer of Claytie's three challengers and was "fighting desperately to keep Mr. Williams's count below 50 percent and force an April 10 runoff."

There was also a grumpy observation from Hance, bemoaning Claytie's TV commercials and campaign spending. "It's like running against Fort Knox."

Largely because of the Williams phenomenon, the foreign and national news media became increasingly infatuated with the election, labeling Claytie the "race's biggest surprise"—a fresh face who sits atop a horse like John Wayne, tips his Stetson when greeting a woman, and is not averse to settling disputes with fisticuffs. "His sincere, blunt-spoken style has more than compensated for a nonexistent political resume," reported one news magazine, quoting Democratic insider Pete Schenkkan: "He's the man on the white horse, the real cowboy who's also a big business success."

George Christian, Pres. Lyndon Johnson's press secretary and a widely respected Austin political consultant, suggested that Claytie "typifies what a lot of people think Texas ought to be."

Interviewed by *The New York Times,* Christian said: "The secret of his success is that he really is old Texas, the genuine article, and a lot of people still want to believe in that." Asked about Claytie's well-earned reputation for settling disputes with his fists, Christian wryly responded that "Texans would rather vote for a fistfighter than a summa cum laude." The nation's most famous newspaper checked in from Houston after catching Claytie "breaking into a raspy rendition of a rodeo ballad" with a country-western band in a small community theater.

"I ain't no greenhorn, I'm still sitting tight," Claytie sang, drawing laughter, the *Times* reported, from a crowd eating fried catfish from paper plates. "By the time he led them in singing 'You Are My Sunshine,' Mr. Williams's followers were primed and ready to hear a message that has catapulted him to front-runner status in a crowded primary field."

The *Washington Post* offered its take on the "Claytie mystique," sounding slightly awed by a candidate "boasting of his fistfights and his taste for beer, talking about how delinquents should 'bust rocks' in prison, hamming it up at rodeos and small-town fairs, harkening back to the good ole days that his daddy talked about, the Texas of myth and legend."

The *Post*'s David Maraniss wrote: "With a virtually unlimited television advertising budget, most from his pocket, and an easygoing western style that seems like a cross between Roy Rogers and Will Rogers, Williams has emerged as the rising political star of Texas this year. It is as though he roped the Republican Party around the right hind leg and hauled it back to his Alpine cattle ranch."

Claytie sensed he had connected with voters during a visit to the annual Houston Livestock Show in the Astrodome. One of his opponents, hometown boy Jack Rains, appeared in the arena and received an impressive round of applause. But when Claytie and Modesta rode out on horseback, the reception turned deafening.

"I mean it was thunderous," he recalled.

On the eve of the primary election, *Time* magazine zeroed in on the "folksy gubernatorial candidate" working a food line at a Tyler cafeteria and rattling off campaign pledges in a "gravelly West Texas drawl." Reporter Richard Woodbury summed up those gravelly pledges: "Double the prisons . . . boot camps for first-felony offenders . . . fight drugs from every direction . . . free college tuition for good kids from at-risk families . . . better vocational training . . . more private-sector jobs."

And no new taxes.

Forecasting a primary victory without a runoff, Woodbury pointed to one poll indicating Claytie could "handily" beat any candidate the Democrats nominated, and said, "Williams has caught on because he offers catchy solutions to complicated problems, with a rustic sincerity that Texans seem to relish." To make his point, he quoted Tyler motel clerk Boris Johnson: "Look him in the eyes, and you have to trust him. There's nothing phony. He speaks common sense."

Weighing in from Europe, London's *Sunday Correspondent,* one of Britain's more staid and prestigious newspapers, suggested that the Brits were following the Texas election like a "splashy new soap opera." *Dallas News* columnist Maryln Schwartz devoted a front-page column to the Brits' obsession with the Lone Star potboiler.

"The star in this show is Clayton Williams, whom they delight in calling 'Blatant Millions,'" she wrote, citing a recent headline in the *Sunday Correspondent* announcing that "Blatant Millions Is Punch Drunk on Popularity."

One of the newspaper's own representatives came to Texas to report firsthand on "Blatant Millions" and followed him to a "Women for Williams" rally. "About eighty belles of varying ages had assembled to voice their approval for Ol' Claytie, and what voices they were," he disclosed. "It was like being closeted in a room with a small army of Dolly Partons. The dense cloud of perfume hanging over the gathering seemed dangerously close to upsetting the ecological balance."

A racier London tabloid ran a photo of Claytie atop a horse and with the headline "From Those Same Wonderful People Who Brought You J.R. Ewing." The story told how he rides the range with "his cowgirl and wife, Modesta."

The Maryln Schwartz column also quoted a Dallas woman just back from a visit to England as saying the newspaper stories make the race sound like the gunfight at the OK Corral.

Though almost everything was flattering or favorable, Claytie didn't care for his comparison to the villainous TV oilman-rancher J.R. of *Dallas* fame. "His portrayal of an oilman as a slick, conniving son of a bitch did more than anything to hurt the image of real oilmen."

Virtually no political campaign escapes without a slew of bizarre developments, and Todd Smith witnessed a number of them as Claytie's traveling press aide. One unfolded during a debate at the Grand Kempinski Hotel in Dallas with the four major GOP contenders present along with a lesser-known candidate named J. N. Otwell, a Pentecostal preacher from Fort Worth.

"I was sitting back with the press and thinking that Claytie was not the most colorful candidate that day because Reverend Otwell kept talking about the gays and the "Lisbons." After a bit, Todd recalled, one of the reporters laughed and said, "I wonder what the Portuguese think about this." To emphasize his displeasure with "Lisbons," the reverend declared: "When God created man on Earth, he named them Adam and Eve, not Adam and Steve."

"Amen!" Claytie uttered.

"So we get in the car, we're leaving the event, and Clayton said, 'I want you to call the campaign. I want to send a check to Otwell.'

And I said, 'What?' And he said, 'I want to send a campaign contribution to Otwell.' I said, 'Clayton, he's running against you.' He said, 'I don't care. I like his style.' He said, 'Do it, do it.' And so when I made the call to the campaign and relayed the message, they thought I was insane, or drinking, and I said again, 'Clayton wants to send a check to Otwell.' And I think they did."

Buddy Barfield recalled no such check being sent, but Claytie's request was not a frivolous gesture. Besides genuinely liking the guy, Claytie figured Otwell had no chance of winning, and he wanted his support in the general election. "He was a good guy, and we became friends," he said. Claytie also was fond of one of Otwell's favorite expressions, which he borrowed on occasion: "It's true that I rode into town on a load of watermelons—but it wasn't this morning."

The primary campaign was humming along on a high note in the run-up to Valentine's Day 1990. A Republican Women's rally on February 13 was a roaring success in Sterling City, where Claytie's mother, Chic, had attended school. The rally was held at a historic home and drew a historic turnout.

"The house was full, the yard was full, and I don't know where they got those five hundred women in little Sterling City," said Denise Kelly, who returned afterward to Midland with Modesta and Claytie's mother to attend a political fund-raiser and rally at the Midland Center. The event was special for several reasons. The crowd included Baby Jessica McClure, the little Midland girl rescued from a well three years earlier in a nationally televised recovery effort. Claytie had sent his plane and pilot to New Mexico to pick up a mining engineer to assist in Jessica's dramatic rescue, inducing Oprah Winfrey to refer to him on her show as "Mr. Private Jet."

The Midland rally also provided an opportunity for Claytie to spend quality time with several close friends he hadn't talked with in weeks because of campaign obligations. Nephew Clay Pollard and his wife, Jeanne, were also in town for the political gala, and Clay was struck by how everyone was so upbeat. "The campaign was going well and everybody was in such an unbelievably good mood," he said.

After the rally, Claytie and Modesta gathered for an extended chat with a small group of friends and employees, among them "Executive Sidekick" Bob Smith, Williams Companies president Jamie Winkel, and Randy Kidwell, the former president of ClayDesta Communications who was returning to the company. Aaron Giebel, a close friend and member of Claytie's bank board, and Williams Aviation Company pilot Ken Mardis also attended the rally.

Besides personal matters and politics, the conversations that night focused on business meetings in Dallas and San Antonio the next day and who was flying where and how. Clay and Jeanne Pollard overheard Jamie Winkel telling Claytie, "We need the MU-2 tomorrow. We've got a bank issue. We've got to go back to Dallas and so we need to use that plane."

"Sure," Claytie replied. "Whatever you need."

The plan was to take board members of ClayDesta Bank to Dallas for their session, then fly to San Antonio to visit the company's exploration office. Since Pollard had a scheduled sales meeting with his new boss in San Antonio, his wife suggested that he grab a seat on Claytie's twin-engine Mitsubishi 2, called the MU-2. Jeanne Pollard knew that Modesta, as a director of the bank, would be making the trip to Dallas and that Clay always enjoyed being with her and flying on one of Claytie's planes. Modesta had told her mother that she would be on the Dallas flight. But Clay reluctantly decided he'd better fly commercial to ensure his arrival in the Alamo City in time for the midmorning meeting with his new boss. Meanwhile, Randy Kidwell had made commercial reservations since he was going to Dallas on business. But at the rally, Winkel suggested Kidwell travel with them.

The next morning, February 14, Claytie called the Midland office from his home all aglow over the previous evening's success and the opportunity to spend time with friends. "Wasn't last night just grand?" he gushed to Denise.

They reviewed his schedule for the day and ended the brief conversation.

At practically the last minute, Modesta decided that with several other ClayDesta directors going, it was not imperative that she attend the Dallas meeting. Meanwhile, another company executive, Paul Latham, intended to make the Valentine's Day flight, but several events forced a change in his plans as well.

And so it was that shortly after seven o'clock on a cold, overcast winter morning, the plane called MU-2 lifted off from a private Midland airpark bound for Dallas. Aboard the sleek little craft were pilot Ken Mardis, fifty-two; Jamie Winkel, forty-five; Aaron Giebel, sixty-three; Bob Smith, sixty-two; and Randy Kidwell, thirty-seven.

After the triumphant and joyous rallies less than twenty-four hours earlier, the group was almost certainly upbeat as it winged its way toward Big D and Love Field, about three hundred and fifty miles east.

Early on, pilot Mardis attempted to get a forecast from the Automated Flight Service Station in San Angelo, but the station's computers were down. Mardis was flying on instruments, indicating that clouds obscured visibility. What the pilot may not have known was that ice was building on the wings.

Suddenly crippled by the icing, the turboprop descended from more than 14,000 feet to 9,700 feet in twenty-four seconds. Then Mardis lost control, investigators would determine, and the plane plunged toward the ground.

The doomed plane, still flying on instruments, slammed nose first into a field roughly thirty-five miles east of Abilene, killing everyone instantly.

At exactly that moment, Clay Pollard's commercial flight was landing in Dallas before continuing on to San Antonio, where he would learn of the crash.

Word that a Williams plane had disappeared spread swiftly across the state and country, creating chaos and touching off mounting fears and frantic phone calls throughout Williams companies and families.

Who was on the plane? And who was not?

A reporter called the Midland office, asking Denise Kelly if Claytie's plane had crashed. "Of course not," she snapped. In Modesta's nearby office, Brenda Chambers fielded similar calls. "Denise," she shouted, "that's the second call I've had from a news reporter asking me to verify that Clayton's plane had crashed!"

Before she could reply, Denise's phone rang again. It was an official of the National Transportation Safety Board asking the same question. "My heart just froze," she said. She took his name and phone number and said she'd check and call back. She contacted Aubrey Price, the chief pilot of Williams Aviation; he knew nothing about a crash. "Denise," he said dismissively, "you know Williams is in Midland and I'm standing here looking at the jet."

"But where is the MU-2?" she pressed.

"I'll call you right back," Price promised, and did less than a minute later. "Where's Williams?" he asked grimly. "It's the MU-2."

Brenda remembers wanting to cry, but she had no time for tears. "We had to find out who was on the plane."

When Modesta's mother heard the news report, she thought her daughter had gone down with the plane. When Randy Kidwell's Cadillac was spotted at the airpark, it was assumed he was on board the Williams plane. Brenda recalled the moment Denise phoned Randy's wife, Suzanne, and calmly asked in her "perkiest" voice: "Hey, Suzanne, we were just wondering if Randy took a Southwest flight to Dallas this morning?"

"No," she replied. "He decided to catch a ride with Jamie."

Denise thanked her, hung up, and fought back the tears. Because Randy Kidwell was Clay Pollard's recent boss, it was feared Clay also was on the MU-2. Clay, meanwhile, was in the opening moments of his meeting in San Antonio when someone summoned him to a phone. "Clay, Clayton Williams's plane crashed," the caller said. "He's gone down."

Clay thought: "Claytie and Modesta!"

At the company's Fort Stockton office, Wynona Riggs answered a call from the Federal Aviation Agency: "Do you have a plane in the air this morning?" Aware of no such flight, she advised the caller to contact the company's aviation department in Midland. Soon Wynona's husband walked in the office, saying: "I talked to Johnny May, and he heard a rumor that one of your planes is down."

Claytie, meanwhile, was at home in his favorite chair near the swimming pool when he got a call from his chief pilot, Price. "I'm afraid the plane has gone down somewhere near Abilene because it disappeared from radar," he said.

"Claytie just went white," Modesta said. She retreated to the bedroom, dropped on her knees in prayer, and quickly realized her vision turned black. "To this day, I felt like the Lord was saying, 'No, they're gone.'"

And to this day, Claytie has never again sat in his favorite spot out by the pool.

Tearful and traumatized, Claytie and Modesta left almost immediately for the homes of their friends' families, starting with Jamie Winkel's wife, Carol, and Randy Kidwell's wife, Suzanne.

"The plane crash was the worst thing we ever went through," Wynona Riggs said. "And nobody took it any harder than Claytie."

"Clayton was just devastated," Denise remembered. "Absolutely devastated. To see how he reacted to the tragedy was a defining moment. He felt like it was up to him, single-handedly, to bring some comfort and hope to the wives and families."

When Claytie had talked with Denise that morning before the crash, he spoke repeatedly about how pleased he was about the special gathering with his friends the night before. "I had not gotten to sit down and visit with just my friends right here in town for so long," he said. After the crash, Denise said, "He would hold on to that last good-bye as almost a parting gift."

Likewise, she said, he never took anything more seriously than the remarks he prepared for the eulogies he delivered that week at the First Baptist Church. Some worried that he would not be capable, emotionally, of handling the eulogies. "They said if he can get though this, he can handle anything," Modesta remembered. And he did so beautifully, friends said, with "strength, tenderness, sweetness, kindness, and compassion."

He bid a teary farewell to the "laughs, the hunts, and the campfire songs" they all had shared through the years, noting: "We weren't related by blood, we weren't related by marriage, but we were bound by love, by respect, by achievements, and by some battle scars."

In a closing prayer, he asked the Lord to "give us the strength to comfort one another, to love one another, and to move forward and live our lives by the example these five dear men set."

It was a long, sad week of funerals, eulogies, tears, and mourning amid speculation that Claytie might drop out of the governor's race. He did not, of course, in part because every widow insisted that he press on. Modesta knew, however, if she had been aboard the plane as planned, it would have been different: "I don't think Claytie could have made it through. I just think he would have cratered. We are soul mates."

The NTSB headquarters in Washington subsequently reported that the pilot had little experience in the Mitsubishi MU-2 turboprop and had failed, both before takeoff and during flight, to get a comprehensive weather forecast. After an early attempt to get weather information from the flight station at San Angelo, he made no further efforts, investigators said.

"Excessive accumulation of structural icing on the aircraft's wings, stabilizers, fuselage, and engine inlets" caused the pilot to lose control of the aircraft, the report said.

According to a safety board spokesman, "Planes are not equipped to fly with a buildup of ice on them unless there is de-icing equipment operating." He said freezing temperatures were occurring that day at ten thousand to twelve thousand feet, and the aircraft was cruising at fifteen thousand feet. The MU-2 was equipped to fly in icing conditions, but "the status of de-icing equipment wasn't determined due to impact-fire damage."

However, a civil jury later took a definitive look at the facts surrounding the crash. Claytie and Modesta sat through every day of the trial to lend support to the families and, they hoped, help influence the jury. The panel ruled that Mitsubishi was liable for the icing problem that caused the crash and awarded the families of the five victims millions of dollars.

Eulogy for five friends killed in 1990 plane crash

"With the award money and our insurance, which was good insurance, the families were taken care of financially," Claytie said, adding remorsefully, "but that didn't replace a loved one."

While Claytie struggled to regain his campaign momentum after the crash, his TV commercials received an unexpected reception. His primary opponents were fretting over the ads, and his potential Democratic foes were sounding more impressed and envious than concerned. "Sure, we watched those commercials like everybody else in the state," Glenn Smith, Ann Richards's campaign manager, told the authors of her biography, *The Thorny Rose of Texas*. "And it was our opinion those were the greatest political ads we'd ever seen. They presented a forceful message that defined and framed the candidate in a clear and positive light. Ann characteristically managed to stay focused on winning her own primary, but yes, she was intrigued by Williams and those commercials, which had a production quality that you see in presidential elections and rarely at a state level."

The authors of the Richards book, Mike Shropshire and Frank Schaefer, maintained that Claytie's commercials almost immediately made him a celebrity. "Within a month," they noted, "his name recognition quotient rose from 4 percent in Texas to 88 percent."

They acknowledged that few of Claytie's investments and ventures ever paid off as gratifyingly as that weekend filming session on a rocky mountainside at Happy Cove Ranch outside Alpine. "Milam's spots were overwhelmingly popular, and Williams's bid for the Republican nomination against three other more conventional candidates was won before it ever really got under way," they wrote.

Shropshire and Schaefer quoted a political analyst as saying Claytie "got there with those TV spots early and he sawed the rest of the field off at the knees."

For Todd Smith, Claytie's field media manager, the high point of the primary came about a week before the election. That's when word arrived from the Austin headquarters that Kent Hance had surrendered. The former front-runner had agreed to shut down his campaign if the Williams team would withdraw a devastating TV commercial directed at Hance's campaign ambiguities.

"We were in Amarillo and we got a phone call about three o'clock in the afternoon," Smith said of the Hance revelation. "Clayton and I kind of looked at each other, gave each other a high-five, and Clayton said, 'Let's go find a banana split!' And we drove all over Amarillo looking for an ice-cream store where we could get a banana split to celebrate—basically—the end of the primary campaign."

Sure enough, on March 13, it was official: a GOP primary triumph of landslide proportions. Claytie told joyous Republicans whooping it up in the state capitol that night, "I bet this is the biggest crowd an Aggie ever had in Austin!"

The victory speech was vintage Claytie, right away challenging anyone who still doubted his salesmanship to just look at Modesta, who appeared smashingly radiant and maybe a little stunned when he introduced her as the "next first lady of Texas." He also introduced his mother, Chic, who he said had been skeptical of his gubernatorial bid but insisted that if he actually made the race, "I want you to have a good time doing it."

He reminded his supporters of the promise they made to the voters: "We said from the beginning that we were going to be a campaign of the grass roots, of the neighborhood, of the people. And we've even surprised the experts by doing just that."

Without getting maudlin about the plane crash, he touched on the "tragic loss among our family in the course of this campaign" and he thanked the Republican Party of Texas for "giving me the greatest honor of my life. To be your nominee for governor is a responsibility I respect, a challenge I will cherish, and a cause I will champion." He noted that things had gotten a little "testy" during the spirited primary, "although looking at the Democratic mess makes us look like a bunch of sissies."

He didn't just extend the olive branch to his vanquished GOP opponents, he tossed them the whole tree: "Kent Hance, Tom Luce, Jack Rains—my hat's off to each of you. In this hard-fought battle, you have each shown the people of Texas that ours is the party of the future. Your supporters must be awfully proud of your efforts. And I look forward to working closely with each of you and with your team in the months ahead as we all come together to share our common vision with the people of Texas."

All his life, he said, people have been telling him "nope": "You can't do this. You can't do that." He rejected it then, he was rejecting it now. "In short, we are the party of hope, the Democrats are the party of nope. . . . What's the difference between the Democratic naysayers and we Republicans? Hope . . . hope."

In closing, he said first in Spanish, then in English: "If you're looking for someone who's ready to lead our state into the future, who's willing to fight the special interests for the good of the whole, and who'll give you a day's work for a day's pay, then get ready to meet Clayton Williams, Texan.

"God bless all of you. God bless Texas."

Hardly had the echoes of Claytie's remarks faded when the *South China Morning Post*—not a newspaper normally identified with Texas electoral battles—spoke out on the "John Wayne of American politics."

"The millionaire who has just won the Republican nomination for the governorship of Texas would find the comparison right on target—a standard-bearer of hope, honesty, and justice; a self-made, God-fearing man; and one prepared to do what he must in the name of God, country, and the American Way."

Citing Ronald Reagan as an example, the newspaper said it would be no great surprise to see that macho John Wayne image carry Claytie into the governor's mansion and, "in due course," propel him on to the White House.

Claytie, however, had been compared to the Hollywood icon on previous occasions, such as when he gave his commercial spiels from atop or beside a horse or when he walked through a western ghost town. His response was vintage Claytie.

"I'm John Wayne walking down the street," he said, laughing, "except that I'm short, bald-headed, and ugly."

South China and John Wayne aside, Claytie was physically and mentally exhausted after the primary and the uplifting victory party and speech. He wanted—he needed—a break. But that was not to be. He and Modesta flew to Washington for a White House luncheon with the president and Barbara Bush. Lee Atwater, then chairman of the Republican National Committee, was there. So were Todd Smith and half a dozen Texas reporters, among them Sam Attlesley of the *Dallas Morning News*.

"We came out to do a press conference on the South Lawn of the White House with Atwater, who was walking with a slight limp," Smith recounted. "Did you hurt yourself?" Claytie asked. "No," Atwater replied. "For some reason, about a week and a half ago, I started limping and I'm not sure why." Smith theorizes now that the limp was probably the first indication of the brain tumor that soon killed Atwater.

On a lighter note, one of the reporters asked Claytie what the Bushes served at the Oval Office luncheon. Claytie said he didn't know what it was, but that it had meat in it. Todd thought at the time Barbara Bush would be mildly shocked to learn that her guest, a cattleman, didn't know what it was he'd eaten. But Modesta could identify it only as a meat patty or meat dish with vegetables. She did remember, however, a quip from the First Lady: "Don't be waiting for what comes next; that's all there is."

During that trip to the nation's capital, Claytie's crew engineered a rare face-to-face meeting with President Bush's energy secretary, James Watkins. Watkins was a retired four-star admiral and recognized as one of the fathers of the nuclear navy. For security reasons, reporters remained downstairs while Claytie and his aide rode a glass elevator to the top of the Department of Energy building. Todd briefed his candidate on the way up.

"Now, Clayton," he said, "remember, you're going to be meeting with Jim Watkins, and even though he's the secretary of energy, he does not like to be referred to as 'Secretary.' He still likes to be referred to as 'Admiral Watkins.' You got it? Admiral Watkins. And we're going to be meeting with his deputy, Hinson Moore. Moore is a former Republican congressman from Louisiana. He ran for the U.S. Senate from Louisiana, came very close to winning, but lost his race and is now the deputy secretary of energy."

Claytie repeated the names aloud: "Former Congressman Hinson Moore and Admiral Watkins. I got it."

They entered Watkins's palatial office, decorated with a magnificent photograph of a nuclear aircraft carrier hanging on the wall, and the discussions on energy policy and related topics proceeded swimmingly. Afterward, entering the elevator, Claytie was visibly pleased but also exhausted. The elevator doors opened, camera lights clicked on, and the Texas reporters moved in with tape recorders and notebooks in hand.

Meeting in the Oval Office with President Bush

"How did your meeting go?" asked Attlesley, the *Dallas Morning News* reporter.

"Had a great meeting," Claytie replied. Pausing a moment, he looked at Todd and continued: "I had a great meeting with the ambassador and his assistant, Vincent Price."

Of course, the reporters broke out laughing, as did Todd. Claytie couldn't figure out what was so funny, but he could read a Texas newspaper or two the next day about his meeting with "Ambassador" Watkins and horror movie star Vincent Price.

"It was one of the more comical moments of the campaign," Todd recalls, grinning, "but it didn't faze Claytie."

Meanwhile, back in Texas, the Democrats were wrapping up a nasty, mud-slinging brawl between Ann Richards and Texas Attorney General Jim Mattox. Former Gov. Mark White was a distant third. As the keynote speaker at the Democratic National Convention in 1988, Richards had become an overnight celebrity at the expense of President Bush. "Poor George," she said of Bush the elder.

"He can't help it. He was born with a silver foot in his mouth." Now, in 1990, the feisty, sharp-tongued candidate had won the primary and a runoff with Mattox, but emerged from the process bruised and battered. A headline in the old *Dallas Times Herald* memorably caught the sordid flavor of the Democratic primary: "Richards Wins in Mudslide."

"If it's inevitable, just relax and enjoy it."

20

With his primary triumph, presidential luncheon, mystery-meat dish, and horror-film pal Vincent Price behind him, Claytie would have been content to savor the moment and watch from the sidelines as the Democrats slugged it out in their runoff. "It was all fun, but they just kept throwing work at me," he said. "You've got to go while it's hot. Go, go, go; work, work, work."

Todd Smith would later fault the campaign, but, he rationalized, "We were looking to make news while Jim Mattox and Ann Richards were engaged in a very brutal primary runoff."

So instead of taking a break, the campaign crew turned its attention to a new endeavor—one that appealed to the weary candidate. Claytie would invite reporters to Happy Cove Ranch for the spring roundup: "Let 'em see me working cattle on horseback; let 'em see me working in the pens; let people see that I'm a hands-on guy; let 'em see that I really am a working man." After all, voters in stunning numbers embraced the cowboy image during the primary and now they would get a glimpse of the hardworking cowboy in action.

"At the end of the primary race, Clayton invited those of us who had covered him to his ranch near Alpine for the spring roundup," recalled Kaye Northcott, who reported on the election for the *Fort Worth Star-Telegram*. "He fell into the trap that a lot of neophyte candidates do—thinking they can be friends with reporters. But the system is not set up to take time off for fellowship. I was hoping to have a good time, but you never know when you're going to have to turn back into an ungrateful cur."

Typical of most reporters covering the 1990 election, Northcott respected Claytie and found him personally colorful and his race interesting to cover. John Gravois, then with the *Houston Post* and later with the *Star-Telegram,* would admit that "never before or after have I dealt with anybody that is as completely open and honest about any topic as Clayton Williams." He added, not altogether jokingly, that if he admired any politicos more than Claytie, it was Modesta.

Todd Smith said he believes the press liked Claytie and that he genuinely liked reporters. He was particularly fond of Attlesley, the late *Dallas Morning News* reporter, and once gave him an engraved set of spurs, which Sam reluctantly returned.

"He had to give them back because he couldn't accept a gift from a candidate running for governor," said Todd, who of course was present that weekend Claytie welcomed reporters to Happy Cove. "That really hurt Clayton because he didn't do it to court favor."

In an eerie footnote to the roundup weekend, Kaye Northcott said she was contacted just prior to the trip by a West Texas astrologer who wanted her to write about the woman's political prognostications. "She actually told me that Williams was about to make a terrible misstep and that he should watch his tongue very carefully," Kaye said. "Of course, that was too ridiculous to mention to anyone, so I didn't." But she vividly remembered the spooky forecast fifteen years later.

"We stayed at a hotel in Alpine that night and were transported to his ranch before dawn in a fog," she said. "Claytie and Modesta had arranged for an outdoor breakfast from a vintage chuck wagon at a campsite. The food was still cooking and I sneaked back to one of the vans to sleep a little longer."

The group of roundup-bound news people that fateful Saturday morning in March included Northcott and Karen Potter from the *Star-Telegram,* Gravois from the *Post,* Attlesley from the *News,* R. G. Ratcliffe from the *Chronicle,* and photographer David Breslauer from the Dallas Associated Press, among others. Claytie provided horses for any or all to ride.

But the weather turned rainy, cold, and foggy, restraining planned roundup activities. "The weather really did suck," said Gravois. "It wasn't heavy rain, but it was misty and chilly." Most of the male reporters and all the women retreated to the ranch house or the vans, leaving behind Claytie and his ranch hands and cooks and a handful of hardy scribes. Gravois recalled that only his opposition from the *Chronicle,* Ratcliffe, and Attlesley remained at the campsite with Todd, and they all overheard Claytie talking to one of the cooks about the weather. Although there remains disagreement over precisely what was said, and to whom, the gist of the comment stemmed from a familiar but ill-conceived and politically insensitive joke comparing lousy weather to rape: "If it's inevitable, just relax and enjoy it."

Gravois remembered that "our jaws just dropped, even though he wasn't saying it to us." But now reporters from three major newspapers were involved, including the two cutthroat Houston dailies. Just before the roundup, the *Chronicle* and *Post* were confronted by a similar dilemma over a racially sensitive comment uttered by a local politician. After considerable ethical debate, the comment had made it into print, causing a noisy uproar. "So two out of three of us worked for newspapers that had already made an editorial decision that comments like that are news," Gravois said.

As the three reporters discussed what they heard or thought they heard, Todd intervened with a humorous attempt to minimize the gaffe, insisting that Claytie didn't say rape. "No, he said 'rope, rope.'" Shaking his head at the thought of the "rope" effort, Todd sighed. "They didn't buy into that."

When Claytie learned that a flap had developed over the statement, he was flabbergasted that someone might be writing a story about it: "Oh, I was just talking. . . ." Todd took him to the side and said, "This is a bigger deal than you might think it is, and we're going to have to deal with it."

"What do you mean I'm going to have to deal with it?"

"We're going to have to explain what you meant by that."

Claytie said he didn't recall his exact words but simply was telling a cook or a cowhand that "the fire's good, the weather's bad, like rape; let's relax and enjoy the fire because we're not gonna work cattle."

Before anybody filed or faxed a story, the reporters who heard the remark shared the information with colleagues, Kaye Northcott remembered. "The fellows were pretty sure this was in bad taste and later asked Karen Potter and me what we thought. Being older, I had more tolerance for the crude Texas vernacular than Karen did, but this was, after all, a rape joke. You don't speak lightly of rape when you're running for governor. And it didn't help any that Williams was running against a woman."

The reporters huddled and agreed there had to be a story.

For several hours, the traveling press corps busied itself with Claytie and Modesta and the cowhands branding and castrating cows, then returned to the campsite and confronted Todd. "We told him that we needed to have a serious word with Williams," Northcott said. "I must admit I was feeling awful about the impending storm we were about to bring down on him. I even vacillated, thinking maybe this can be a little bit of a feature rather than hard news. But that was really not an option."

As they gathered around Claytie, someone asked if he thought it was acceptable to make such a rape comment. He said it was just a joke and apologized. "It's not sexist of any sort," he insisted. "If it offended anybody, I apologize. It's a man's world where we were today. Rape is not funny in any way. It's a terrible thing. . . . I was trying to be light and humorous to the men. I am not a sexist. I have women in my upper management."

When asked if some people might find the comment offensive, he told the Associated Press: "I'm not going to give you a serious answer. It wasn't a serious deal. It wasn't a serious statement." The AP also quoted Modesta as saying, "If the word *rape* was in a joke, if sex was in a joke, it was just a joke." In response to a question, she said she considered the reporters' questions unfair, reminding them that Claytie was a gentleman and a caring husband and father.

Leaving the campsite, the reporters headed directly to their hotel rooms to write. They did not talk to one another about how they intended to pitch their stories. But like Northcott, John Gravois was caught in a quandary. "I can't remember how he put it, but Claytie said he fully regretted the comment and he was very sincere in that he did not mean it in the offensive way that everybody took it. And [the rape joke] was the typical kind of comment you would expect to hear around a campfire and a ranch during roundup."

Gravois flirted with the option of downplaying the incident with a "short story." But he knew others considered it a big deal. In the end, like Kaye, he realized he had no option.

"But the remarkable thing," Gravois would recall years later, "was that after all was said and done, after everybody goes back to the hotel and to their neutral corners to get their stories filed, Claytie takes the entire press corps out for a group dinner that night with him and Modesta and the kids."

Claytie wanted to pick up the tab but most of the news folks paid their own way.

"In the midst of all that had gone on," Gravois continued, "Claytie welcomed the very people that he knew were filing stories that could well have ended his political career before it ever got off the ground. . . . The guy was not oblivious to what had happened and he knew it was very serious . . . but he sits down and eats steak with us and acts just as calm and natural."

Describing Claytie's demeanor as amazing, Gravois said: "If I were him, I would have left the press in Alpine and gotten the hell out of there. I wouldn't have been able to meet the press that night."

Northcott was equally astonished with her host's conduct that evening and said it was just one reason she liked and admired him. "Sure, he was an insensitive Aggie cowboy, but he had a good heart and could stand up to his mistakes. By dinnertime, I'm sure Todd Smith, his press aide, had explained the full implications of his blunder and that it would be all over the state the next day. Here he'd wanted to show us his ranch and let us experience a real roundup, and we were about to put his campaign in deep doo-doo over a joke.

Well, he and Modesta and his aides all showed up for dinner and Williams was a delightful host. He didn't pout or snarl. He knew he'd made a grievous blunder, but it wasn't going to get in the way of his being a great host, relaxed and funny."

It dawned on her also that her astrologer's forecast proved jarringly accurate. The next day was Sunday, and the rape joke was splashed across the front pages of most of the major dailies across the state.

The opening shots in the war later known as "Claytie and the Lady" had been fired prematurely that weekend, but they were just Claytie—as he himself said—shooting himself in the foot.

Democratic reaction to the rape "joke" was predictably quick and caustic, whereas Republicans maintained that Claytie was being unfairly criticized. Claytie's supporters struggled to keep the issue in perspective. After all, they argued, the candidate admitted it was just a throwaway remark not meant in any way sexist, and even then he had apologized profusely. Although seldom mentioned by the Texas media, the pithy zinger on rape and inevitability was first uttered decades earlier by a woman—the sophisticated, sharp-tongued New York writer Dorothy Parker. So reported columnist Wesly Pruden of *The Washington Times*: "The remark was graceless when Dorothy Parker invented it in a more grown-up era when men and women felt free to entertain each other by saying wicked things to each other, and it was graceless when Clayton Williams repeated it to a group of reporters in what he thought was the privacy of his back yard. . . . Now feminists are picketing him, little girls are throwing rocks at him, lady dogs are growling at him, lady bugs are biting him, and the columnists are attacking him as if he invented the kind of smutty jokes that newspaper persons tell to make the air in their newsrooms blue. . . ."

Claytie, honest again to a fault, admitted that his critics included his mother, Chic, and daughters Chim and Allyson.

"My mother and my daughters gave me a working over this morning like you can't believe," Claytie told a brief news conference at

Dallas-Love Field that Monday evening after flying in for a political appointment. "My mother said, 'I didn't raise you this way.' My daughters talked to me a little more strongly than that."

But, as he told the *Fort Worth Star-Telegram,* "You can't print that, either."

Claytie pointed out that he had demonstrated his concern for violence against women long before he entered the governor's race. He produced information showing that his companies sponsored a self-defense course for female employees and paid the twenty-five-dollar registration fees for each of them. "Actions speak louder than words," he said. "These were my actions."

Then again, his words weren't bad, as evidenced by his formal apology. "I feel terrible about this," he said in the written statement. "I had no intention in my heart to hurt anyone, especially those women who had been traumatized by rape. Looking back, I realize it was insensitive and had no place at the campfire or in any setting. People who know me or what I've been saying in my campaign know that I feel strongly about criminals who roam our streets inflicting violence on innocent citizens. Rape is one of the most violent types of crimes we are faced with today and will be met with a firm hand if I'm elected governor.

"Once again, I apologize from the bottom of my heart and although I didn't mean any harm, I realize I was wrong."

The next day, daughter Kelvie Muhlbauer, unaware of the furor in Texas, opened the morning paper at her home in Memphis, Tenn., and a startling headline caught her attention. "Texan Apologizes for Rape Comment." She recalled closing the paper and saying, "Oh please, God, not my Texan!"

Several women's organizations and antirape groups seized the opportunity to denounce all things sexist, and a number of feminist columnists weighed in with curt remarks. In Austin, six groups assembled at a news conference, including the Texas Association Against Sexual Assault. The association's president, Sherri Sunaz, dismissed Claytie's apologies as inadequate and said there remained a misunderstanding of the depth of the issue. "The very suggestion

TexasMonthly

JULY 1990 · $2.50

Texas Humor
Just Sit Back and Enjoy It

Featuring

**Clayton Williams' Favorite
Aggie Joke, Joe Bob Briggs,**

that anyone should 'relax and enjoy it' is an outrage to the memory of those who have been murdered and to those who have survived and daily struggle to heal from the effects of this crime," Sunaz said, according to the *Star-Telegram*. "The governor's ability to veto legislation which directly impacts the rights of survivors and potential victims makes sensitivity to these issues critical to all Texans."

Jim Mattox, the acid-tongued attorney general, paused long enough from his drugs and alcohol assaults on Ann Richards to take a couple of potshots at Claytie. "Just because you're in the barnyard doesn't mean you have to act like Clayton Williams," he said. "I just think that women voters are going to remember his attitude about this."

Ann Richards put a slightly different slant on the controversy: "I think that the saddest part of it was Clayton's feelings that it was justified because it took place in a cow pasture. I don't think it makes any difference where remarks like that take place. Until they stop, the feeling is that it is all right to make jokes about violence, and certainly rape is one of the most devastating crimes of violence."

Meanwhile, a number of Republican women spoke out in Claytie's defense, as did Gov. Bill Clements, who sounded more upset with the reporters than with Claytie. "I find it hard to believe that the press would violate an informal meeting of that kind, and I don't think that he had any idea that he was saying something for the record," Clements told reporters. He was half right. It never crossed Claytie's mind that his "joke" would or would not be reported, but he had agreed before the roundup that his comments would be on record. Of course, no one could anticipate the circumstances under which such a joking remark might be made.

The *Star-Telegram* spoke with Tarrant County GOP leaders of both sexes the next day and reported that they described Claytie's rape reference as unfortunate and offensive, but it would not cost him the support of Republican women. "I think he really did not mean it in the way he used the word," said Jane Berberich, a former member of the Republican State Executive Committee and an active member of the Texas Federation of Republican Women. "But it is offensive to women for something like that to happen." Fran Chiles, Claytie's Tarrant County chairwoman, called the comment a "figure of speech," and said it did not offend her. "I don't think, in any way, it was his intention to damage anyone."

Echoing that sentiment, seventy-eight-year-old Republican Executive Committee member Virginia Steenson of Richardson called it just "an old joke, which we've heard a million times." Campaign spokesman Bill Kenyon offered an interesting spin: "Part of the reason that we allow access to Clayton is we want people to get to know him, and that includes warts and all. He's not an expert in the art of sound bites. . . . People have had the opportunity to see that he is a caring man." The *Star-Telegram* account noted also that Kenyon predicted the furor would quickly pass and that Claytie never had feminists' votes anyway: "The feminists are a highly charged, focused liberal political group and are going to support the most liberal candidate, whoever that is," he said.

With the cruel benefit of hindsight, it was probably Governor Clements who made the most flawed forecast of the episode. While conceding that Claytie's remark was unfortunate, and predicting victory in November, Clements said, "I am sure that he will be more cautious in the future. I'm positive of this."

Claytie, cautious?

It was not an auspicious start, but Claytie's campaign polls indicated that after the roundup mishap he had bounced back from a brief downtick and would enter the governor's race as the favorite against either Democratic contender, Richards or Mattox. In what some branded the most "vicious" bloodletting in the state's raucous political history, Richards won the April 10 primary with nearly 60 percent of the votes, collecting 639,126 to 479,388 for Mattox. And though she emerged more than a mite muddied, Richards proved once again she was a tough, savvy candidate not to be taken lightly. She was determined to be the first woman governor of Texas since Miriam "Ma" Ferguson more than half a century earlier, and her previous political track record was impressive. A teacher, an activist, and a former Travis County commissioner, she had served two terms as state treasurer, winning the 1986 election without opposition.

Texans would soon be introduced to what an Associated Press political writer famously described as the wildest and woolliest Texas governor's race ever.

Someone else christened it simply "Claytie and the Lady."

Even before the general election shifted into high gear, Claytie's accessibility and forthrightness generated new accusations of sexist insensitivity. This time, however, he knew he was speaking on the record, and again John Gravois of the *Houston Post* was a pivotal player.

Responding to rumors that Claytie had visited brothels as a youngster in Fort Stockton and at A&M, campaign officials alerted the Austin press corps that he would address the issues upon returning from a trip out of state. In fact, he was in Scottsdale, Ariz., that April weekend at the All-American Wildcatters convention. The first thing Gravois did was call his Houston desk and report that Claytie had agreed to discuss the issue with reporters. "Why don't we go find out where he is on the out-of-state trip and go try to talk to him?" he asked his editor. That's how it was that Gravois walked into the plush Phoenician resort in Scottsdale one Saturday and smack dab into Claytie, Modesta, Amarillo oilman Boone Pickens, and former U.S. Secretary of State Henry Kissinger.

There were no press secretaries or campaign officials to cope with, but Gravois knew the typical politician would have summoned hotel security and had him unceremoniously escorted from the resort grounds. But this was no typical politician. Claytie figured out at once why Gravois was there, excused himself, and he and Modesta joined the reporter in a quiet hallway of the hotel. To the reporter's amazement, Claytie "began to lay out everything," taking control of the story and recounting how as a teenager in Fort Stockton and a young college student at A&M he had visited prostitutes.

He explained, as the *Post* reported in a copyright article the next morning, a Sunday, that visiting "Boys Town" on the Mexican border was a West Texas cultural rite of passage from boyhood to manhood.

Modesta, as forthright and supportive as ever, confirmed the cultural validity of that statement and added her own assessment: "What he did before we were married is certainly his business. That doesn't bother me at all."

Claytie told Gravois: "I've never claimed to be a perfect man. It's part of growing up in West Texas. . . . It's like the Larry McMurtry book *The Last Picture Show*." As for visits to the infamous "Chicken Ranch" at LaGrange, he said, "It was kind of what the boys did at A&M." That was a difficult statement for critics to challenge if they'd seen the Broadway musical or Burt Reynolds movie *The Best Little Whorehouse in Texas*. They were based on West Texas author Larry L. King's article in *Playboy* that immortalized the LaGrange brothel, a near-century-old institution about an hour southwest of College Station.

But Claytie went one step too far in his attempt to be open and honest about his youthful indiscretions. "It was different in those days," he told Gravois, using a familiar cattle breeding expression to make his point. "The houses were the only place you got *serviced* then."

Once again, the reaction was swift, noisy, and nasty, though less from the Democrats than the newspaper editorials and columnists. This time the venerable *Washington Post* jumped into the fray with columns by Judy Mann and Mary McCrory and a news story by Mary Jacoby writing out of Austin. Both Mann and McCrory, while resurrecting the rape joke, were justifiably incensed with the connotation they attached to the "servicing" comment.

"The most you can say for the contest for the governorship of Texas is that the voters cannot claim to be bored," McCrory wrote. "In Texas, where excess in pursuit of higher office is no vice—as volume two of Robert Caro's biography of Lyndon Johnson, *Means of Ascent,* so vividly attests—the focus has been on sex and drugs and personal history. In an era of exceptionally rotten and negative politics, the Lone Star State seems to be going for the gold in slander and bad taste."

Jacoby, in her news story, did point out an assertion by campaign spokesman Kenyon that Claytie's candor about prostitution would not damage his campaign. "I think that's one thing that's played to our benefit," he said. "Clayton is candid and tries to tell the truth. He's not as crafty as many politicians. . . . And we had two choices when we started this campaign: either put clamps on him and run a more traditional campaign, or we could let Clayton be Clayton and understand that we would take some bumps along the way."

Back in Texas, the editorial tone was typified in part by a comment in the *Star-Telegram:* "If the Republican gubernatorial nominee had a better grasp of what is insulting to much of his audience, and a better choice of words, his honesty and frankness about his own past might be refreshing."

The Richards campaign took an ambivalent stance—of sorts—about Claytie's revelation.

"He implies that women are here to 'service' men. That kind of an attitude is as insulting to men as it is to women," spokesman Glenn Smith told reporters. "In recent months, the Republican nominee has made several comments which taken together drive this wedge between men and women, and I think that's unfortunate." That said, he asserted that the Democratic candidate herself did not wish to comment on Claytie's revelations. "His private behavior is best left to him and his family," said Smith with perhaps a trace of haughtiness. "We don't believe it's a legitimate subject for discussion in the context of a public, political debate."

Only a handful of people knew that the whole Scottsdale brouhaha could have been avoided if Kenyon had listened to Claytie's executive assistant, Denise Kelly. When he called the Midland office on behalf of Gravois and others, she told him the Wildcatters convention was not campaign-related and that reporters did not need to know his location. When Denise learned that the press secretary had given out that information, she asked Kenyon when he was leaving for Arizona to handle media control.

"Oh, I'm not going; none of the reporters are going," she quoted him as responding.

"But you gave them the information where he was staying," she said.

"But they are not going," she recalled him saying.

"I'm done with the campaign. I quit."

21

Though Claytie's self-inflicted miscues of March and April commanded barrels of newspaper ink and more air time than most natural disasters, he rode out the storm. His cowpoke image, brutal honesty, and what *Time* called his rustic sincerity had connected with voters in an unprecedented fashion. And nobody knew it better than Ann Richards and her campaign workers. After the primary and heading into the hot, intense summer, polls put Claytie's lead at twenty points — and more.

Taking nothing for granted, Claytie asked friend and adviser Davis Ford to work the Aggie vote while his wife, Gwen, assisted with the Travis County–Austin campaign.

"I got the easy job," said Ford, explaining that virtually all Aggies loved Claytie. But it was a challenge for Gwen, he quipped, because the word around Texas was that there remained only two Communist cities in the entire world: "Havana and Austin."

By early summer, according to Richards's biographers, her pollsters placed her a whopping twenty-seven points behind Claytie. And even by late summer, *Texas Monthly* reported, she had not shaken off the "negatives" of her knock-down, drag-out primary victory. The magazine said Jim Mattox had "fixed Richards in the minds of many voters as a divorced, dope-smoking liberal with a rabid lesbian following."

The so-called negatives of the two candidates was such that when *USA Today* did a major story on the 1990 election it quoted a Texas newspaper as worrying editorially that the national image of the Texas gubernatorial race bore a strong resemblance to the "Geraldo Rivera show of national politics." But the summertime state conventions would become high points for both candidates, and change was in the air.

Mary Beth Rogers, a close friend of Ann's, succeeded Glenn Smith as campaign chairperson for the general election and "proved to be a stabilizing influence on the campaign," authors Shropshire and Schaefer wrote. Explained Smith, who stayed on as a consultant: "After the primary, and all of the tension involved with that, Ann decided that she felt more comfortable with Mary Beth Rogers running the show. Mary Beth, more than me, was somebody Ann could confide in. There was no animosity involved in the change. I understood."

Some, including the new campaign chair, traced the turnaround of the conflicted Democratic Party to the state convention in Fort Worth in June. "We really rejuvenated ourselves in that convention," Rogers said. Ann's inspirational speech was greeted with cheers, shouts, and stamping of feet, and her performance and the convention itself "proved to be the rallying point that launched one of the biggest comebacks in Texas political history," biographers Shropshire and Schaefer said. "For with the rank and file solidly behind Ann, Mattox and his supporters, and some of [Mark] White's supporters although not White himself, agreed to back Ann Richards in the campaign."

Two weeks later, the Republicans took over the same Tarrant County Convention Center in Fort Worth. The GOP assemblage was not far removed from a conservative-flavored love-in. For his assistant Denise Kelly, Claytie's appearance and speech at the convention was a defining moment, one that brought tears to her eyes. She was on the stage with the family on that June afternoon and it seemed that tens of thousands of Republicans were clamoring to see their candidate.

"It looked like a rock concert," she said.

Scenes from his life played out on a giant screen above the stage and "John Wayne–type music" blared in the background. When

Claytie suddenly appeared, the crowd started screaming and hollering and trying to shake his hand, hug him, or just touch him. Denise could not help but remember that slightly more than a year earlier, as a political unknown, Claytie was knocking on doors, telling folks he was thinking of running for governor and asking them for support—which was not always forthcoming.

"And now they adored him," she said. "People cheered and screamed and hollered and there were all these ovations throughout his speech. He was never better."

All things being equal, Buddy Barfield thought, Claytie could ride the wave of new Texas conservatism to victory in November: "The state had become more conservative, more Republican." And he knew that Ann's flaming liberalism had "really angered the Republicans."

But in the governor's election of 1990, nothing could be taken for granted.

It was a tough summer on everyone. Barfield was upset that the press, particularly the national press, could not introduce Claytie in any story without resurrecting the weather-rape comment, if not the bordello capers and occasionally even the mythical "honey hunts." The "honey hunts" purportedly involved young women scattered around the ranch as sex targets for hunting guests, but the story was blatantly false and never became a serious campaign issue.

Still, said Barfield, "They just pounded us and pounded us. The campaign team became shell-shocked in a lot of ways." Before Labor Day, Claytie's lead had dwindled briefly to two or three points. But it was not from a lack of effort on the candidate's part. The campaign staff was working him night and day and often to the exclusion of his exercise breaks, which Claytie felt were vital to keeping him alert and reducing the likelihood of his misspeaking again.

"Clayton liked to exercise in the morning," Todd said in relating a little-known story that the press would have loved. "Lots of times he blamed the campaign for scheduling him too tightly and not giving him enough time to rest and exercise and do the things he felt he needed to do."

One day Todd and Claytie checked into the Embassy Suites in Dallas and walked to the nearby offices of a prominent media-specialist company for a training session. As the conference got under way, Claytie said, "Give me a second," excused himself, and walked out the door.

"Is he taking a call or something?" someone asked.

"I'll go check," Todd said.

He spotted Claytie out in the hallway walking toward the elevator.

"Clayton, where are you going?" he asked.

"I'm done."

"What do you mean you're done? We've got another two hours with these folks."

"No. I'm done."

"You don't want to do this anymore?"

"No, no, no, no. I'm done with the campaign," Claytie said. "I quit."

He grabbed his overnight bag and his hat and headed back to the hotel.

"Clayton," Todd said, "where in the hell are you going?"

"I quit. Call the campaign and tell them that I quit. I'm done. I've told them not to schedule me as tight as they are. I need to have my rest. I quit."

"Clayton . . ."

"You call Buddy Barfield and tell him I quit."

So Todd called Buddy Barfield from the lobby of the hotel.

"How's it going?" Barfield asked.

"It's not going very well."

"What do you mean?"

"Clayton just quit."

"You mean he quit meeting with them?"

"No, he quit the campaign."

"Where is he now?"

"He's at the Embassy Suites."

Todd said he looked up to see Claytie running up and down the stairs, exercising. Actually, he was running up the stairs, taking the elevator back down, then running back up the stairs again.

Telling Barfield he would call him back, Todd interrupted the exercise session.

"Clayton . . . ," he began.

"What?" he blurted, then added with a growl: "Did you tell them I quit?"

"Yeah. Buddy's wanting to know what he should do."

"Well, tell him he better get his ass up here."

So Todd called Buddy and said, "Buddy, we're done for the day, I think, so you better get up here."

"Oh, God," Buddy said.

Of course, Claytie reengaged, but only after receiving assurances that he'd get more time for exercise and a lighter schedule.

"It was typical Clayton," Todd sighed. "That was his way of rebelling."

As Claytie explained once, "That was the fatigue factor. I made mistakes because I was tired, and I was getting pretty grumpy and pretty sick of it. I said, 'Lord, let me out of this, win, lose, or draw. I just want out.'"

It didn't help the campaign's mood when the Richards team turned one of Claytie's off-the-cuff remarks against him in a commercial, but he maintained he was innocent. Asked early on if he'd rather run against Jim Mattox or Ann Richards, he said, "I'd feel much more comfortable running against a man." In the same context, he was quoted as saying if Ann won the nomination, he'd handle her just like he did his cattle: "I'll head her, I'll hoof her, and I'll drag her through the dirt." Claytie insists he wasn't referring to Richards with his "head 'em and hoof 'em" remark. He said he was talking about streamlining state government and how, as governor, he intended to straighten out the bureaucracy. "It's like working cattle," he said. "You rope 'em, heel 'em, and drag 'em through the dirt."

But critics leaped on that one as another intemperate example of his feelings toward women.

After the brief late-summer downturn, Claytie's campaign picked up new momentum with another TV blitz that restored what appeared to be a comfortable lead. "By the middle of September we were back about twelve or fifteen points up," Barfield said. Money posed no problem as the November showdown approached, although Claytie would pour an estimated $8 million of his own cash into the campaign. Todd Smith said one of his favorite "Claytieisms" was an observation made earlier in the campaign: "You know, I used to hate asking people for money. But after I put the third million of my own money in the race, it got easier."

One of the qualities that Todd most admired in his traveling companion was that Claytie rarely took himself too seriously, although one episode at the ritzy Anatole Hotel in Dallas left even Todd shaking his head. "I don't know if Claytie even knows this or not, but when we'd check into a hotel, I'd go give them the credit card and get our two rooms," he said. "They'd usually give him the presidential suite or one of the very nice rooms, and Clayton was just looking for a place to go to bed and didn't appreciate the fact that he was in a swanky hotel room. He'd be in bed in five minutes. I was twenty-eight years old and single, and I'd say, 'Here, Clayton,' and I'd give him the key to the room they gave me, and I'd take the presidential suite."

But this particular night they had scheduled fund-raising calls from the hotel the next morning and needed a room with access to multiple phone lines. About 11:30 that night, half an hour after checking in, the desk notified Todd that neither of the two rooms had two-line capability and they needed to move to different rooms.

"I was two floors above him, so I went down and knocked on his door and told him, 'Clayton, we're gonna have to move.' And he said, 'Why in the hell are we going to have to move?'" After an explanation, Claytie agreed, but not happily.

"I'll go grab a key and be right back," Todd said.

When he returned, Claytie opened the door wearing a T-shirt, his cowboy hat, his cowboy boots, and a pair of boxer shorts decorated with little red hearts—a Valentine's Day gift from Modesta. "Let's go," Claytie announced, slinging his overnight bag over his shoulder. "Let's just go. I'm not changing." To Todd's relief, they made it to the elevator without encountering anyone.

"So I push the elevator button, the door opens, and there's a group of ladies on the elevator. And they just stared at him. The nose, the ears, the hat—everyone knew what Clayton Williams looked like. I mean we had spent $13 million or $14 million at that point. And he tipped his hat and said, 'Ladies.' They walked off the elevator and he walked on, and they just turned around and stared at him as the doors were closing."

Recalled Todd: "I had this fear for days that I was going to be reading about this in the *Dallas Morning News* or the *Star-Telegram*. I can't imagine any other candidate for governor, during that period or since, who would have even contemplated doing such a thing.

"But it didn't faze Claytie."

> *"A handshake is a sign of trust.*
> *I withdrew my trust."*

The September upswing provided Claytie's campaign team a welcome boost of confidence, but both sides worried that an eleventh-hour bobble could swing the election. As September rolled to a close, Ann contended she had pulled within six percentage points of the lead—a claim not substantiated by the Williams pollsters. Claytie dismissed the figure, saying, "I hope she didn't go back to drinking again."

Ann, a recovering alcoholic who had just celebrated her tenth year of sobriety, was not amused.

"It is unfortunate that my opponent's desire to be clever and cute in his remarks continues to cloud his judgment and behavior," she said via a news release. Press spokesman Chuck McDonald was less tactful, labeling Claytie a "fraudulent, honking goose."

It was mostly a minor tempest in an antique teapot, and Claytie refused to apologize. But his campaign issued a typed statement quoting him: "I was caught by surprise with these phony numbers from the Richards camp, and it was a poor choice of words in this particular circumstance."

The final face-to-face meeting between the two candidates was looming, a joint appearance at a Greater Dallas Crime Commission luncheon at the Anatole Hotel. During the second week in October, just before the luncheon, a story appeared in Texas newspapers suggesting vaguely that Claytie's Midland bank had laundered drug money and that the Richards campaign was demanding answers.

Although the story was without merit, it deeply offended Claytie, even hurt him, because drugs were a personal concern as they related to his elder son. Additionally, the drug issue had served as both catalyst and cornerstone of his gubernatorial bid.

"The money-laundering story was not something people were talking about on the campaign trail yet, but it was something the campaign team was concerned about," Todd Smith said. "And so we had a meeting that morning at the Embassy Suites Hotel by Love Field. . . . We had Dick Dresner and Jay Townsend, Buddy Barfield and Bill Kenyon, and we were sitting in the hotel restaurant strategizing about how we were going to deal with this issue."

Kenyon reminded the troops that the late Sen. John Tower, offended once at a personal comment by Bob Krueger, famously refused to shake hands with his Democratic opponent at a joint appearance. Tower went on to win the close 1978 reelection. "Well, what do you think?" someone asked, and it was decided that Claytie would refuse to shake hands with Richards at the Crime Commission luncheon.

As they headed downtown, Claytie, in the front seat, leaned back and said to Todd, "I just don't feel right about not shaking her hand." Neither did Todd. "Well, Clayton," he said, "I may not have been as forceful as I should have been during that meeting, but it's a different scenario from the Bob Krueger–John Tower situation."

Todd cited three reasons. "Number one: She's still a woman and this is still Texas, and we have spent up to this point $13 million trying to create the perception of you being what's good about the old Texas. She's running a campaign about the new Texas, and if we come in and do something that's going to be viewed as discourteous violating the Code of the West, I think it's not going to sit well with folks.

"Number two: She's the elected state treasurer.

"Number three: We have the rape joke situation, and this just enforces it."

When Claytie repeated that he did not feel right about spurning her handshake, Todd said, "Clayton, your first instincts are usually the best, and if you don't feel right about it, don't do it."

"Yeah, but the campaign guys think we ought to do this."

"Clayton, you do what you think you need to do, but I don't think you should do it."

Claytie said, "I agree with you. I'm not going to refuse to shake her hand."

As they pulled up to the hotel, Todd remembers thinking, "OK, we're not going to do this no-handshake deal." He was relieved. They entered the ballroom, one of the biggest in Texas, and Todd veered toward the media, where the line of cameras was the longest of the campaign. A huge crowd, estimated between eight hundred and a thousand, had gathered for the climactic joint appearance. The scene struck Todd as surreal: a giant cowboy hat above the crowd moved down one side of the ballroom and a white bouffant hairdo moved along the other.

At the front awaited a group of reporters and a herd of TV news cameras, including CNN.

As they reached the front, Claytie hopped up on the stage with a number of cameras focused on him. He spotted a friendly face, John McKissick, who headed the Crime Commission, and said: "John, watch this. There's going to be a confrontation."

Todd said that "suddenly my eyes just got big and my heart sunk."

He watched Claytie approach Ann, who turned and said, "Hello, Claytie." Without acknowledging the greeting or her outstretched hand, he said: "I'm here to call you a liar today."

"I'm sorry, Clayton," she replied.

Claytie continued: "That's what you are. You've lied about me; you've lied about Mark White; and you've lied about Jim Mattox. I'm going to finish this deal today, and you can count on it."

He told reporters later he refused to shake her hand because "a handshake is a sign of trust. I withdrew my trust."

At the back of the ballroom watching the bizarre drama was Tom Pauken, an employee of a Dallas venture capital company. He had volunteered to help Claytie in his campaign. He had, however, become disenchanted with the professional handlers, the "highly paid, politically hired guns" who he said pushed aside the volun-

teer advisers and, in his opinion, consistently provided bad advice. Now, one of those "hired guns" asked him what he thought about the handshake saga.

"I think you just lost the election," Pauken said. The campaign aide turned and, wordlessly, walked away.

A sampling of the newspaper headlines the next day caught the flavor of the handshake flap: "Williams Snubs, Bashes Richards" . . . "Claytie Slings Accusations; Ann Says He's Lost Control" . . . "Williams to Richards: 'I'm Here to Call You a Liar.'"

The *Dallas Morning News* led off its page-one story with a forthright introduction.

> Republican Clayton Williams branded his Democratic opponent a "liar" on Thursday, prompting Ann Richards to ques-

tion whether the GOP candidate has the temperament to be governor.

The exchange, which came before the Greater Dallas Crime Commission during a rare joint appearance, stemmed from Ms. Richards's efforts to link Mr. Williams to a federal investigation into alleged drug money laundering. . . .

The *Fort Worth Star-Telegram* had a little different slant:

DALLAS — Clayton Williams called opponent Ann Richards a liar in a face-to-face confrontation yesterday and refused to shake her hand as a luncheon crowd of about eight hundred watched.

Later, in a speech to the group, Williams compared Richards's tactics to those of Sen. Joe McCarthy, who destroyed careers in the 1950s with accusations of Communist ties.

When the luncheon ended that Thursday, reporters swarmed the candidates, and Claytie's campaign team beat a hasty retreat. But Todd Smith realized only one viable exit existed. Bill Kenyon rushed up: "Todd, I think we gotta sneak him out some way." Because Kenyon was one of the staff officials who had proposed the nonhandshake, Todd balked: "You sorry bastard, you got us into this mess, now you ask me to turn and run and hide?" As he tried to lead Claytie out, they were inundated by cameras, microphones, notebooks, and tape recorders. "There must have been fifty reporters," Todd said. "It was awful."

When they finally reached their car, Claytie offered an instant analysis of the hotel confrontation and its hectic aftermath.

"I don't think that went very well."

"We went from twelve points up to four points behind," Buddy Barfield later revealed, citing his pollsters' results and grumbling over the national attention the flap received. Bill Cryer, Ann's spokesman, told Kaye Northcott in Austin that "our office calls, particularly in Dallas, have been overwhelming. A lot of people are saying they're taking their Clayton Williams bumper stickers off and putting on Ann Richards."

Claytie routinely accepted most of the heat for the campaign mistakes, often justifiably. But after the handshake miscue, several key players rushed to his defense, including Buddy Barfield, Todd Smith, and Denise Kelly. Even Claytie had certain misgivings about his campaign advice. "Kenyon was the one who came up with the idea of not shaking Ann Richards's hand," he said. "It never would have occurred to me, but I was dumb enough to do it."

Said Todd: "In Clayton's defense, the nonhandshake went against his nature. It was not something he felt comfortable about." But, he said, by nature Claytie was accustomed to listening to people he considered experts. "And so I think that he felt that even though his own best judgment said, 'Don't do it,' his campaign team had said, 'This is what you need to do.' And so he felt that he was going to be betraying them and violating their trust and confidence and wisdom if he did something other than what they suggested." Sometime after entering the ballroom and walking toward the stage something told Claytie, "I need to do this," Todd theorized. "I don't know if it was when he saw her hairdo or when he first caught a glimpse of her." But obviously something triggered that reaction after his pre-ballroom discussion with Todd and his decision outside the hotel to follow his instincts. "Clayton, I think, was put in a very bad situation, and I think he got very, very poor advice from the campaign team," Todd reiterated. "I wish he had followed his own best judgment, his own intuition, and not done it. But I think that was the day of the campaign that we started losing Republican women. And this was on top of the rape joke."

Barfield, again in defense of Claytie, said the campaign itself toward the end was like a football team that got worn down in the fourth quarter. "We weren't crisp. . . . We weren't on our game at that time." He acknowledged that besides the rape comment and the bordello story it was "not right for a man, no matter how bad it is, to go up and say you're not gonna shake a lady's hand."

Denise said flatly the handshake controversy was a campaign mistake, not a Claytie mistake. "I think you have to be true to what your heart tells you," she said. "It is not Clayton to get down on that level with anybody like that. . . . And he never felt comfortable with it."

That his opponent was a woman magnified the snub. It appeared Claytie was rude, discourteous, and disrespectful, Denise said, and he was never, ever any of the three.

Barfield said the campaign made some quick, effective TV and radio adjustments and Claytie, though fatigued, stepped up his own personal appearances and activities. They weathered an unnecessary gaffe over the only constitutional amendment on the ballot—one which Claytie had cast an absentee vote for while admitting in a TV interview he did not understand. But polls indicated it was still a classic horse race entering the final weekend before the November 6 election.

And then along came "The Train Trip from Hell."

It began as "The Harry Truman Whistle-Stop Tour" and wound up by late afternoon as "The Devil's Express." At least that was Todd Smith's assessment of one of the last major campaign swings designed to carry his stubborn, refreshingly honest candidate to victory. Buddy Barfield cited polls indicating that Claytie had reclaimed a tenuous edge moving into the final weekend of the campaign and the journey by rail through Central Texas could cap things with an innovative bang.

Although overworked and exhausted, Claytie remained upbeat. President Bush would be flying in over the weekend and he and GOP Sen. Phil Gramm planned a final campaign push on Claytie's behalf Sunday and Monday before the Tuesday election.

With a group of political writers aboard, the train trip began at 8 A.M. in San Antonio and included stops in College Station and other towns before winding up in Houston at 6 P.M. "We put a group of reporters on the train with no communications, which probably made them antsy," Todd recalled grimly. "But it got off to such a good start that senior press aide Kenyon left the train early, which, in hindsight, triggered concern on the part of Denise Kelly, among others. "They should have insulated Claytie," she said.

Said Todd: "On the first stop: OK, this is an interesting, beautiful setting; neat train, neat concept, kind of whistle-stop tour. . . . But by the time the train got to the next to last stop, College Station, the reporters had had enough of the train, and they started asking some tough questions."

Ann Richards had been chiding Claytie about not releasing his income tax returns, and he was asked about it for probably the fiftieth time of the campaign. Claytie's standard response was that it would take a couple of eighteen-wheelers to haul around all his tax papers. "The question that should be asked," he would add, "is this: If Ann Richards is elected governor, will she impose a personal income tax on the people of Texas?"

But this time, Todd said, there was a follow-up question: "Well, Clayton," the reporter wondered, "is there any year you have not paid taxes?"

Pausing a moment, he replied in part: "I'll tell you when I didn't pay any income tax. It was in 1986, when our whole oil and gas economy collapsed." Honest as usual, he was saying that he didn't pay any income tax that year because he had no income; he was admitting no wrongdoing. Oil had dropped from forty dollars a barrel to less than ten dollars a barrel, and he was scrambling just to survive—something many in the oil patch did not do. His explanation, however, was misinterpreted, though it was less Claytie's fault than the media's. Todd switched on the TV in his hotel room that night just in time to catch the CNN anchor saying, "Scandal in Texas: Republican gubernatorial candidate admits to not paying taxes in 1986."

Newspaper headlines in Dallas and Fort Worth on November 4 were strikingly similar and, some said, similarly misleading, implying that Claytie had done something illegal or at least irregular:

The *Star-Telegram:* "Williams Says He Didn't Pay Taxes in '86"

The *Dallas Times-Herald:* "Williams Didn't Pay Taxes in 1986"

The *Dallas News:* "Williams Didn't Pay Income Taxes in '86," with a subhead: "Richards Chides Foe for Using 'Loopholes'"

Fateful train tour

After likewise attaching a sinister spin, the Richards campaign hopped all over Claytie's revelation. "He said it was a bad year," Richards asserted. "It was a bad year for a lot of Texans in 1986. I paid my income tax in 1986, how about you?"

The Democrats got on the air quickly with a commercial contending that while millions of average Texans were paying taxes, Claytie was taking advantage of "loopholes for the rich."

With the wire services, AP and UPI, distributing the story nationwide, the tax episode circulated all weekend over TV and radio as well as in newspapers, and Claytie's campaign took a terrific beating. Barfield said polls underscored the volatility of the election, indicating that Claytie's lead of six to eight percentage points evapo-

President Bush and Claytie deplaning Air Force One

rated between Friday and Saturday night and that Ann had actually moved ahead by several points.

"To see that kind of swing overnight . . . ," Barfield said, his voice trailing off.

Still, he said, Claytie bounced back, no doubt because of help from President Bush, who campaigned with him at huge rallies in Tyler, Waco, and Houston. Claytie attended church with the elder Bush in Houston and was at the president's side in Waco when he got off one of the best self-deprecating lines of the closing days. The *Dallas News* quoted Bush as quipping in his opening remarks at the rally that the GOP traveling team was running late because "Claytie and I both set off the metal detectors with our silver feet."

The president urged voters repeatedly to put Claytie in the governor's mansion so the Bush White House would have someone to work with in building a better Texas. Claytie did not dwell on the explosive income tax issue, but Senator Gramm put it in a clever context during the election-eve rallies.

"I knew in Washington that deep down in their hearts the Democrats wanted to tax every penny you earn," said Gramm, who was coasting to reelection to a second term. "But Ann Richards has added a new dimension to tax and spend as the Democrats' slogan. She wants to tax income you don't earn. She wants to tax when you lose money."

And so it was that going into election day, a *Houston Chronicle* poll disclosed that the race was too close to call. But Barfield knew the Williams campaign polls revealed that Claytie was a point back and still rebounding from the Saturday night figures.

"We didn't know how it was going to break," he said.

Claytie arose early on election day and joined President Bush and some of his supporters at the Houstonian Hotel for a Mexican breakfast of tacos and migas. He then flew to Dallas, visited the workers at a busy phone bank, and winged his way to Austin to await the electoral verdict at the stylish Stouffer Hotel on the city's northwest side.

He didn't wait long.

Ann seized the lead as the early returns trickled in and slowly widened it. The mood among the crowd assembled in the hotel ballroom shifted from festively optimistic to pensively pessimistic, although some held out hope. "Everything we hear is razor-tight," Bill Kenyon told the *Morning News*. "Some polls show us ahead, some show us behind, some show us tied." A television update on the giant TV screens touched off a round of cheers and Aggie war whoops when results from the Panhandle and West Texas showed Claytie ahead.

But long before that fleeting flash of good news, Denise Kelly entered the team's command post in Claytie's hotel suite and found staff members already rewriting a victory speech into one of concession. She thought that was premature, and told them so, but the campaign pros told her it was a lost cause.

"The polls closed at 7 P.M. and we knew by 8 or 8:30 we were in trouble," Barfield said.

Someone asked her to go downstairs to meet Governor Clements and his wife, Rita, who had just arrived to see Claytie. Denise and husband Richard intercepted the couple, escorted them into the elevator, and ascended in awkward silence up to the suite. "I just can't believe it," Clements said.

As they entered the hotel suite, Rita rushed to comfort Modesta, and a fuming Clements demanded Claytie call for a recount. "No," Claytie said. "The lead is too much, and that's the way it is."

At 10:45 P.M., Ann Richards walked into another hotel ballroom overflowing with jubilant Democrats, hoisted a T-shirt proclaiming "A woman's place is in the Dome," and announced: "This is a night of celebration." She said she was winning heavily in the Democratic strongholds of South Texas and predicted victories in East Texas, the major cities, and even some counties in the Panhandle.

For Denise Kelly, one of the piercing memories of the evening was another trip in the service elevator—riding with her husband and Claytie and the Williams family from the presidential suite to the back entrance of the ballroom minutes before the concession speech. "Very quiet. No sniffles, no joking, nothing—just ear-shattering silence."

At 11:10 P.M., with a tearful but strikingly beautiful Modesta at his side, Claytie conceded the costliest governor's race in Texas history—as high as $50 million, with Claytie outspending Richards by nearly two to one—and he surrendered with uncommon graciousness. "Modesta and I thank you from the very bottom of our hearts," he told the GOP faithful. "We thank you, and we thank the thousands and thousands of Texans who share our dream of making Texas great again. . . ."

Telling his supporters he was sorry he let them down but that he did his best, he said: "I will always cherish the faith you had in me. . . . I don't know what the future holds for Clayton Williams, but I hope I can be of service to our Republican Party and to our great state."

An emotional Denise thought Claytie a picture of strength, restraint, and statesmanship as he extended his congratulations to Ann and offered her his support. The crowd booed repeatedly at the sound of her name, and Claytie reprimanded his supporters each time. "No, no, you owe me this courtesy," he said when they interrupted his concession remarks. "The bad news is we lost," he said at one stage. "The good news is, it's not the end of the world." When his supporters interpreted that as a hint that he might possibly run again, they began chanting "'94, '94, '94." Flashing his signature grin, Claytie cracked: "I'm an Aggie, but I'm not crazy!"

At the conclusion of his concession speech Claytie introduced family members, who, like daughter Allyson Groner, were crushed by the loss but proud of their candidate's gracious response. "It was devastating to all of us," said Allyson, genuinely amazed that her father was comforting his supporters instead of them comforting him. "He just rose above all the political b.s. and showed what a truly wonderful human being he is. Even though his heart was broken, and all our hearts were broken, he just did a marvelous job."

As the evening wore down, Claytie nodded toward Todd Smith, one of a handful of non–family members on stage. Claytie introduced his young traveling companion. "He and I have spent hours and hours and hours together for the last two years. Come up here, Todd." Claytie hugged him, and the former undercover agent burst into tears. "I was crying like a baby. I really was, and it was tough."

But Claytie had one more surprise for him before they parted company. "While Clayton didn't wear his religion on his sleeve, he was a deeply religious man," Todd recounted, "and he kept a book of Scriptures on the plane with him." Before flying back to Midland, Claytie approached his aide and said, "Todd, I didn't want to show you this before." He then produced a calendar with a scripture on it for November 6, election day.

"Clayton told me he had flipped ahead and read that scripture verse before the election and that he basically had become comfortable with the fact he was going to lose. That was his signal from above that he should start preparing for defeat."

Claytie's revelation was a jolt.

"I just didn't have the heart to show this to you before," Todd recalled him saying. "I didn't want you to see it because I knew that you were still hopeful that we could win, and I didn't want you to think I'd let you down and that I'd given up. I hadn't given up. But I was at peace with losing because of that."

The Bible verse Claytie showed Todd was a scripture familiar to Christians around the world: "Forgive them, Lord, for they know not what they do." Fearing that he might be sounding presumptuous, and refusing again to take himself too seriously, he later added with a grin: "On second thought, they do know what they do!"

> *"I was a little political before I got political. When I got political, I wasn't worth a damn."*

With nearly 3.9 million votes cast, Ann Richards won by fewer than one hundred thousand. She collected roughly 49.4 percent of the vote; Claytie, 47.2 percent, and a third-party candidate, 3.4 percent.

The Richards camp cited as pivotal "a surge to the polls in minority-dominated South Dallas, supplemented by heavy support from women voters in the usually archconservative north end of the county." Buddy Barfield agreed that the biggest loss—hardly surprising—was in Dallas: "Dallas was the area where we always had the biggest hurdle because we were not cut out of the fabric of what Dallas looks for in a candidate." Citing the Dallas women's vote, he added, "We lost a lot of Republican women that traditional Republican candidates should have gotten." Clearly several miscues figured in the upset, and Claytie was quick to accept blame for most of them. But the campaign advice and decision making was not always the best, as several team members conceded. The spurned handshake was a monstrous example.

Buddy Barfield speculated that the most critical mistake was the campaign strategy after the resounding primary triumph. "We should have gone underground until about August and done nothing but raise money," he said. After peaking early, the campaign lost its edge and its crispness toward the end, when Claytie was overworked and worn down.

The astute political observer George Christian agreed that timing was the key to the Richards rally. "She peaked at the right time and he didn't," Christian told reporters. "Her campaign had nowhere to go but up and his campaign had nowhere to go but down."

Lost in the euphoria of the overhwhelming primary success was the effect the plane crash had on the general election. "The sad, sad tragedy of the plane going down had a tremendous impact on Clayton and on that campaign," said state cochair Carole Rylander. "The plane was full of his friends . . . and he just actually shut down for weeks after that. I was making the talks. He wasn't. He was hunkering in with those families."

Barfield called the plane crash a "huge, huge event" in the lives of Claytie and Modesta as well as in the life of the campaign. "Clayton had lost some of his close personal friends who were also part of the campaign advisory board," he recalled. "These were people he had worked and played with so many years. And I think this hurt us in the general campaign to not have some of these individuals as a sounding board and a leveling factor for Clayton." Claytie's longtime friend and attorney, Tom Scott, likewise thought the traumatic Valentine's Day tragedy might have been the turning point in the campaign because of the loss of his friends' wise counsel.

No doubt Claytie's miscues also proved costly. "His self-inflicted wounds bled him to death," maintained Austin consultant Karl Rove, who had worked in Kent Hance's losing primary campaign and would later become the lightning-rod architect of Pres. George W. Bush's political fortunes. Yet focusing on Claytie's gaffes as the reason for his loss, his supporters say, overlooks that it was his honesty, candor, openness, enthusiasm, and accessibility that won him countless votes as the only major "nonpolitical" candidate in either the primary or the general election.

Claytie being Claytie, he often joked about some of the advice he received. "I can't tell you how many people told me, 'Claytie, you're too honest to be a politician.' And Phil Gramm told me, 'Claytie, you're not mean enough to be a politician.'" With that huge grin, he added: "Maybe I should have listened to them."

When the subject of the rape joke arose, he would respond with a Claytieism: "If the Lord wanted me to be governor, He wouldn't have brought in that storm."

Although Bill Kenyon absorbed his share of the heat, he was generally on target with an oft-repeated assessment about the necessity of letting Clayton be Clayton.

Claytie once offered his own refreshingly convoluted perspective: "I was a little political before I got political. When I got political, I wasn't worth a damn."

Perhaps not surprising, Kent Hance had campaigned hard for Claytie after the primary, describing him as a "real Texan" and a "likable guy" who simply "outspent" his GOP opponents. He told an old journalist friend that Claytie was "one of a kind," that they "broke the mold" after Claytie. Hance pondered that statement a moment, then quipped: "That probably was not all bad."

Even though he occasionally viewed some elements of the media as his enemy, most were quite fond of Claytie and, especially, Modesta, of whom John Gravois said: "She is like a movie star. I mean she is the type you see in movies and read about in books. I have never known a woman like that in real life. For every time Claytie would amaze me, she would amaze me more." The political writer Kaye Northcott admittedly liked Claytie and adored Modesta; she considered the blunt, outspoken candidate very much a gentleman—"in his own way." Barfield said later that he'd probably lost only a couple of the sixty or sixty-five campaigns he'd worked, but that Claytie was one of the two or three individuals he most respected. "From a purely political standpoint, his greatest weakness as a candidate was that he was not a politician." Barfield joined the chorus that agreed Claytie's honesty and directness were at the heart of his character and business strength but ultimately hurt him as a politician.

"And from a campaign perspective, you couldn't have asked for a better political wife," he said. "Modesta's just a jewel. . . . It wasn't just Clayton, it was Clayton and Modesta — they were a pair and a team and it was always approached that way. Anything you asked her to do, she'd do it . . . and everybody she met fell in love with her." Although the author of several devastating stories about Claytie, Gravois admired and respected him as both a candidate and a person. "Never before or after have I dealt with anybody that is as completely open and honest about any topic like Claytie is," he said. "The man would sit there and talk to you about anything you wanted to talk about, and no other politician that I have ever dealt with has been like that."

He said Claytie's tactic for confronting the ugliness of the campaign was to tackle it head-on, and he called it ironic that voters say they want their politicians "to be honest and speak their minds . . . and when they get it they don't want it." Gravois, now the political editor of the *Star-Telegram,* said he could not recall Claytie being bitter or ugly about any of it. But he did remember with a laugh that the candidate did come close on election night, jokingly pointing him out "as the guy who lost the election for us."

Claytie's concession speech inspired an intriguing annotation. "We did tracking polls a day after the election and they showed that if the election had been held the next day after people had seen and heard his concession speech, he would have won," Todd Smith said, adding that Ann was elected with less than a plurality. "I think people saw a side of Clayton when he was conceding on election night that they'd never seen before. They were touched by it."

Barfield said another week "without any kind of mistake by the campaign and we could have been four or five points ahead."

While Claytie and the staff stuck around Austin a little longer, a brokenhearted Modesta, who had come so close to becoming the state's first lady, flew home in a private jet. The loss had taken a terrible emotional toll, which she described as crashing into a brick wall at high speed. Richard and Denise Kelly drove her to the airport. Denise, sobbing uncontrollably, watched the plane until it disappeared in the distant November sky. Richard attempted to comfort her, but he too was caught up in the trauma of the moment. "The wrong woman is leaving Austin," he said softly.

Those who have come to know Claytie and Modesta well insist that he would have been a hardworking, business-sensitive, and entertaining governor, and she a spectacular first lady.

"He would have brought to the table a personality and background that would have been a very healthy situation for Texas," said Governor Clements. Despite appearances sometimes to the contrary, Clements called Claytie a serious, cautious, shrewd, and thoughtful investor who does his homework and demands good information even if he has to pay big money to get it.

"It's Texas' loss really," he said.

As one of Claytie's campaign cochairmen and in 2006 an independent candidate for governor herself, Carole Rylander Strayhorn could speak from a unique perspective. "I believe Clayton would have been an excellent governor," she said. "I think he would have surrounded himself with the best and the brightest. He does that in his business, too." She also was impressed with his energy level—"the Energizer Bunny is still going"—and his passion. "He cared passionately . . . and he loved the people and he was doing this for all the right reasons."

Disagreeing sharply with the Richards campaign, she said nothing even vaguely ulterior or self-serving tainted Claytie's bid for the governor's office. "There was nothing in it for him. He didn't need to be governor of Texas. He wanted to be governor of Texas."

Speaking as one who was with the candidate night and day for nearly two years, Todd Smith said, "I think he would have been an interesting governor, a great governor, a consensus builder." Claytie, he said, truly believed that the future of the Republican Party was building support for the Hispanic community and that he would have done so quickly and effectively. "Clayton demonstrated during the communications fight with AT&T that he was able to go out and build consensus and find compromise and bring people together, and that's the kind of governor he would have been."

Modesta modeling at a campaign function: Claytie always said he overmarried!

Smiling at the thought, he said Claytie also would have been a colorful state leader: "I told people they would have seen Clayton in a pair of bermuda shorts and his cowboy hat out barbecuing on the lawn of the governor's mansion and that there would probably have been touches of maroon added in various places to the white mansion." Asked about that once, Claytie said, "Yeah, I would have made it fun. I would have tried to do fun things."

Before returning to his Houston office, Pat Reesby attempted to console his boss just hours after the election loss. "You know, Pat," Claytie responded reassuringly, "when things like this happen, a man just needs to step back and look at the bright side."

With Reesby wondering just what that might be, Claytie said: "Tit bars and poachin'."

"What!?" cried Reesby.

"Tit bars and poachin'. For the past two years, while this damned campaign has been running, I haven't been able to go to tit bars and I damn sure couldn't do any poachin' on my ranches."

While seldom one to play the "what if?" game, Claytie agreed with those who believed he would have worked harmoniously with the Democratic leadership. Most were already friends or friendly, thanks in large part to the efforts of the former Texas House Speaker Billy Clayton. "We beat AT&T by virtue of going to the liberal Democrats under Billy Clayton's guidance," Claytie recalled, referring to the Austin legislative skrimish on behalf of ClayDesta Communications. "It would have been very natural for me, once elected. I wouldn't change my principles, but my principles weren't all that much different from Bob Bullock's or Pete Laney's or Gib Lewis's, all Democrats."

In 1990, Speaker Lewis himself said, Texas Democrats and Republicans were much less partisan than the national parties, and Claytie was a master at unification. Although a dedicated conservationist, Claytie confessed that he would have been at a loss in unifying the environmentalists, whom he disdained and distrusted as much as trial lawyers. With his broad experience as an entrepreneur in oil, gas, ranching, farming, communications, and banking, he most certainly would have been ultrafriendly to Texas business. "But by the same token, education has always been important to my family," he said, "and it would have been important to my administration, particularly higher education and making those opportunities more widely available."

Before leaving Austin, Claytie rounded up his campaign staff and descended on El Jalisco's restaurant for a postmortem on the election and an unofficial "drowning of sorrows." Denise Kelly, husband Richard, and Modesta's assistant, Brenda Chambers, had just returned from the airport, and Denise was still anguished over Modesta's brokenhearted departure for Midland.

"Clearly, she was fragile and hurt and had no interest in staying in Austin one minute longer," Denise said. "She just wanted to go home."

Brenda remembered Modesta asking them both to please make sure they got Clayton on the plane home safely. Denise and Brenda, neither much of a drinker, were not participating in the "drowning" of the moment but were quietly commiserating. Then a waiter appeared with a pair of flaming drinks. "Apparently," Denise concluded, "the campaign staff wanted us to truly bond with them and become blood brothers. I'll never forget Brenda and I looking at each other and realizing we *had* to 'take one for the team.'"

With everyone cheering and clapping, they picked up their fiery beverages, gulped them down, and then celebrated with high-fives. The entire joint erupted in applause, with Claytie looking on proudly at his latest flush-faced "team players." Brenda recalled, "The events at the bar are scorched into my mind." As subsequent rounds of "Flaming Coyotes" appeared at the tables, the mood took on a more festive gala. But it was illusory.

"When we got to the plane with Clayton that night, he must have felt like it was finally OK to let his feelings all come out," Brenda said. "He was disappointed to his very core, and we grieved with him all the way home. Later, when the smoke cleared a little, I remember thinking that we had Modesta and Clayton back again and we didn't have to share them with a million other people for a while.

"We could all be ourselves again and heal together."

Years passed before the full impact of the Williams campaign and the candidate himself would be fully scrutinized and recognized. The 1990 campaign, in fact, profoundly changed the Texas GOP and Texas politics. And in a bizarre twist of fate that no one could have foreseen, Claytie's defeat, by extension, altered the course of U.S. and world history—for the better, he insists, though not everyone would agree.

"Had I won, George Bush would not be in the White House today," he told a reporter a short time after the terrorist attacks of 9/11 in 2001. It is difficult to dispute that premise, since Richards was governor and seeking reelection when George the Younger, Claytie's friend and fellow conservative, defeated her.

"If I had won in 1990, George wouldn't have run against me in 1994, with a Republican in the governor's office. Most likely, George might not have ever entered politics. . . . I think fate was involved . . . and, well, you never know what fate holds."

Claytie and his supporters are among the tens of millions of Americans who would contend that the younger Bush emerged as a strong, decisive leader in the wake of the 9/11 terrorist attacks and that his actions provided a calming and reassuring influence on a stricken country. "I'm very relieved to have George and all those good men and women up there today in this trouble we're in," says Claytie.

By the same token, critics might wonder if Bush were not in the White House, would the United States have invaded Iraq in 2003 and would America be torn asunder years later? How would another president, Democrat or Republican, have coped with a world seemingly short-circuited on all fronts—ranging from natural disasters such as hurricanes, tsunamis, earthquakes, and flooding to mudslides, volcano eruptions, bird flu, and mad cow disease? And from manmade disasters embracing everything from corporate fraud, immigration disputes, and congressional scandals to cartoon-inspired rioting, world hunger, and international terrorism?

Maybe that friend of former U.S. House Speaker Jim Wright was correct after all. Because Claytie didn't win the governor's race as he should have, the friend insisted, "Whatever troubles we have today are Clayton Williams's fault!"

More than fifteen years after the 1990 election, Todd Smith, now a highly respected Austin political consultant, could offer an insight to the Williams political legacy like few others. "I think one of the reasons that Carole Strayhorn thought she had a shot in the [2006] Republican gubernatorial primary was because she saw in 1990 that Clayton Williams was able to bring four hundred and twenty-five thousand people who had never before voted Republican into the Republican primary.

"And I see some of those people every day as I work as a political consultant, as a lobbyist, and as I travel around the state. I see people who are very actively engaged in Republican politics who were not involved back in 1990, 1989, 1988."

Before Claytie's race, he said, the Republican Party was the "Country Club Party," and while Claytie was probably the wealthiest of the candidates, he was not a "country club" Republican. "He was able to bring people that were ClayDesta Communications customers or employees, people whom he knew and met through his Brangus cattle operations, people who had worked for Clajon Gas— people who had never been involved in politics—he was able to bring them into the party. . . . We had people who were just excited about his campaign, and they have not left. They've been there ever since and have become the backbone of the Republican Party.

"I think that's just one of his legacies."

Carole Strayhorn, who called herself a "populist conservative activist," was no less emphatic. "I really believe that Clayton Williams positively changed the Republican Party in Texas," she said. "He brought new people into the party, into the primary. I think that's true all over the state and particularly true in rural Texas and East Texas. I think there are a lot of folks who called themselves Democrats, and they're Independents who had not voted in a Republican primary but who did with Clayton running for office. . . . Clayton brought them into this party and they are there to this day. I don't know anybody who does better at connecting with people one-on-one or with a group. He was very inspirational, the sort of person you can tie yourself to in a windstorm, the first person there in good times or bad times. When the people met him they knew they had a friend for life. He deserves a lot of credit for where the party is today."

Strayhorn, a three-term Austin mayor, said she spoke across the state as one of Claytie's campaign cochairs "and about everywhere I'd go, there would be an Aggie that would meet me. The breadth and depth of the Aggie loyalty is just incredible, too."

Ironically, Strayhorn bolted the Republican Party and campaigned as an Independent candidate in her own race for governor in 2006, won by GOP incumbent Rick Perry.

In a front-page column years after the 1990 governor's race, Gary Ott, editor of the *Midland Reporter-Telegram,* highlighted Claytie's ability to connect with individuals or groups. "Back in my earlier life, I used to run into him occasionally at a favorite watering hole," he wrote. "He always slapped me on the back and had something funny to say. He had a way of making me feel I was the only guy in the place." Ott told of a late-night guitar-picking and singing session at a popular hangout called simply The Bar, with Claytie leading the frivolity as always. "He's a backslapper. He's a storyteller. He's a jokester," Ott said. "It is the image — or personality — of Clayton Williams that appeals to me. He is what I think of when I hear the word *oilman.*"

After his gubernatorial victory in 1994, the younger Bush paid Claytie the highest of compliments regarding his impact on Texas politics. "I could never have gone to rural Texas and performed as well as I did had you not preceded me," Bush said. "You laid the groundwork." Later, an East Texas legislator, Sen. Todd Staples of Palestine, told him much the same thing at an A&M–University of

Oklahoma football game. "One of the reasons that I became a state legislator is because you opened the gate for 'Bubba' and the Yellow Dog Democrats to move on and become Republicans," said Staples, later elected Texas Agriculture Commissioner. "You laid the groundwork for Republicans in East Texas. We could never have done it without you."

By nature, Claytie was never comfortable discussing such compliments, but he did acknowledge that "I had a role in history, and so I'm gratified." Then he quickly added: "Now sometimes if I had to choose between getting my $8 million back or being a part of history, I'm not sure what I'd do."

He does not deny that he was "part of the evolution of Texas moving from a Democratic state to a Republican state—from conservative Democrats becoming Republicans." Still, he says, the beginning of that evolution could be traced to the 1950s and the reign of Gov. Allan Shivers.

Claytie allowed that he was a unifier who helped make it OK for "Bubba" to be a Republican, even while admitting he really wasn't the Bubba he'd proclaimed all along. "But I have been a worker most of my life. As a third-grader, I was working at the farm, irrigating when I was in the seventh or eighth grade. I identified with work. I worked with Mexicans at the time, the so-called wetbacks of that era. They weren't part of my family, but they were nearly part of the family. I've worked with Bubba. And then as I started building pipelines, I was with working men. As a rancher, I was with working cowboys. So it was easy for me to identify with the average working man. I was comfortable with the labor unions; I might not have gotten their vote, but they wouldn't have been my enemy, per se. There was no acting. It was natural."

At the same time, he knew he didn't hit it off with most of the stereotypical "Dallas women," that they were somehow different. Aides would whoop at Claytie's familiar request when Dallas bound: "Modesta, get my Dallas suit."

He took pride in his disdain for counterfeit sophistication. As he once told the *San Antonio Light:* "Do you know anybody who likes a snooty, arrogant, rich guy? I made an effort to be a nice guy. . . . You can be a man of achievement and not be an arrogant snoot." Claytie spoke occasionally of the wife of an avid Republican who voted against him. Yet, when they later met socially, she told him: "If I had known you, I would have voted for you. But I just saw the 'Bubba' image and I didn't really like that." Claytie realized he probably could never be all things to all people, but, he grinned, "if I had to choose, I'd be on Bubba's side."

That was not idle chatter. After all, this was the guy who, when accused of wooing the "Bubba" vote, famously declared: "Hell. I am Bubba!"

> *"He made mistakes along the way, but he's a class act who took his lumps with dignity."*

It is ironic that the best definition of "Bubba" as it pertained to the 1990 election sprung not from the pen of a Texas writer but from a Canadian reporting on the Williams phenomenon for *The Globe and Mail,* Canada's national newspaper.

"To fully understand Clayton Williams's campaign for governor of Texas, it is necessary to dwell for a moment on the concept of Bubba," Colin MacKenzie wrote in a front-page story from San Marcos. "A Texas variant of the southern redneck, a Bubba is a straight-talking, hard-drinking, hunting and shooting kind of guy whose views on most matters of social policy tend to rigidity. Bubbas are a distinct part of life here, and while they are patronized in some circles, there is a general feeling that Texas would not be Texas without them."

The article appeared in June when, as MacKenzie put it, Claytie had transformed his populist appeal for a return to traditional Texas values beyond the Bubba vote into a twelve-point lead on his Democratic rival. "Along the way, he has committed monumental gaffes, swept aside his buttoned-down Republican rivals, spent a fortune, and, apparently, had a great time," MacKenzie wrote.

"He also seems to have won the heart of Texas."

A day after the election, Rena Pederson, editor of the *Dallas News* editorial page, knocked out a column pinpointing the "highs and lows" of the long, volatile statewide campaigns. Naturally, it focused on the governor's race and was generally lighthearted. But some of her observations bear repeating because they tended to highlight certain voter perceptions, for better or worse.

Best new buzzword: *Business Week*'s profile describing Claytie's "cowrisma."

Best bumper stickers: "I'd Rather Smoke Dope with Ann than Have Sex with Claytie" and, second place, the maroon-and-white sticker "Better a Roper than a Doper for Governor" (complete with Aggie misspelling). Third place: "I'll Shake Hands with Ann."

Best TV coverage: KERA-TV's *Voter's Revenge* broadcast, with homemade videos from voters. "Especially apt," Pederson said, "was the pseudo-candidate with the last name Neither, whose slogan was "Neither is the best candidate. If you must vote, vote for Neither."

Dumbest macho comment: Claytie's purported brag that he would "head and hoof her and drag her through the dirt."

Most flagrant appeal for the Bubba vote: Ann's dove-hunting trip and fliers showing her with a rifle and camouflage ammo vest.

Most incredible campaign scene: At a Richards rally at the University of Texas at Austin, rowdy students reportedly alternated chanting "[bleep] Ann" and "[bleep] Claytie." Meanwhile, Pederson said, representatives of the gay caucus tossed condoms into the crowd with their own chant, "[bleep] safely."

Best exit line: Claytie, explaining why he would not run again in 1994: "I may be an Aggie, but I'm not crazy."

Best campaign advice: Claytie's mother, Chic, who told her outspoken son: "Keep your mouth shut." (Hardly had those words been uttered when Claytie confided to a reporter about one of his personal flaws: "I would have made a horrible girl—I can't tell anybody 'No!'")

Perhaps significantly, in view of the women's vote, was this verbatim observation:

Least-known candidate info: "That despite his tough-guy image, Clayton Williams cried when he had to fire longtime employees during the steep slump of the 1980s. That despite his 'insensitive to women' image, Mr. Williams has over the years entrusted female employees with key responsibilities in his business operations. The first of his fourteen employees to become millionaires was a woman who had worked for his company twenty-three years."

As distressed as he was over the election, Claytie handled the loss much better than Modesta. After all, he was "used to drilling dry holes." Not so, Modesta.

"I took it awfully hard," she said. "It really broke my heart."

As bad as she felt, Modesta reserved her deepest disappointment not for herself but for her husband and those who worked so hard on his behalf. "He is such a good man, such a good person," she said. "He has such a great mind and a big heart. He stood for God, mother, and country, and he was creating new ideas on how to run the state's business. He is such a leader, and people will follow him. I used to tell him to be careful where he led them, and not to take them over a cliff."

Although politically shy early on, Modesta learned to cope with the political abuse and the press attacks, both the fair and the unfair. "I could take it when we could fight back and tell our side of the story," she said. "But when we couldn't tell our side of the story, and the other side had won, it just infuriated me. Made me so mad, it made me cry."

True to the meaning of her name, Modesta modestly maintained that she could never match the accomplishments of Rita Clements, whom she considered a spectacular first lady. But she already had selected her "pet project": working with abused children.

In her statewide travels, she said, she discovered countless abused children, to an extent that defied belief. Especially so since she came from such a loving, caring family and now nurtured one herself.

"Then to go see these babies with cigarette burns all over them and bruises where they have been slapped and hit and had atrocious things done to them. I said, 'Why, why, why?' Almost all of it traced back to drugs," Modesta recalled. "I really wanted to dig deeper into it because I felt something needed to be done . . . about the abused children. I have always loved feeding the hungry and doing things like that, and I've been doing it for many, many years. Carole

Claytie with his mom during the campaign

Rylander helped me with that. One day Carole and I went to a home, a school actually, for minority children. Some of the kids were doing their dances for us and showing us the things they could do, and there was this one little girl, a beautiful child, with her head bowed. I went over to her and asked if she'd like me to hold her. She just grabbed me. She just wanted someone to hug her, somebody that she wasn't scared of; just someone to pay attention to her.

"I will never forget that."

Modesta was pleased that her daughter Chim has been a volunteer with CASA, Court Appointed Special Advocates, which works through the court system on behalf of abused or neglected children. "Chim did that in Austin and she started doing that here in Midland. It's interesting that she kind of picked up where I left off with the abused children."

Biased though he may be, Buddy Barfield believes that not only would Modesta have been a trail-blazing activist in the governor's mansion, but that she and Claytie together would also have been "a grand first couple," that he would have accomplished much for Texas and she would have emerged as one of the state's great first ladies. "Years have gone by . . . but I still look back and I think it would have been incredible for the state of Texas if we'd won," Barfield said. "The part that still hurts me today is the perception of Clayton that was created by the political campaign. It is nothing like what he's really like. That part you can never undo, and that's probably the thing that hurts me the worst—knowing that who he is, what he's done, the kind of person he is—it's not even close to the perception that was created by the political campaign."

Political editor John Gravois expressed similar concerns, that the historical concept of Clayton Williams might be based on a handful of miscues that wrecked an otherwise noble and notable political performance. "The image of Claytie as a bumbling boob from West Texas is misleadling," he said. "He made mistakes along the way, but he's a class act who took his lumps with dignity. He respected other people and wanted respect in return. It would be a shame if he's not remembered for such qualities."

Five

A New
Millennium:
No Slowing
Down

Induction to the Petroleum Museum Hall of Fame, 2005

"I know Claytie can find a way out of this."

25

On that spring 1991 flight to Houston—the bankruptcy flight—conversation remained as scarce as free money. The foursome aboard the company jet—Claytie, Modesta, and executives Paul Latham and Mel Riggs—grappled with their private thoughts, quietly, thinking of their mission: getting the best advice possible from some of Texas' top bankruptcy lawyers.

In less than a decade Claytie had tumbled from the Forbes list as one of the nation's wealthiest individuals to one now overwhelmed with debt—$90 million and counting. The election had consumed him, so much so that he had ignored the home front: his company, his finances, where his rigs were drilling, what some of his people were up to. Now came payback.

The Williams family name, long associated with vision, integrity, and success, seemed certain to be sullied in the messiest of ways: bankruptcy. To Claytie, the mere mention of the word corroded the soul, extinguished the spirit. The ultimate betrayal.

The flight was as somber as a dear friend's funeral, which only made the party's reception at the Houston airport seem like an Irish wake. As the four climbed into their cab, the driver immediately recognized Claytie and struck up a chatty conversation. Claytie responded as jovially as possible. The cabbie rattled on, blissfully immune to his pensive passengers. The irony was not lost on Paul: the celebrity passenger with whom the cabbie was so smitten, having stepped off of his private jet decked out in his familiar cowboy hat and boots, was headed downtown to meet bankruptcy experts.

Mel noticed Modesta still wore her worried look, and concluded it was concern less for the company than for Claytie. Her troubled expression he interpreted as a desperate desire to help him, but she didn't know what to do or say.

Nobody did.

The elevator ride to the lawyers' office evoked an exercise in silent contemplation, but Mel could see the wheels turning in Claytie's mind: "What am I doing? Why am I here?"

As the meeting unfolded, two lawyers put the best face possible on bankruptcy, and the Williams party concluded that they had done their job well. They were reassured. But then, unexpectedly, an older attorney entered the room. Pete Maley had counseled the late John Connally when the former Texas governor and U.S. presidential candidate had been forced to confront his own bankruptcy demons in the late 1980s. Sugarcoating nothing, Maley laid out simply but forthrightly the consequences of the bankruptcy filing and how it could affect Claytie and his company. In the eyes of many, Chapter 11 is a heavily traveled escape route for deadbeats dodging financial responsibilities. Though not always valid, the image is difficult to shake. Claytie listened without a word, but just the appearance of the older man triggered thoughts of his father—and a spark of defiance.

"No," he said to himself. "No bankruptcy." The wheels were spinning again.

The meeting broke up after two and half hours without a decision. But as they left, Paul and Mel thought Claytie appeared less troubled, almost relaxed. They drove to the airport, scrambled aboard the plane, and took off for West Texas. Conversation was minimal. Shortly before the sleek little jet touched down in Midland, Claytie spoke.

"We're not going to do this," he said, catching everyone off guard. "We'll handle this like we have everything else. We'll work our way out of it."

Mel Riggs, left, and Paul Latham looking at a deal

His words stunned everyone. Although no one challenged his decision, everyone aboard was privately coping with troubling questions. A short time later, Claytie summoned his high-level troops to his office. He informed them that they would devise a workable plan to somehow, some way pay off the debts and salvage the company without bankruptcy protection. Mel Riggs and Paul Latham remember Claytie exhorting executives with the familiar refrain: "Boys, let's make it happen."

Most were surprised if not shocked. Modesta was thrilled. "I know Claytie can find a way out of this," she said upon leaving the meeting.

She later explained: "I've known him to hit bottom several times, and I know that he can always pick it up and bring it back to the top. He has so much energy and so many wonderful ideas about how to do things."

Bankruptcy did look imminent, she admitted, and if that had been Claytie's decision she would have accepted it and worked through it with him. But she by no means had lost confidence in her husband.

"I know why he felt that way. He felt like everybody was down on him, and everything he did was going south. He was so hurt. But losing confidence in him? Never."

A moment later, she added: "Never!"

Denise Kelly had noticed that when the bankruptcy issue arose, tears flooded Modesta's eyes. Modesta explained that early in their marriage she had promised to follow Claytie anywhere—as long as he did the right thing.

"This," Modesta said, "was a time when it came down to doing the right thing, and he did it."

Denise was particularly impressed by her boss's challenge to his employees. It reminded her of the words from a song, *Into the Fire:* "When the world is saying not to, by God you know you've got to!" The song was from the Broadway musical *The Scarlet Pimpernel* and was the English nobleman's battle cry to rally the troops during the French Revolution. "It's no wonder that it made me think of Clayton because I've seen him rally the troops almost daily for many years."

Longtime friend Tom Moore always contended that Claytie was at his best when the chips were down, his back against the wall. If true, now would be the time to prove it.

With bankruptcy fading in the rearview mirror, Claytie and the gang gathered for a breakfast meeting to begin forging a recovery plan. Although they knew the turnaround would not come overnight, if at all, they confronted the dilemma head-on and optimistically.

"We'd been in tough times before and worked our way out," Claytie said, and everyone accepted, if not welcomed, the challenge. No member of his management team wanted to admit defeat.

"Claytie had always told us to never give up," Mel said. "His philosophy is that in any situation, you're not in trouble as long as there's one more thing you can do. And if you think hard enough and work hard enough, you *will* find it."

What they discovered was that though burdened by mounting debts, they had assets they could sell to buy time with banks and service companies. Assets included airplanes, artwork, odd lots of real estate, cattle from three ranches and feedlots, and a calf crop.

There was good news and bad news. The bad news included the necessity of layoffs, which Claytie dreaded. But the good news was that the financial picture, while grim, was not as forbidding as feared. The problem was not a lack of assets but liquidity. Cash flow was insufficient, and debts continued to grow.

"The vendors represented the most immediate problem because we were behind quite a bit on meeting our payables, and they were the ones capable of putting us in bankruptcy," Mel explained. "The vendors did all our drilling, and we had a very active drilling program up to that time."

Debt troubles stemmed directly from the inflated Pearsall reserves. Claytie's company had drilled ninety-three horizontal wells in the Pearsall Field and lost money on the last forty or fifty. "Our bank loans were collateralized but the vendors weren't, and if they started demanding their money, our house of cards could crumble and we'd have automatic bankruptcy," Claytie said. "Furthermore, we had maxed out our bank loans and couldn't borrow the money to pay our vendors." The banks, however, did not call the outstanding notes. "They weren't helpful, but they stayed with us. They could have been worse."

As for the miscalculated reserves, "It was a shock," Latham said.

"Most of it was happening while I was running for governor," Claytie said. "I was going around the state telling people that 'the best fertilizer is the footprints of the owner,' but I wasn't making any footprints at home."

With problems coming from contractors, vendors, and even his own bank, it could have been disastrous, he said. "Imagine," he added, shaking his head, "had I been elected governor, and then had this hit me."

Paul agreed: "That would have been very public and very embarrassing."

Perhaps not surprisingly, it was Claytie's reputation that opened the doors to recovery—the very reputation he was struggling so desperately to salvage when he spurned the quick-fix charms of Chapter 11. It was a reputation that reached legendary proportions in the 1980s when he worked his way through hundreds of millions in debts.

"We've always paid our bills," he asserted, "though not always on time." Looking back on the crisis of the '90s, Claytie said the company "simply drilled and sold its way out of trouble." But that was just part of a compelling story.

The battle for survival would be fought on several fronts over nearly three years amid even sporadic downturns so common and bedeviling to the high-risk energy business.

"I remember it wasn't a very fun time," said engineer Greg Benton, who with geologist Sam Lyssy played a key role in the recovery. But Benton also recalled one of the lighter moments when returning by private plane one evening after a meeting with the vendors. Claytie, who played an active role in the vendor campaign, "broke out the hootch" and everyone was drinking and having a good time except a lawyer who had hitched a ride back to Midland. A thunderstorm was tossing the plane around and Claytie, noticing that the lawyer was "white-knuckling it," gleefully said, "Drink up, boys, because we may plant this son of a bitch!"

But it was a time of often unpleasant decisions, including selling a West Texas ranch near Marfa, scattered oil production, and any number of noncritical assets. One operative word: *consolidation.* Claytie closed offices, slashed overhead, and reduced the workforce. Employees who remained took pay cuts. When the market collapsed in the fall of 1991, an early attempt to take the company public failed.

At the heart of the two-part recovery plan was an option offered to the drilling and service companies and suppliers, the so-called vendors, and other creditors. One part dealt with satisfying current debts; the other dealt with compensating vendors for future drilling.

The most immediate concern: vendor debt.

"Vendors were saying, 'Hey, we want to get paid!'" Mel said. Debts were rising and account payables were falling 90 to 120 days behind. Banks were also pressing for money lent against oil and gas reserves. They wanted the payable problems fixed, but for their own well-being; the last thing they wanted was to force the company into bankruptcy.

"The danger at the time was the vendors," Mel said. "We offered them a couple of different options. . . . I knew the consequences; I knew we had to make it happen."

The company offered 80 percent of the amount owed to each vendor if creditors and the service companies demanded immediate payment. If they chose to wait, the company provided promissory notes for full payment, plus interest, over two years.

Some opted for the cash discounts, having heard the bankruptcy rumors and aware that if the company went down, the notes were worthless. Others chose to gamble. It took only three months for all parties to reach agreement.

With the vendor problems solved, the next move was to establish a vendor-financing program, or "vendor packaging," so the company could continue drilling. The company had done vendor packaging twice previously, in the 1980s, but not under such dire circumstances. The program, Mel said, involved everyone it took to drill a well—drillers, well-servicing companies, pipe and mud suppliers, contractors. Vendors agreed to drill the wells without immediate payment, in effect sharing the risks in exchange for income from future production.

"The reason they were willing to do this," Claytie said, "was because their rigs, equipment, and people were idle. So, by combining our leases, operational abilities, and some cash with their people and equipment, we were able to accomplish the needs of all parties."

Claytie's credibility with these vendors was critical, Mel said. "They had done so much work for him and he had paid them for years, and they gave him the benefit of the doubt."

Nobody disputed Claytie's track record, but vendors drawn to the financing program scrutinized it carefully. It was not a slam-dunk. For instance, in 1992 Claytie and his representatives traveled to Houston to explain their financing package to a group of twenty-five vendors. In an "impressive hour-long presentation," Mel said, Greg Benton laid out the program, including an update of such details as the company's oil reserves and cash flow and the probable reserves for the wells they proposed drilling.

Vendors didn't exactly seize the opportunity.

"It was a largely skeptical audience," Mel recalled, "until this one man—a pipe man named Bill Dillard who'd worked with Claytie before—finally stood up and said, 'This guy says he can do it, he can do it.'"

With that unsolicited vote of confidence, everybody hopped aboard.

"They did believe Clayton had integrity and that he would pay them," Mel said. "They also knew that if they could help him get back on his feet that he would drill more wells and they would benefit from it."

Benefit they did.

"To make it work," Claytie said, "the guy who had the leases, which was us, needed to give the drilling companies enough incentive to make them feel like it was worth it to them."

The problem was the volatility of oil prices, not whether the well was going to produce, Claytie explained. "Would the well pay out? In this time period, oil prices went up, and the wells paid out better and sooner than we thought. We kept selling things and consolidating and getting down to where I owed *only* $10 million to the vendors. So that really helped get us through a difficult period."

In spring 1993 the company launched a second attempt to go public. It was an intense time, flying across the country and even abroad to woo investors. Once, in London, at a lunch with a Paine Webber representative, Claytie was touting the merits of the Austin Chalk play, which did not impress the Paine Webber man.

"As the debate raged on," Mel said, "Claytie stands up and is leaning across the table to make his point to the guy. There is a glass of red wine there and Claytie's tie is floating in the wine. He made his point—and had a two-toned tie, which he never realized."

Said Claytie: "It's called focus."

Eventually the effort to go public succeeded and the crisis was history, though consolidation and recovery efforts continued. The result was a leaner, meaner Clayton Williams Energy Inc., a public company rebuilt from ground zero, consolidated in Midland in 1994, with its founder not just back in the mix but back on top of the mix.

Claytie and his senior management agreed that the resurrection of the company could be traced to the closing of the San Antonio office and the consolidation in Midland. "That is what started making the company work," Paul said. "There was too much exploration going on in San Antonio. Nobody knew what the hell they were doing."

Added Claytie: "I had lost control. It's hell for a control freak to find out he didn't have control." But with the consolidation, "I could get on top of things again."

Reputation intact, the Benevolent Dictator, as his staff affectionately christened him, was ready to move forward with renewed vigor and gusto. There remained wells to drill, mountains to climb, rivers to fish, dragons to slay.

And assets to sell. . . .

Although a casualty of the postelection financial plight, the Jones Ranch figured in one of Claytie's more illuminating escapades of that troubled period. The ranch lay north and west of Marfa, a small West Texas town immortalized as the site where the movie *Giant* was filmed. The 1957 classic featured Rock Hudson as a wealthy rancher–accidental oilman with a beautiful wife and a special affection for Mexican laborers.

Sound familiar? The wife was Elizabeth Taylor and the antagonist was maverick oilman Jett Rink, portrayed by James Dean.

In real life, while preparing the Jones Ranch for sale, Claytie came frightfully close to torching the town of Marfa.

"We'd had some big rains in '90 and '91, and it had rained to the point that the grass was mature and dirty looking," Claytie said. "So in the spring we decided it was time to burn off the grass and knock back the brush. When the grass comes back, it's gonna come back green and pretty, and the ranch is gonna sell better."

Accompanied by Modesta and several ranch hands, Claytie burned off a couple of pastures and moved on to a pasture about seven miles north and a little west of Marfa. A south wind was blowing, away from town, and the crew was burning a protective "fire lane" south of a road from the Jones ranch house.

"We look up and here comes a black, ugly storm, rolling in low and right at us," Claytie said, estimating the winds as high as fifty miles an hour. "And we lose control of the fire. Then, suddenly, the storm turns and moves from north to south, and there's nothing but grass between the fire and Marfa. No roads, no nothing. I mean this was damn frightening."

Modesta called it a "devilish type storm, truly demonic, because it just turned black, and it twisted, and it started blowing the opposite direction toward Marfa."

"Oh hell! Look at that!" Claytie remembered saying. He also remembered thinking, "My God, all I need to do to be finished is to burn down Marfa. With all this other crap that's happened, now here's your gubernatorial candidate who just burned down Marfa. . . . On top of everything else. I come back, I'm nearly broke, I'm trying to sell the ranch, I'm trying to burn it to make it look better, and then here comes this damn storm. . . ."

Added Modesta: "It was so scary because we knew it could burn down everybody's houses, kill people, and destroy everything else."

A bull was standing on the side of a mountain watching the fireworks when the storm turned, she said. "I'm afraid he jumped every fence between here and Marfa or he was barbecued. We never saw him again."

With the fire out of control, the wind driving it toward town, and no way to stop it, the couple turned in desperation for divine intervention. "Dear Lord," Modesta pleaded, "*please* help us. We need your help right now. *Please* bring rain or do something to put out this fire."

Claytie pitched in: "Lord, we got to have help."

It began to rain.

"It was like the devil was fixing to burn down Marfa," Claytie recalled, "and God said, 'No, we're not through with Williams yet.'"

The rain doused the flames, sparing Marfa and Claytie's reputation.

"If you don't think God hears your prayers . . . ," Modesta said. "Well, that was one day that we knew, that we were absolutely 100 percent sure that He had heard us."

"I'm gonna get a baseball bat and beat the son of a bitch to death."

Claytie's postelection recovery remained in full swing even after the 1994 consolidation and downsizing. With Paul Latham and Mel Riggs already in place, Claytie's Midland-based, frontline recovery unit included son-in-law Jerry Groner, a lawyer-landman, along with engineer Greg Benton and geologist Sam Lyssy. Groner would assume the title of vice president of land and lease management; Benton, senior engineer; and Lyssy, geological and exploration manager.

"We were a damn good team," Claytie said. "We made some mistakes, but we also made a lot of money."

Lyssy characterized the recovery as a runaway roller coaster with Claytie at the controls and his foot pressed to the floorboard. "It is either on the accelerator or on the brake—sometimes both at the same time," he said. Groner, who joined the company in 1990, likewise touched on the "intense" ups and downs, but said his sixteen-plus years with Claytie had provided industry exposure equivalent to thirty or forty years with the oil majors. Benton said, "I learned that Clayton could do stuff that I didn't think was possible." He cited the successful vendor financing. "When he explained to me how we were going to get the vendors—whom we owed money—to continue to provide services without immediate payment, I thought there is no way these people are going to do this." Benton said he learned to give the boss the benefit of the doubt, and despite recurring disagreements and intense debates, the recovery forces trusted one another and pulled together. Ultimately, he said, that's what got them through the tough times.

The successful 1993 public offering coupled with other vigorous recovery efforts had given Claytie breathing room, and he believed the "real danger" had passed. But after going public, exploration activities in Argentina and West Texas both lost money, and unstable oil prices contributed to a staggering drop in the price of the company stock, from around eighteen dollars to less than three dollars a share within eighteen months.

That was the bad news. The flip side was that Claytie sold the Floresville ranch and its purebred registered cattle and wisely used the proceeds to purchase a bundle of his company stock at bargain prices.

In December 1994, Claytie sold ClayDesta National Bank, which he'd recapitalized twice, the second time with a healthy chunk of investor funds. Then, just four months after the bank sale — and overriding Modesta's protestations — he sold ClayDesta Plaza, the family treasure. He had little choice: "The building had too much debt, and we were forced to sell it or ante up a substantial amount of money that I didn't have."

At the team's first strategy session, Claytie had announced, "Boys, we're down to our last bullet. We can't afford to screw up." Now Sam Lyssy's thinking, "Claytie just sold the building we're in; we really are down to our last bullet."

By 1995 management concluded it had tried just about everything, striving to take big steps forward but mostly going backward. Now there was no room for error. With few options, Claytie decided to go back into Giddings, the southeast Texas field that in 1979 yielded the oil and gas production that helped establish Claytie for two years running as one of *Forbes* magazine's wealthiest Americans. "We're cutting back everywhere to focus on Giddings," Claytie announced. "This is it. This is what we will live or die with."

Years later, Claytie would recall that his companies drilled 307 horizontal wells in the Giddings and Pearsall fields between November 1989 and July 2006. In the crucial recovery period of the early

'90s, he was the number two driller of horizontal wells in the United States behind Sun Oil Company.

"We had to make it work and we did."

By 1995, Claytie had made virtually all his key personnel changes, and his core group was moving forward again. There would be stumbles, such as productive but noncommercial wells, and some mixed "2-D and 3-D seismic shoots," oil lingo for the sophisticated geophysical technology used to help locate commercial exploratory targets. Claytie endured one more layoff, another big drop in oil and gas prices, a fourth vendor package, and the sale in 1997 of the Sullivan Ranch in Wyoming. Claytie deeply regretted the ranch sale because of the vast improvements he'd made there over the past decade, most notably the fishery and the dams and the trout-filled lakes.

"But," he said, "that was the last sale it took to get me in a position of good solvency."

The Wyoming sale also marked the end of the consolidation movement that began fifteen years earlier with the 1982 sell-off of oil and gas assets to Petro-Lewis for $110 million. "It took me fifteen years to undo all the doing I did," noted Claytie. But consolidation finished with a flourish, said Paul Latham, who was particularly impressed with a unique, eight-hour auction devised by Claytie and fashioned in part after the liquidation of assets he and Johnny May used to end their partnership in the 1960s. Claytie gave the two potential buyers eight hours to keep bidding up their offers, and when the low bidder refused to bid higher, the last one standing bought the ranch.

While initially skeptical of the concept, Latham said, it added an extra $2 million to the proceeds. A second bonus was Martin Sullivan's agreement to stay on with Claytie to handle calf sales from other ranches.

To this day, trout-fishing trips to the Wyoming ranch remain an annual tradition and sometimes include lunch at a Casper restaurant favored by Claytie called Pork-n-Bee's. The restaurant marquee: "Worst food, service, and prices in town."

In 1997 a news story appeared about an ancient Williams controversy that had split Fort Stockton more severely than Claytie's divorce. The issue, first arising more than half a century earlier, had threatened to erupt during the governor's race of 1990, but never became a major campaign issue. The controversy, which lingers even today, centered on Comanche Springs, the recreational heartbeat of Fort Stockton and the favorite hangout of Claytie and his childhood friends when they weren't playing war or swiping watermelons.

The 1997 news story appeared in the *Austin American-Statesman*. It remains one of the few public or private accounts devoid of the emotional and political allegations clouding the issue. The story, by Ralph Haurwitz, indicates as much with its introduction: "If they were selecting a poster boy for the rule of capture, Clayton Williams would be a likely choice. Or perhaps not. Times and people change."

As a West Texas farmer, oilman, rancher, and Republican candidate for governor, Claytie reigned as the most prominent beneficiary of the rule, Haurwitz reported. As Haurwitz explained, the so-called rule of capture was a legal principle that allowed landowners to pump essentially unlimited amounts of underground water even if it dried up springs, streams, or other wells fed by the subsurface supplies.

"His father and a few other farmers near Fort Stockton in West Texas won a landmark court case in 1954 that upheld their right to pump ground water for crop irrigation" wrote Haurwitz. "The pumping dried up Comanche Springs, a popular swimming hole and the supply for irrigation canals used by more than 120 farms. The springs, which had gushed for thousands of years, ceased continuous flow in 1962, and the spring-dependent family farms were wiped out. Fort Stockton lost its recreational centerpiece."

The article acknowledged that Claytie was now—in 1997—suggesting a broader view: while still supporting the rule of capture, he believed farmers should not stand in the way of thirsty city residents.

"That kind of talk is heresy in many of the state's rural quarters," Haurwitz wrote.

"If a drink of water and bath give more value than irrigating cotton, then that's where the water should go," he quoted Claytie as saying. "The argument, I think, should be more over compensation to the person who has the water."

Claytie contended that water should be treated as a commodity, with landowners able to sell their holdings. If water is needed for drinking and a landowner refuses to sell, he said, the government should have the right to seize it, provided the landowner is paid. Claytie acknowledged that his family's pumping contributed to the loss of Comanche Springs, but added that with the state's population rising and demand for water increasing accordingly, the challenge was to find a balanced policy: "In a democracy you've got to have some meeting of the minds."

Claytie recalls that at the height of the controversy the waterless irrigation farmers sued his dad and the other farmers in the Belding area alleging they had drilled into a "well-defined underground stream" and that the irrigation farmers had first claim to the water.

"It was a bitter suit with many hard feelings and split our little town for some years," he recalled. "My dad was never proud of drying up the springs, if he did, but he did believe that a landowner had the right to the oil, gas, water, and other minerals under his land, the so-called law of capture."

The Supreme Court of Texas ruled in 1954 that the law of capture would prevail. "My dad was always distressed over this suit and the animosity it caused in Fort Stockton. It was the main reason he was defeated for county judge in 1954," Claytie said.

Reviewing the newspaper article later, Claytie updated the 1997 *American-Statesman* story with events of the last decade: "I think it's important for people to recognize that I did not inherit this land from my dad. When I was in the army, he and several others sold their land to different farmers who drilled water wells and put the land into farming. It was those farmers who developed the Belding Water Field. Contrary to the facts, some articles suggest that I was involved in the field because of inheritance. I acquired the farmland and the water rights that I now own there by buying different tracts from unsuccessful cotton farmers. Over the years, I have put together a large farm with substantial amounts of water, but it's important to me for people to know that I did not inherit it. I simply bought it back piece by piece from different landowners."

Likewise, he said, the Haurwitz information about the rule of capture and unlimited pumping is no longer true today because of modifications by the legislature and by newly created water districts. Local ground-water districts now have the right to regulate the amounts of water that can be produced within the district, and in Claytie's case it is a total of forty-three thousand acre feet of water a year. "I can pump only that amount of water."

The emotional events of 1997 spilled over into the spring of 1998 and included, most notably, the critical illness of Claytie's mother, Chic. She was receiving around-the-clock nursing care at her daughter Janet's home in Midland. Claytie flew to Tennessee on March 30 for medical tests of his own, minor surgery, and a visit with daughter Kelvie and her family. When he kissed Chic good-bye before leaving, he was not certain he would see her alive again.

When he returned April 6, it was obvious that his mother's death was imminent. After several sleepless nights, Claytie, frustrated, decided to drive to Fort Stockton on April 13, the day after Easter. Chic died at 4:30 P.M. that day, and he returned home immediately. Meanwhile, he'd run out of antibiotics and was encountering postoperative problems.

After a memorial service on the 15th and the funeral on the 16th, Claytie resumed his business commitments, but he was physically and mentally drained from sleepless nights. Aggravating everything was a painful staph infection resulting from an elbow injured a month earlier on vacation. Trying to relax, he took grandson Joshua Groner fishing on his boat in Fort Stockton. And on Sunday, April 26, after frustration, anger, and stress over dropping his glasses and a friend's knife into the lake, he suffered a transient ischemic attack. Known medically as a TIA, it is defined as a temporary interruption of blood flow to the brain but is not a full-blown stroke.

He and Joshua made it back to shore, where Joshua used the car phone to call for help.

Four weeks later, Claytie sat down at his desk to write a letter to an old friend, Karl "Buddy" Butz. They had not communicated since 1987 when their businessman-banker relationship—and friendship since childhood—inexplicity went sour after an initial exchange of letters about their dispute. Over the years Claytie wrote several letters to Buddy, trying to make amends, but he never got an answer. Modesta once even called Buddy's wife, Connie, about their husbands' estrangement. "I don't know why Buddy doesn't respond to Claytie's letters," Modesta recalled Connie saying.

Thus, on May 29, 1997, Claytie wrote another letter to Buddy, who was now retired and living in the Central Texas town of Iredell.

> Dear Buddy,
> Almost ten years have gone by since the falling-out we had over the sale of Clajon Gas Company. Neither one of us lied to each other; neither one of us cheated or misrepresented anything to one another.
> I have gone back and reread my letter to you and yours to me and it looks like we were two different people talking about two different things. This had to be one of the biggest misunderstandings of my entire life. I value very deeply the memories of our long-term friendship and would like to try again to renew this friendship. "Forgiveness is one of the great tenets of

Christianity." I've forgiven many people who have transgressed against me. I have forgiven you and I ask you to forgive me for whatever I did to upset you.

The Fort Stockton High School reunion is coming up in July. It sure would please and delight me if we could touch base sometime in the future.

Your friend,
Clayton W. Williams Jr.

This letter, too, went unanswered.

It was little wonder, after the events of spring 1998, that Claytie soon became a member and ardent spokesperson for the Community Bible Study in Midland. Over the years, Denise Kelly said, Claytie has encouraged others to join them in Bible study. Smiling at the thought, she added: "Once, when I heard a longtime friend of Claytie's react in surprise that he was such a student of the Bible, Claytie openly replied, 'Don't give me too much credit; I'm cramming for finals!'"

As the twentieth century moved toward a climactic close, Claytie's recovery team was focused and working alternately with both vendor and company financing. Drilling operations had shifted to the Cotton Valley Reef Complex in Robertson County and the Pinnacle Reef trend that lies deep beneath the Austin Chalk. The subterranean reef roughly parallels the Texas Gulf Coast, though more than a hundred miles inland.

Upon successful completion of the 3-D seismic project, the first Pinnacle Reef test was a thirty-five-mile "step out" to Marathon's reef gas production. The prospective reef was only ninety acres.

"The well was a Pinnacle Reef discovery but had limited gas flows, and tests indicated we had hit only the edge of the reef," Claytie said. Chronicled one industry newsletter about Claytie's 1998 entry into the Pinnacle Reef: "So many fortunes were lost in the heart of the play surrounding Buffalo [Leon County] that we thought no one was even bothering anymore." But, according to the publication GPR: "In typical Clayton Williams fashion, the J.C. Fazzino #1 is the rankest of wildcats, in the range of twenty to twenty-five miles south of the former end of the trend."

No doubt, conventional thinking might assume Claytie would find validation in the strike, collecting his royalties, playing it safe, and laughing all the way to the bank. After all, he had once again spent generously where others feared to open their wallets.

But Claytie wouldn't know conventional if it bit him in his boxers. The J.C. Fazzino #1 had only whetted his appetite.

After completion, the well flowed at 9.2 million cubic feet of gas a day—eventually it would be flowing at 15 million cubic feet daily—and the GPR report said tubing pressure was, in the jargon of the oil patch, 8,800 psi, "a quite stupendous pressure reading." Claytie, the newsletter said, believed the well had only penetrated the edge of the reef.

"The fact was that this well depleted rapidly and we needed to drill another well," Claytie said, "but oil prices had fallen below ten dollars a barrel and we couldn't afford it."

It was then that Claytie and his team formed their fourth vendor package with service companies like Schlumberger, Nabors Drilling, Smith Bits, M-I Drilling Fluids, and Dowell. Their payment would come from production if the well produced. "We had the ability to cover the miscellaneous cash costs in the well," Claytie said, "and the vendor well [J.C. Fazzino #2] was completed in July 1999, flowing 25 million cubic feet a day with potential future gas reserves of 15 billion cubic feet."

The Fazzino #2, he said, had aimed "for the reef's core."

Several other Pinnacle Reef tests were drilled with varying success, but, said landman Groner, it was "the well we did with the vendor package that in my mind got us out of the woods."

Had it not been successful, engineer Benton noted, the vendors would not have gone forward.

Claytie discussing strategy with, left to right, *exploration manager Sam Lyssy and board members Digger Smith and Bob Parker, 1999*

Now they were rolling. A Cotton Valley wildcat back-reef test well appeared to be a dry hole, but Claytie insisted they drill deeper—"into the unknown." This, too, would be a major discovery, drilled not on science but on what the team labeled "guts and balls." It also revealed a layer of Jurassic sand, which would later become known as the Bossier sands. It was a precursor of one of the biggest gas plays of the new century.

The Cotton Valley discovery well, logged in January 2001, foreshadowed an uncommonly eventful year for Claytie and Modesta—a year once again sprinkled with literal heights and hellish depths. Claytie would complete a well he called "the best one I ever drilled in my forty-plus years" and also reclaim the family jewel, ClayDesta Plaza. Those heights and depths merged during a September sheep hunt when the world travelers were perched atop a faraway mountain overlooking Afghanistan—oblivious to the 9/11 terrorist attacks back home. Less than a month later he and Modesta would celebrate his seventieth birthday scaling the highest peak in Texas just hours after America began the retaliatory bombing of Afghanistan in the aftermath of 9/11.

It was also a year in which Modesta would endure a beastly assault that Denise Kelly asserted was as ironic as it was painful: "She has traveled the world over hunting for dangerous animals, and then right here at home she becomes the hunted. If she'd run to the wrong door . . ."

On what she described as a beautiful and sunny winter day in 2001, Claytie's globe-trotting, big-game-hunting wife suddenly became the hunted in a horrifying ordeal that stretched the boundaries of belief.

"I've chased wounded bears through the brush, I've tracked lions on the sand through the brush, I've been charged by a wounded cape buffalo, and I've come through a leopard charge with only a blood blister on the top of my toe," Modesta said in recounting the incident. "Lots of travels to lots of strange places and many hair-raising events. However, I was unprepared for what happened the afternoon of January 6, 2001."

Arguably the foremost female big-game hunter in the world, Modesta was mauled by a crazed deer.

A crazed *pet* deer.

The animal was one of a pair of twin bucks born to a whitetail doe named Beamer, who was rescued as a baby after being abandoned at one of Claytie's Fort Stockton farms. Beamer had the run of the Midland home and developed an insatiable taste for Modesta's flowers, those inside as well as outside the house. Beamer was joined early on by a mule deer buck named Ranger, a distressed fawn also retrieved from Fort Stockton. In time, Ranger bred Beamer and produced twin bucks—RB for "Ranger's Baby" and BB for "Beamer's Baby."

"Beamer was an excellent mother and nursed the twins as well as any deer you've ever seen," Modesta said. "However, every once in a while when she got tired of them, she would come to the door and wait to be let in to become a house deer again. Ranger would deer sit."

The next year Beamer and Ranger had another set of doe twins—Sweet Jane and Sweet Pea. "What a beautiful family, mother and dad and two sets of twins," Modesta said. "As they matured, the bucks' horns grew quite well because they were fed everything from dog food to all the table scraps they could eat."

But Ranger eventually became too rowdy and was put out to pasture. Then RB, the larger of Ranger and Beamer's twin bucks, attacked his reflection in a window one night, cutting himself badly and breaking a leg. He had to be put to sleep. Thus, in January 2001, the household herd consisted of Mama Beamer, the surviving son BB, and the two does.

"Actually," recalled Modesta, "it was pretty quiet and pretty nice. The deer and our horses kind of vied for their cookies every day, but fortunately there was enough to go around."

She was at home alone at the couple's north Midland residence that fateful January afternoon, recalling that Claytie was on a two-hour drive to the High Lonesome ranch for a weekend of working cows. "Things had been pretty hectic through Christmas and New Year's, so he gave me the weekend off," she said. "This was my quiet time."

Following an exercise session, she glanced out the window and saw that BB, agitated and in rut, had rounded up the three does and was leading them away from the road where a jogger was running with a big dog.

"He brought them to the house at a run and he was huffing and puffing quite a bit. I had the screen door open just enough for the dogs to come and go to the exercise room where I was and this left it open for Beamer to dash into the house, where she felt perfectly safe. When Beamer got into the house and BB couldn't come in, it made him extremely mad. He started butting the doors and he would run around to the other side and butt the window. I surmised that probably the testosterone hormones were raging."

As she did twice daily, Modesta picked up her bucket of treats and went out to feed the deer and scratch BB behind the ears to calm him down. As she started to feed him, he butted her with his horns, knocking her down, gashing her beneath one eye, and ripping her ear.

"I was surprised but not scared," she said, although at first she thought the deer had put her eye out because she couldn't see. Before she could gather her thoughts, BB hit her again, then attacked her with his horns.

"Somehow I managed to get myself away from him and I ran behind a small bench that was on the patio. He followed me and . . . knocked me up against the rock wall. Then he butted me again with his horns and literally picked me up, getting his horns into my flesh pretty deep, and threw me down again."

As the enraged buck assailed her ferociously with hooves and horns, Modesta realized he would kill her if she didn't somehow escape.

"I knew there was no possible way of getting up and outrunning him, so I just started rolling as hard and fast as I could and rolled underneath a bench. BB kept on butting me and the bench, but I had plastered myself at the back of the wall and put my head up under the bench as far as I could so that he would not be able to hit me anymore."

She lost consciousness. When she awoke, BB was nowhere in sight. But she spotted a deer by the door leading into the kitchen. Half blind and terribly mangled and bloody, she dashed for the door into the exercise room, aware that if BB caught her he could kill her. She made it, but then blacked out.

"I don't remember anything until I later got into my bedroom." She crawled into the bathtub to wash away the blood and didn't realize how seriously injured she was until she looked in the mirror. "Yikes," she remembered thinking. "It looked like the worst monster in any scary movie you've ever seen."

The phone rang. It was Claytie calling from the road to check on her. He recalled this exchange:

"How you doing, baby?"

"Not too well."

"What's the matter?"

"I had a little accident with the deer, but I'll be all right. Just go on to the ranch."

He turned around and headed home.

Modesta called daughter Allyson for help. "Allyson and Jerry and three of my grandchildren—Anna, Joshua, and Jered—all came to the house. The kids couldn't believe that their 'Destee' looked so horrible."

They got Modesta into Jerry's pickup without incident, but the kids had to run out the backside of the house to another vehicle to avoid being attacked by the still-agitated deer. Arriving at the hospital in shock, Modesta spent six hours in the emergency room while doctors checked out a concussion, sutured fifteen injuries on her head and body, repaired her split ear, sewed up the gash beneath her eye, and treated her for a cracked tailbone.

While lying there being "beautifully sutured," as she put it, an animal control officer showed up to question her. More accustomed to dog attacks than deer attacks, the dumbfounded officer said: "Well, I've never heard this before. I've got to call my supervisor."

When Claytie arrived, Modesta remembered, he was "absolutely livid," and she worried that he would strangle BB with his bare hands. But that wasn't quite what he had in mind.

"I'm not going to shoot him," Claytie said. "I'm gonna get a baseball bat and beat the son of a bitch to death."

Modesta, fearing "another go-round of men and wild animals," quietly instructed Allyson to call estate manager Ray Ramirez and ask him to "do away with the deer." While Modesta would spend nearly a month recuperating from her injuries, the world was spared the spectacle of Claytie furiously stalking a rutting buck around north Midland with a baseball bat.

As a "reminder to all wild animal lovers," Modesta later wrote a brief account of her bizarre encounter. "You can pick them up and love them from the moment they are born, bring them in the house, care for them for years, and at any moment they can turn on you. I hope people can learn from my mistakes. Be aware that this could happen to anyone anywhere."

"Back in the Saddle Again"

27

On May 22, 2001, Clayton and Modesta Williams celebrated their thirty-sixth wedding anniversary, an event that ordinarily would not command front-page headlines. But Claytie seldom embraced ordinary, as the *Midland Reporter-Telegram* would lustily attest.

"Claytie Rides Again," proclaimed the headline on a story chronicling the event, which was also covered by three local television stations. Accompanying the newspaper headline was a color photograph of a Stetson-waving, Aggie-whooping Claytie atop his horse, and with a smiling but less flamboyant Modesta and members of his "posse" riding at his side, including friends and two former Texas Rangers. A second headline announced: "Clayton & Modesta: Back in the Saddle Again."

Back they were.

After two decades of high and low drama, staggering financial ups and downs, and an incredible mix of heartwarming and heartbreaking events, the irrepressible Claytie and his effervescent wife chose the anniversary date to formally reclaim the business plaza, now known as ClayDesta Center and Twin Towers. The showplace 183-acre office, retail, and banking complex in north Midland had been among the most personal casualties of the monstrous debt load that in the early '90s threatened to topple the Williams empire. Reluctantly, he had sold the cosmopolitan, six-story complex about a decade after it had opened with all the fanfare one would expect of Claytie. After all, one could argue persuasively, it was the prime business address in this oil-sated West Texas city of just under one hundred thousand.

"It's probably one of the bigger things we've ever done—certainly the most permanent and beautiful," Claytie told reporter Ed Todd. "And I think it contributes a lot to the Midland community and the area. We were really not very happy that we sold it. We are durn happy to be buying it back."

Nobody was happier than Modesta, who traced her own business career to the design and building of the plaza and towers, which, she said, was truly a labor of love.

With his scaled-back financial empire under control, Claytie and his handpicked local investors were rescuing the complex from Nevada magnate Ralph Engelstad. And Claytie was ready to celebrate, which, even at age sixty-nine, he would do with customary exuberance. It was a showy spectacular orchestrated by Joe Milam, whose communications and political commercials for Claytie had wowed advertising moguls from coast to coast.

As Claytie and his "posse" galloped up to the crowd gathered at the office park, Jody Nix and the Texas Cowboys, a popular western swing band, greeted them with the Gene Autry classic "Back in the Saddle Again."

Midland's civic hierarchy was almost as thrilled as Claytie and Modesta over the reclamation of ClayDesta Center, because it symbolized the turnaround of not only one of the city's most widely known citizens but also the city itself and much of West Texas.

As Modesta once said, ClayDesta opened not only a new area of Midland but also a new era that changed the dynamics of the city's real estate.

"He [Claytie] exemplifies the West Texas spirit of making good things happen, always looking for ways to achieve and to make Midland better and to make his business stronger," said Mayor Bobby Burns, as quoted in the *Reporter-Telegram*. "The ClayDesta properties being back in the hands of Clayton and Modesta will be great for Midland."

Echoed Midland Chamber of Commerce chairman Mike Conaway, later elected to the U.S. Congress: "It's a win for everybody in Midland to have those buildings managed in Midland again." When someone asked retired Texas Ranger Jesse Priest why he was there participating in the festivities that day, he responded with one of Claytie's fondest compliments. "Well," said Priest, "he's always been one of us but he never got above us."

Within a year, the plaza occupancy zoomed from 63 percent to 100 percent. (The complex today houses the headquarters of Claytie's public oil and gas company, Clayton Williams Energy, and Claytie's grandiose personal office, which remains almost as beguiling as his atrium, although there still are no "Brobdingnagian philodendrons" or "deracinated interstellar colonists" in sight.)

For his part, Claytie made no secret of his displeasure with the way owner Engelstad had operated the center. Before Engelstad, it was a showcase for symphonic affairs, fund-raisers, and charitable and social events. Once it was the site of a widely ballyhooed "String of Pearls" black-tie cattle sale, which, thanks to Claytie's high-watt showmanship, lured *CBS Morning News* to town.

Modesta was even less pleased than Claytie with Engelstad's indifference toward her commercial jewel.

"This was just a building," she snipped. "Things started looking a little shabby, and he wouldn't let people have parties or weddings or anything, and we had built this building to be part of the community."

Now, addressing the crowd gathered outside ClayDesta for the horseback reclamation escapade, Claytie was cheerfully caught up in the moment. After all, he and Modesta had celebrated their twenty-fifth anniversary during the political campaign with a hugely successful party in the plaza atrium.

"We are very happy to buy it back and to run it like we want to, like we did in the old days," he said, his infectious grin lighting up the makeshift stage as the band played and revelers in Levis, boots, and western hats danced in the streets. "We always had in mind that the center would be a major part of this community." He was so

Claytie presents Denise Kelly her twenty-year award at ranch party ceremony

jubilant that he promised the crowd, "We are even going to have nice, soft, toilet paper again."

Modesta, too, was quietly bubbling with joy. "It was just like getting a long-lost kid back," she said.

While the recovery campaign had been long, difficult, and erratic, Claytie maintained his tradition of celebrating triumphs, however big, small, or illusory. On one such occasion in the 1990s, he decided to toss an office party at a Midland bar on the trendy north side and told Denise Kelly to line up the entertainment.

"Like what?" she asked.

"Maybe a belly dancer," he suggested. "Just make it happen."

At the anointed hour, after male and female guests had quaffed sufficient mood-modifying beverages, the music signaled the arrival of an exotic dancer. With Claytie and the guys eyeing the stage expectantly, out pops the dancer—a male stripper!

With the gals all screaming and clapping, the guy shed his shirt, then proceeded to strip, not down to a G-string but to his Spandex bicycle shorts. Denise stole a glance at Claytie. "He looked at me . . . ," she said, breaking up at the memory. "It was priceless."

When relating the story later, Denise adopted her most innocent demeanor and said, "He told me to get somebody everybody would like. And after all, there were more women there than men."

Modesta's assistant, Carolyn Sandlin, called it "equal-opportunity entertainment" and added wryly, "There's laws about that stuff."

"Consider the hunting trip over and get the hell out of Dodge."

After a series of major hunting excursions in Canada, Alaska, Mexico, and the continental United States, Claytie and Modesta had embarked in 1974 on their first overseas big-game adventure in Asia.

"We went to Afghanistan, and that was like the end of the world," Modesta recalled. They found everything fascinating—the people, the animals, the terrain, their hotel in Kabul, and even the mountain campsites. With an interpreter, they roamed the country by land and air, in a four-wheel-drive vehicle and atop small Arabian horses. In quest of the fabled and majestic Marco Polo sheep, they rode the long-haired wild oxen called yaks up and down the barren, rocky valleys and mountains at altitudes up to eighteen thousand feet.

"It just got stranger and stranger," Modesta remembered.

It was a unique adventure, and through the years the globe-trotting duo hunted big-horn sheep, elephants, crocodiles, grizzly bears, polar bears, lions, leopards, rhinos, and dozens of other exotic wild game on six continents and in nineteen countries.

In the early years of their marriage, she said, they hunted black bear, moose, and caribou in Alaska, but, more important, it was there they met the hunters whose stories were the basis for what became an "obsession" with sheep hunting.

Like wild animals staking out their turf, the couple often left their mark in surprising places. Claytie's Democrat friend Gib Lewis, the former Texas House Speaker, tells of the time he was hunting in Russia and stumbled upon a cabin in the mountains overlooking the Caspian Sea. "There we were, halfway around the world, the weather's miserable, and we find this little old cabin and there's an autographed rock. It said, 'Claytie and Modesta Williams, Midland, Texas.' We found out later they'd been there about two months earlier and written on this rock with a felt pen."

Establishing themselves as world-class hunters, both took the required four North American sheep for the coveted Grand Slam and the twelve species necessary for the rare Super Slam of trophy sheep hunting. Modesta was the second woman in the world to achieve the Super Slam.

So it was hardly surprising, despite the ongoing financial recovery campaign, that the new millennium found "Midland's most adventuresome couple" back in Asia in hot pursuit of additional trophy sheep. Each took a Transcaspian Urial mountain sheep in Turkmenistan north of the Afghanistan border.

It was during this trip, north of the Iranian-Afghan border, that they encountered hordes of big military trucks and Turkmenistan soldiers. Surly, uniformed officers jerked open their car doors on several occasions and stared at the hunters, sometimes demanding to see passports. Eventually, they learned the soldiers were looking for members of the Taliban, the militant religious sect linked to Saudi millionaire and international terrorist Osama bin Laden.

Shrugging off the interruptions, they caught a plane and flew on to the second hunting site in search of a different species—the Afghan Urial mountain sheep.

That was why on an early September evening in 2001 they sat atop a mountain in Turkmenistan on the Uzbekistan border overlooking Afghanistan. Modesta said they had been warned not to venture up that mountain because of security concerns, but she insisted on seeing the breathtaking panoramic view.

"I could see the big river that comes out of Afghanistan about ten miles below us," she said, reminiscing with Claytie about their first foreign hunting trip together some twenty-seven years earlier. "When we first hunted Afghanistan, we had a military escort take

Claytie in Mongolia with his trophy Altai Argali sheep and local guides, 1977

us in, and we stayed some nights in little 'subforts' for protection from the Afghan bandits, who still prowled the region in 2001."

They returned without incident that night to their Turkmenistan campsite and the next morning descended the mountain at daybreak to the highway below. There they rendezvoused with the game warden and driver who would take them to catch a flight to Ashgabat, the nation's capital.

Back home, it was September 11, and America had been reeling for hours from the terrorist attacks at the World Trade Center towers in New York, the Pentagon in Washington, and the related plane crash in Pennsylvania.

Unaware, of course, that the world's attention was focused as well on Afghanistan and this Asian region, the Texas couple climbed into a car with no idea that the hunters might suddenly become the hunted. The driver began speaking to a member of the hunting party, a Russian outfitter named Vladimir Treshchov, in an Asian dialect. By the look in Vladimir's eyes, Claytie and Modesta sensed immediately that something was wrong.

Finally, Vladimir spoke. "I have a lot of news and none of it is good," he said, attempting to explain that airplanes had flown into the towers and the Pentagon and that thousands were dead. Modesta thought it must be some terrible airplane accident.

It was no accident, she was told.

"You must have it wrong," she said. "That's not the way it goes."

Claytie and Modesta had no way of knowing that daughter Chim and executive assistant Denise Kelly, among others, had been trying desperately to reach them and get them out of harm's way.

"One of our biggest fears," Denise said, "was that a successful American oilman and his wife were right there . . . and what kind of prize they would be for Osama bin Laden." She huddled with company officers and contacted or fielded calls from the Texas governor's office, the U.S. State Department, and a White House staffer. She sought help and advice while trying to reassure a frantic Chim.

At age twenty-five the youngest of the five Williams offspring, Chim called the office in tears.

"Where are Mom and Dad?" she demanded.

"Well, Chim, they're still out hunting," Denise replied as calmly as possible.

"Have you talked to them and do they even know what is going on?"

"No, but we are going to get them home."

Rowdy McBride, one of Claytie's friends and a member of the hunting party, had flown into the Turkmenistan capital earlier and was the first of the group to arrive at the Sheraton Hotel, where he spoke with Denise by phone.

"Where are Claytie and Modesta?" she asked.

"Out at the hunting camp," he said.

"Do they even know what has happened?"

"No."

She relayed the gist of the advice from state and federal sources: "Consider the hunting trip over and get the hell out of Dodge."

Government sources suggested flying to Europe as quickly as possible, preferably to Frankfurt or Amsterdam. Claytie and Modesta, meanwhile, had heard enough from their driver and Vladimir to conclude that bin Laden had orchestrated an attack on American soil, and reportedly was in Afghanistan. While in no apparent immediate danger, they knew being in a Muslim country was hardly the safest place on earth.

Not yet grasping the magnitude of the attacks, Claytie was reluctant to cut short their hunt despite orders from the State Department. With unbridled enjoyment, hunting companion Rowdy McBride tells the story of Claytie's confrontation with a U.S. Embassy official in Turkmenistan.

"It's time to go home," the official said.

"No," Claytie resisted. "She's got her sheep—and I don't have mine yet."

According to McBride, Claytie was chagrined that Modesta led him in the career taking of trophy sheep—twenty-one species to his twenty—and was determined to stay to hunt another day. But the State Department, embassy officials, Modesta, Denise, Chim, and common sense eventually prevailed, and Claytie would grudgingly head home short one sheep.

When she and Claytie finally arrived in Ashgabat at midafternoon local time, Modesta spotted an American flag at half-staff. "I just came apart right then." Escorted to their room, they picked up CNN on television.

"The first time we saw the images of those planes going through the buildings we—we just couldn't imagine it," she said. "It couldn't register. It couldn't get through. . . ."

As Claytie fielded phone calls, Modesta watched with mounting dread as the story unfolded on TV. She realized the world had changed in a flash, that her children and grandchildren would never know the innocence and freedoms she had experienced since childhood.

"With the new fear and uncertainty, they will never have it again," she fretted. "I think my deepest hurt was for the whole country, that it had completely changed overnight."

Chim broke the spell when she finally got through by phone.

"Mom, don't you go out shopping!" she commanded, urging her to stay off the streets and out of the crowds and to keep a low profile. "No," Modesta assured her, "we will not go out and I will not go shopping."

That was before Claytie insisted they go shopping for Asian rugs, which they did. They found the city calm, the streets quiet, the people of Ashgabat friendly, and the flag at the U.S. Embassy aflutter at half-staff. The calm of the city contrasted sharply with the valid concern, worry, and anxious travel alterations that were rapidly being made in Texas to get the hunters back home.

"Unbeknownst to the Williams party," Denise said, "it was difficult to get them booked on a flight out of Ashgabat to Frankfurt and they would not be able to continue on to the United States for two days as all flights departing Frankfurt were full. A hotel reservation had to be secured in Frankfurt before the airline reservations could be confirmed."

Denise received little encouragement about finding a vacant hotel room, but as luck or fate would have it, the first hotel she called in Frankfurt, a Sheraton, produced an unlikely windfall. "I was surprised to find an incredibly fluent English-speaking reservations assistant," she said. "And they had three rooms for the hunting party. Consequently, the airline reservation confirmation was also immediately completed."

By necessity, all the travel changes were instigated without an opportunity to consult the travelers, who originally intended to fly on to Moscow for a brief Russian vacation after the hunt.

"Normally, all travel arrangements are handled and approved by Modesta—but this was not normal," Denise noted. "It was imperative that these changes be made, whether they liked them or not, in order to get them out of there. The State Department had made that clear to me."

Their flight from Ashgabat to Frankfurt was uneventful, and after two nights stranded in Germany, they prepared to board a Lufthansa jetliner bound for Dallas on Saturday morning, September 15. But their ordeal was far from over. It would be six and a half hellish hours at the airport, delays caused in part by the guns and ammunition stored in their luggage. Airport police got involved at one stage, and a final security check even unfolded on the tarmac as the plane waited to depart.

At liftoff, they joined fellow passengers with shouts and cheers of relief and delight, a joyful sound repeated when the plane touched down in Dallas ten hours later at a largely silent and deserted Dallas–Fort Worth International Airport. "We were the only passenger jet, along with two freight planes, landing at Dallas," Modesta said. Because U.S. commercial flights had not resumed, a chartered plane whisked them to Midland, returning them home four days after the cataclysmic events of September 11, 2001. A banner hanging from their doorway welcomed them "back to the U.S.A."

Said a reflective Modesta: "This has been like something out of a science fiction novel or movie, a moment I will never forget."

Less than a week later, Claytie's team in the field logged in a gas well known as the Lee Fazzino #2. This was an offset, or development well, resulting from the gutsy, "wild ass" discovery well of January 2001 that had been successfully "drilled deeper into the unknown." Geologist Sam Lyssy, ever the optimist, quickly branded the new Fazzino a winner. Engineer Greg Benton, ever the conservative, was not so exuberant about the seventh well in the reef series. But he soon realized they had a real moneymaker in the Fazzino #2.

Barely a week into production, Claytie bounded into Benton's office to inquire about the Fazzino. There was this exchange:

Claytie: "How big is it?"

Greg: "Well, it is good."

Claytie: "How good? Is it ten billion [cubic feet of gas]?"

Greg: "I would say, oh, yeah, it is ten b's."

Claytie: "Twenty b's?"

Greg: "Yeah, I think it is twenty b's."

Claytie: "Thirty b's?"

Greg: "Yeah, I think it is thirty b's."

Claytie: "Forty b's?"

Greg: "I think Sam finally found what he's been looking for."

Claytie: "Let's go get drunk and celebrate!"

To many, Lee Fazzino #2 simply reinforced the oil industry's admiration—if not awe—for Claytie's derring-do, for the Pinnacle Reef Trend had become little more than a bone yard for oilmen, a repository of broken dreams and busted bank accounts.

Fazzino #2 came in flowing 40 million cubic feet of gas a day with ten thousand pounds flowing tubing pressure; it would produce an estimated 45 billion cubic feet over its life. Such a well, with gas at $3, would gross in the neighborhood of $135 million. Even with drilling costs up to $7 million a well, Claytie and the gang could afford a lot of cold beer, and probably even a couple of new Aggie flags atop the rigs.

Describing the Fazzino #2 as the best well in his forty-plus years in the oil patch, Claytie and the recovery team found themselves in an unusual position. "We had a big cash flow but we were prospect poor," he said, explaining that the Fazzino #2 was the peak of the Fazzino activity "and we found we had little more Chalk to drill." With money burning a hole in his pocket, "We were reaching to find somewhere to put our cash flow."

After a succession of missteps, they began reaching in the right place.

Aside from girls, beer, and singing with mariachi bands, Claytie and his irrepressible lifelong crony, David Ligon, seldom agreed on anything, most definitely the facts of a good story. But with the Pinnacle Reef providing a huge cash flow, Claytie recalls challenging Ligon to celebrate their seventieth birthdays in 2001 by climbing the state's tallest mountain together.

"I don't think I want to do that," Ligon purportedly replied.

"We did it when we were sixteen years old and we can do it again when we're seventy," Claytie remembers saying.

Ligon recalls it somewhat differently, that the two were partying in the summer of 2001 and Claytie asked him, "Have you ever climbed Guadalupe Peak?"

"No, I haven't, but do you want to try it?" Ligon says he replied, and Claytie asked, "Why don't we do it?"

Claytie went into training at once, but Ligon soon began having second or third thoughts.

"I'm not sure my knees are going to make it," whined the Windmill Man, whose knees rarely interfered with his travels around the world as a highly regarded windmill technician.

"You've got to do it with me," Claytie declared. "You've just got to."

Then, ten days before the climb, Claytie cornered his unsuspecting executive assistant: "Denise, you and Richard are going with us, aren't you?"

And so it was that on October 8, a month after the terrorist attacks of 9/11, Claytie and the Windmill Man and a small entourage of semihearty souls set forth toward the summit of 8,749-foot Guadalupe Peak in far West Texas. The troupe included Modesta and daughter Chim, who was celebrating her twenty-sixth birthday; Denise and husband Richard Kelly; and Ed Todd, the Midland journalist whose stories and photographs would help sort out the fact and fiction of Claytie's and Ligon's mountaintop adventure. Also trudging up the winding, rocky mountainside were Ligon's daughter Vicki and his helicopter pilot, Russ Hill; Claytie's Fort Stockton farm manager–foreman, Frank Velasco; lifelong friend Sam White; and a Midland acquaintance, Charles Noel.

Just hours earlier, American warplanes had begun retaliatory bombing of Taliban targets across Afghanistan, and the nation was now at war with Osama bin Laden and al Qaeda. Modesta remembered that the terrorist assaults and the American response were very much on everyone's mind that day and she wondered what the rest of her life might be like.

Is it going to be all terrorism or are we ever going to be able to live normal lives again? What's going to happen? Are we going to go up totally in smoke?

"I think at that time everybody was clinging to their family and their loved ones and wondering what tomorrow would bring," she said. "And I think it made that moment with our friends and our daughter all the more precious. Chim had been so worried about us on 9/11, to the point of screaming and crying and becoming hysterical. But now she had her momma and daddy with her up there and we bonded even closer because of the perilous times. We realized how fragile life is and that we don't know what's going to happen tomorrow."

Called Signal Peak by old-timers, the top of Texas rises from Guadalupe Mountains National Park about two hundred miles west of Midland and only a short hop from Ligon's Nickel Creek Ranch.

"Up and back down to the Pine Springs trailhead, the trek is an 8.4-mile roundtrip," Ed Todd wrote. "It is a rocky, narrow, challenging, and splendiferous trail along tiers of natural beauty and steep canyons. . . . The rise and fall of the land mass is marked by maple, oak, juniper, ponderosa pine, madrona, and other trees and by shrubs and wildflowers and cacti and moss."

Among the critters inhabiting the wilderness of the national park, Todd noted in his *Reporter-Telegram* article, were elk, mule deer, wild sheep, raccoons, wild turkeys, vultures, black bears, mountain lions, jackrabbits, coyotes, golden eagles, peregrine falcons, and other birds.

Claytie scaled the mountain in three hours and twenty-five minutes, pausing only once to belt out an old-time Aggie "raccoon" song, "You Asked Me How I Knew." Modesta, then fifty-eight, reached the peak in two hours and fifty-nine minutes, while Chim led the way in two hours and twenty minutes. Ligon was back there somewhere, but once atop the peak he pointed across the rugged park and announced, "I live right over there."

Lifelong friends David Ligon and Claytie: two crazy old geezers

He told Todd: "When you get to my age and are still able to do what you want to do, that's more important than anything else. That checkbook doesn't amount to a hill of beans. Health and attitude is what counts."

At the top of the mountain, the climbing party found a silvery triangular monument, a tribute to the pioneers of the 1800s who passed below the mountains and to the aviators of the 1900s who flew over them. Proclaiming rather proudly that "Nobody gave this [climb] to us, we earned it!" Claytie penned a poignant message for posterity in a guest book contained in a metal box left for climbers.

> *Oct. 8, 2001: My 70th birthday and the 26th birthday of my daughter Chim. An intense moment for Modesta, Chim, and I. We thank God for our life, for our country, our freedom, and the life we have been blessed to live.*
> *The U.S. and allies attacked the Taliban of Afghanistan yesterday. God Bless the USA.*
> *— Clayton W. Williams Jr. — Midland, Fort Stockton & Alpine, Texas.*

Claytie and his mountain-climbing gang took time for reflection at the summit before beginning the trek down, and Denise sounded prouder for her boss than herself. "He is just as sure and steady as a mountain goat," she told Ed Todd.

Claytie laughed off the praise: "They say when you're a *tortuga* [turtle], you've got to go steady, because you don't have any spurts." And for someone who has drilled as many dry holes as he has, he pointed out, you've got to have a sense of humor, the capability to laugh at yourself. "It gets you through the hard times." But turning briefly reflective, he touched on his passion for work and accomplishment and a lifetime of going full-throttle. "There's a joy and satisfaction in continuing to work, because you feel of value. You're contributing. You're doing something. And I like that." He said he took on the mountain challenge on his seventieth birthday to prove that he could, even though he was confident that he could and would do so in a reasonable amount of time.

After their conquest, the climbers gathered at Ligon's ranch for the mandatory party. Sufficiently served, Claytie insisted before dinner that a prayer was in order, to bless the food and the time spent together on this memorable day.

Richard Kelly would recall later that they bowed their heads and Claytie said, "God, forgive me. I'm drunk!"

Ligon's version of the prayer was a little different, as usual.

"You left a bunch out, Richard," he said. "Clayton blessed everything on the ranch and went on and on and then said, 'Damn it, Lord, I'm sorry I got drunk. But it's that damn Ligon that did it!'"

Said Denise, "Clayton was *so* sincere."

"Oh, he *was* sincere," Ligon conceded. "And let me tell you what. If you're gonna talk to God, ignore all that other stuff and by damn, just talk to God. And that's exactly what he did: 'Damn it, Lord, I'm sorry I got drunk.' By God, you can't tell it any more honorably or any more honest. And then he leaned on me and said, 'That damn Ligon did it!'"

Added Ligon: "That was the damnedest prayer I ever heard."

Not content without the last word, Claytie asserted that "Ligon's like garlic. He should be taken only in small doses."

"We bought $300 million worth of seismic data for $7.5 million."

As 2001 surrendered itself to historians, Claytie and his exploration team had emerged from recovery mode. "We're back growing again, in intermittent spurts," he said. Armed with an abundance of the scientific 3-D seismic data—and gathering more—they were prowling now for even bigger, better, but elusive prospects.

"It has always been difficult to drill a well and get rich, and it is more difficult than ever now because the shallow deposits of oil and gas have been drilled," Claytie said. "It is a tough business, and I'm particularly proud that our group has made a living wildcatting. Since the early '80s, most of the people who've made money in the oil business did so by acquisition—buying companies in trouble or buying the castoffs of the major oil companies. We never did that. In hindsight, I wish I had but that wasn't what we did. We are accustomed to risk and risk management, and that's what an exploration company does."

For sure, the post-Fazzino era was no picnic, but at least it produced a steady cash flow.

"After we maxed out our Chalk and Fazzino area, we debated where to go from there," Claytie recalled. "We took the cash flow and we went here, there, and yonder, and really didn't do any good with it."

This period included unsuccessful wildcats in Mississippi, South Texas, California, and Arizona and a drilling venture in New Mexico that developed some "nice" production. But it soon became clear the immediate future of the company lay in Louisiana, for several reasons. One was expensive 3-D seismic technology purchased at bargain basement prices from a couple of cash-strapped companies caught up in the economic downturn of the late 1990s.

In 1998, Claytie and crew developed a relationship and friendship with North American Schlumberger, which had purchased a large seismic acquisition interpretation company called Western Geco. "In the economic troubles that evolved in the late '90s, Schlumberger was generating no income from its Western Geco acquisition," Claytie said. "Their company was at a standstill, and Pat Reesby [who headed CWEI's Houston office] and I got the idea of maybe buying their whole seismic data set."

Early efforts to work out a deal failed. But when the economic woes of the energy industry continued, he and Reesby arranged a meeting with Schlumberger president Maurice DuJols and executives of his subcompanies, particularly Jim White, who headed Western Geco.

"Tell us what you'll do," DuJols asked. "What would you pay for the three thousand miles we have in the transition zone where you have been doing some work?"

Claytie calmly pulled from his pocket an offer of $7.5 million — $2.50 per mile. DuJols looked at Jim White and said, "Jim, is that all right with you?" White gave the go-ahead.

"We made a deal in that room, and we bought $300 million worth of seismic data for $7.5 million," Claytie recalled happily while admitting that he didn't actually have $7.5 million.

"We were able to do it because, number one, they let us have a year and a half to pay the money, and, number two, we had the cash flow from the Chalk and the Fazzino complex. We also committed to pay them two hundred thousand dollars for every well we drilled in the seismic package. Anyhow, the timing was absolutely perfect." That was because many of the companies that somehow survived the wrecks of the '80s had encountered new economic challenges in the late '90s and were not exploring when oil prices tumbled to nine dollars a barrel.

"The whole industry was having fits," Claytie said, and his timely acquisition of the cut-rate scientific data would be another instance of what colleagues called his oil-patch "guts and vision."

In January 1999, as luck would have it, Claytie had been the keynote speaker at the NAPE oil prospect exposition and he took a gloomy message to his contemporaries. "I told them if you did not really enjoy the oil business, you should change careers because the future looked dim." But just days later, the price started moving up as if it would never retreat.

"So what do I know?" he shrugged.

The Louisiana exploration operations during this critical re-building period were under the supervision of the Houston office headed by Reesby, an LSU Law School graduate committed to Louisiana's exploration prospects. Besides the superb seismic database and his ties to LSU, Pat said his prejudice toward Louisiana exploration was traceable to a sandstone reservoir in the prolific Miocene-aged rock that extended beneath the southern Louisiana marshlands. It has produced more gas on a per-square-mile basis than any other reservoir in the nation, he said.

"It is a good, clean reservoir . . . with phenomenal reserves and a high flow rate," he added, while describing the seismic database Claytie had acquired as "probably second to none."

Better still, as a veteran of the Williams roller-coaster rides, Reesby was a natural leader at rebuilding. His introduction to the company in 1981 was etched in his mind, occurring when Claytie was splashing around happily in Austin Chalk gas and oil from the Giddings Field.

"Oil had spiked up, gas prices were up, and Clayton was in the midst of a great expansion," Reesby recalled. "Sam Pfiester was the exploration manager, and everything was growing so fast that Sam needed an assistant just to try and help him keep up with where we were buying leases, where we had prospects, and where we were planning on drilling wells."

Years later, during the recovery efforts in the mid-1990s, the Houston office shrank to two—Reesby and his secretary-wife Martha. "She was the only one willing to work for the wages we had to offer."

But in 2000, Claytie and Pat began establishing a new core area of operations in the southern part of the state. They assembled over the next couple of years a team of experienced consulting geologists and geophysicists to identify drilling prospects in the Miocene Trend of south Louisiana based on the enhanced 3-D seismic technology. They soon had acquired 3-D seismic data covering a total of fifty-four hundred square miles, some purchased as cheaply as a penny on the dollar—making it even better than the Schlumberger–Western Geco deal.

"We could not have been as aggressive in supporting Pat in south Louisiana without the Fazzino well, which funded it," Claytie said, recalling that during one run of bad luck the Houston/Louisiana operation drilled seven straight dry holes in a ten-well package. Discouraged and blaming himself, Reesby told Claytie: "This is not working and I don't know why. Let's quit here and take that money and find something else to do."

Once again badly bent but not broken, Claytie insisted on drilling the remaining wells, saying: "I don't know how to pick them any better than you do, but it is a numbers game. Let's roll the dice."

Two of the last three wells were "outstanding," Reesby said.

Now, little more than two decades after the giddy Giddings years, the circumstances were vastly different. But Claytie was again the aggressor, his laserlike attention focused on Reesby's operations in the Plaquemine Parish area of southern Louisiana. "That's where the Mississippi River flows from New Orleans down to the Gulf," Reesby says. "All of that stretch on both sides of the Mississippi is Plaquemine Parish."

By the end of 2003, the company had drilled thirty-five exploratory wells in south Louisiana, with fifteen completed as discoveries. In 2004, CWEI had a 100 percent working interest in three new discovery wells and a percentage of two others.

Most important, the cash flow from the Louisiana play along with the Fazzino and Chalk production figured prominently in the company's ability to raise the equity in May 2004 to purchase Midland-based Southwest Royalties Inc. Southwest was a privately held energy company engaged in oil and gas exploration mostly in the Permian Basin of West Texas and New Mexico. Claytie called the $210 million purchase a "damn significant event in the history of CWEI" and declared: "It gave our company some stability we never had before. Southwest Royalty had very long-life oil reserves."

The acquisition provided the company a material presence in the historic Permian Basin, extended its reserve life from three and a half years to seven years and allowed CWEI to rebalance its drilling portfolio between exploration and development prospects.

"We went into the public market to acquire the equity to purchase Southwest Royalty," Claytie said, "and as usual, the barracudas on Wall Street took a big bite out of my ass. We thought we would get twenty-nine or thirty dollars a share, but the barracudas chased us down to twenty-two dollars."

However disgruntled he was over the toothy, sea-faring predators, he was not surprised: "I have scars all over my body from Wall Street."

The timing did appear dazzling, because six weeks after closing the deal, the price of oil started its historic and steady move upward. "It looked like a brilliant move, but it really wasn't, because three-fourths of the production was hedged at twenty-five-dollar oil and five-dollar gas," Claytie revealed. "But it is long-lived production, which sounds good on Wall Street. . . . Those hedges don't expire until September '08, and at that point the company will probably be worth double what we paid for it.

"So it was a good deal."

On the home front, the best recovery news was unfolding behind the scenes and had little to do with oil, gas, cattle, or consolidation. Clayton Wade, who had completed the boot-camp hitch after his postelection arrest in 1990, had conquered his drug problem, graduated with a political science degree from Texas A&M, married a lovely Aggie co-ed, and by 2004 worked part-time for his dad at the Alpine ranch. And topping it all off, he and wife Kristy welcomed their first child, Aubry, born in March 2005.

"It cost him some years, but he finally kicked his drug habit," Claytie said happily. "His drug fight's been a major factor in our lives, and it was a principal reason that I ran for governor."

Talking candidly with a reporter in 2004, Clayton Wade admitted that the family he'd rebelled against so fiercely as a teenager had remained supportive throughout his ordeal but that conquering his "nightmare" had been a long, intense, and difficult journey. Being the son of Clayton Williams was a mixed bag, he said. "He's a great teacher, and that's what he wants to do, to teach people and pass on what he knows, and there's no doubt he knows a bunch. . . . Look at the things that he's done for me and at the things he's done for everybody else around him. But you know, he wasn't a soccer dad, to put it as mildly as I can. It's a double-edged sword. There's good and bad. . . . It can be tough."

Besides a supportive mom and dad, young Clayton said another factor in his recovery was that such people as Wynona Riggs, Nancy Carpenter, and Denise Kelly never gave up on him. And like Claytie's grandmother Mernie, young Clayton's grandmother Chic thought he could do no wrong. "She took up for me even when I didn't deserve it," he said, smiling at the recollection.

"I wasn't a bad person; I was just a wild person. I had to learn on my own. I just had to see the dark side, I guess."

By the mid-2000s, the Pearsall reserves crisis and the bankruptcy scare were distant memories, but for some, the 1990 election was not so easily dismissed. At an Austin "roast" for Karl Rove, Pres. George W. Bush's political troubleshooter, Rove took a shot at Claytie. He referred sarcastically to the "intellectual" candidate from Midland, which a miffed Claytie interpreted as labeling him a "dumbass from West Texas."

Since Rove was the honoree and a friend, Claytie didn't even consider slugging him, but he did remind himself that "I kicked your ass when you represented Kent Hance in the 1990 primary." Claytie also found solace that evening in a favorite quote, by Theodore Roosevelt: "It is not the critic who counts, not the man who points out how the strong man stumbles. . . . The credit belongs to the man who is actually in the arena, whose face is marred by dust and sweat and blood, who strives valiantly, who errs, who comes short again and again, because there is no effort without error and shortcoming . . . but who spends himself in a worthy cause . . . and who at the worst, if he fails, at least he fails while daring greatly, so that his place shall never be with those cold and timid souls who knew neither victory nor defeat."

On a cheery note, Claytie's company disclosed in a generally upbeat annual report that it spent $117.8 million on exploration and drilling activities in 2004 and estimated similar expenditures of $124.1 million in 2005. Reflecting the high level of activity in Louisiana, the company said it planned to spend more than $50 million there in 2005 on drilling and completion activities. This would include $17.6 million for additional seismic and leasing data.

The team Reesby and Claytie began assembling five or six years earlier now included some twenty professionals — geophysicists, geologists, geological technicians, engineers, and landmen, plus consultants and a clerical staff.

It wasn't the heady years of 1979–81, but it wasn't bad. It was good enough that, once again, at the company Christmas party Claytie handed out thousands of dollars in drawings and bonuses to his employees and scholarships to their children.

The ambitious projections of the year 2005 did not take into account an episode that began with a grand coup at the annual meeting that year of NAPE, the North American Prospect Expo. With guts and a suspect three-hundred-thousand-dollar personal check, Claytie secured a big block of acreage in the vicinity of what appeared to be a major discovery in the Utah "overthrust." Then, with sons-in-law Jerry Groner and Greg Welborn in tow, Claytie flew to Utah to buy leases, among them a parcel of acreage owned by a sheep rancher named Nielsen. But it was a "messy" deal to begin with, in part because another buyer had the inside track. Undeterred, Claytie explained to Jerry and Greg that they would strive to meet with the rancher before lunchtime and perhaps be invited to join the family for the noon meal. "Rural people, if they feed you and share with you that hospitality, you probably will make a deal," he said. The scheme worked, with Claytie and Nielsen conducting a lively conversation over lunch about castrating sheep with their teeth. "Son," Nielsen told him, "I have done that, too."

After establishing such unique rapport, Claytie heard nothing from Nielsen for more than a month and was sorely disappointed that his dinner-table and barnyard diplomacy had failed. Not so. It was a miscommunication between two deaf old dogs. "It turned out," said Claytie, "that he was hard of hearing, and of course I'm hard of hearing. The old man wanted to deal with us all along. What I told my sons-in-law about a landowner feeding you was true—it just took a little longer than I expected to make the deal."

The partners in this project were the Yates family from Artesia, New Mexico, and Herbert Hunt from Dallas. With maybe a smidgen of smugness, Claytie added: "We began drilling that area in the fall of 2006."

Back in Louisiana, meanwhile, the company's drilling prospects expanded beyond the south to a northern area near Shreveport and then on eastward to an Anadarko field in Jackson Parish. Said Claytie: "We have substantial leases on three potential big fields, and this could be the next leap forward. This could do for us what the Austin Chalk did in '79."

That, insist his friends, would be a historic hoot: ricocheting from the postelection brink of bankruptcy back to the Forbes 400. "Hell," said one of his old drinking buddies, "he could run for governor again!"

"The heart of Muster is the heart of Texas A&M, and the heart of the Aggie experience."

The pageantry was spectacular, a cheering, chanting, emotional throng afloat in a sea of red, white, and blue — and maroon. The Aggie Band and the Singing Cadets appeared even more stirring than normal, commanding twelve thousand–plus Aggies and former students to their feet for rousing renditions of *Texas Our Texas* and *The Star-Spangled Banner*. Four Aggies clad pristinely in uniform whites paraded through Reed Arena to adorn the stage with American and Texas flags.

The occasion was Aggie Muster, the most important and inspiring tradition at a university that prides itself on its legacies and traditions. Each year on April 21, San Jacinto Day, it honors all Aggies who have died in the past year. Besides the campus ceremony, the Association of Former Students also organizes several hundred simultaneous Aggie Musters around the world. "It's the common bond we have with each generation," said Ann Melson, a member of the Muster 2005 Committee. "In my opinion, Muster is the absolute exemplification of the spirit of Aggieland."

Speaking as the Muster programs subchair, Melson explained that the keynote speaker for the April 2005 Muster was chosen because he defines what it means to be an Aggie.

"He is the essence of dedication and passion for the university," she said.

Camouflaging his nervousness behind a proud smile, and dazzling in his maroon sport coat, Clayton Williams Jr. arose that

Williams: Muster a standstill in time to look back

By Melissa Filbin
THE BATTALION

Clayton Williams Jr., Class of 1954, said his most memorable Muster was right before World War II when he attended with his dad, Class of 1915.

With the nation once again at war, Williams said the tradition of mustering troops and Aggies is important.

"Muster is a standstill in time to look back at Aggies, loved and lost," he said. "I think of friends no longer here, of my father, of my roommate."

Williams, the keynote speaker at Muster 2005, graduated from Texas A&M with a degree in animal husbandry and went on to serve two years in the Army and work in oil, ranching, communications, real estate and teaching. But his greatest achievement, he said, is his family.

The campus headquarters for the Association of Former Students is named after Williams, who said he was overcome with emotion when asked to help build the Alumni Center.

"(This is) the greatest story in my broad experience," he said. "I cried when they asked me. Of course I accepted."

In 1986, with oil prices high and the final payment on the Alumni Center due, Williams joked, he cried again.

"I had financial strains," he said. "To pay the last building payment, I had to sell my largest, most successful company, Clajon Gas Company,

EVAN O'CONNELL – THE BATTALION

See Williams on page 4

Clayton Williams Jr., Class of 1954 gives the keynote address at Muster 2005 Thursday at Reed Arena.

Muster Speaker at Texas A&M, College Station, 2005

spring night to deliver a speech he had anguished over more than four months.

Designed to "present the true spirit of A&M," he had never worked harder on a speech. And it showed.

"Howdy!" he hollered. "Come on . . . Howdy!"

"Howdy!" the audience responded, rattling the roof of the packed arena.

He thanked Kim Harris of the Muster Committee for his formal introduction, told some familiar self-deprecating jokes, and recognized university president Dr. Robert M. Gates, Corps Commandant Gen. John Van Alstyne, retired Maj. Doc Mills, and other dignitaries and the families of departed Aggies.

After a special greeting to the family of his friend Gordon Tate of the 1954 class, Claytie launched into a speech that would trigger perhaps an unprecedented flood of congratulatory letters, phone calls, and e-mails from Aggies young and old.

His speech, though not lengthy, cut immediately to the theme of the evening: "The heart of Muster is the heart of A&M and the heart of Aggie traditions." This is that speech, his finest, in its entirety:

> Of course, when I was a student here, my best grades were not in English. But, one thing my English prof did tell me has stuck with me to this day. One thing — the word *unique*. There's no such thing as very unique, or sort of unique, or extremely unique, or kind of unique. Something either is or it is not unique. In all the world, there is no other word like *unique*.
>
> Well, let me tell you, friends, Texas A&M . . . is . . . unique.
>
> In defending that claim, let me tell you why Texas A&M is *not* unique.
>
> It's not unique because it has great teaching facilities.
>
> It's not unique because it has a great research program.
>
> It's not unique because it has a fine faculty.
>
> It's not unique because it has a good football team or a large football stadium.
>
> No. Texas A&M is unique because of the way we feel toward each other, the way we feel about our school — unique in the pride we feel about ourselves. It is particularly unique because of these traditions that we have carried forward for so many, many years. We Aggies celebrate and maintain our uniqueness. And, Texas A&M is unique because of the way its graduates have served this state, this nation, this school, and our fellow Aggies.
>
> Aggie Muster is not just one of those traditions; it is our greatest tradition! It is one of the highest honors of my life to

have been invited to speak at this campus Muster. I offer my sincerest thanks to the Muster Committee. These kids are really neat. You have paid me a compliment, greater than you know.

Muster has come a long way since the early days of the A&M College, when cadets first gathered at the San Jacinto battle-field where we gained our independence from Mexico. It has continued to grow and evolve over the years.

While growth and evolution are often necessary for tradi-tions to remain relevant, I would ask you not to become fo-cused on the event of Muster, or the process of Muster. I would ask you to focus on the meaning of Muster. Meaning some-times is lost as a tradition grows. I ask you to focus on what's the heart of Muster. Because the heart of Muster is the heart of Texas A&M, and the heart of the Aggie experience.

To really understand the meaning of Muster, let's look back at its origin. The word *muster* is a military term meaning to as-semble a military unit, to bring its members together to fight in some emergency. For most of our history, America did not maintain a large standing army. It relied instead on the raising of state militias to meet whatever emergency faced the pioneers and the settlers as the years go forward. In the Revolutionary War we had the Minutemen to face the British. To face Indi-ans, we called in the Texas Rangers. Citizen-soldiers have been called on in our history to form their units to muster. The mus-ter roll would be read.

Our Muster evolved from this tradition, but with a uniquely Aggie modification. The annual calling of the roll at our Muster remembers all those who have departed our ranks.

And therein lies the key to what Aggie Muster is really all about. It's about people. It's about our heart. It's about remembering.

When we call the names of the departed, we remember them as individuals and as Aggies. We honor their contributions to our lives—and to Texas A&M. While we may not have known them personally, we say "here" for them in our heart because they will always be part of the heritage of Texas A&M. As these names of others' sons, daughters, mothers, and fathers are called, we think of our own sons, daughters, fathers, and yes, even our grandparents.

At the same time, Muster can be a very personal and individualized experience for each of us, because it gives us the opportunity to recall those Aggies who have had a great and direct part and a beneficial effect on our lives, but who are now among the departed.

This year, my thoughts are with all those Aggies who are defending freedom around the globe. I think of other Aggies I have known—Aggies who are personal heroes to me and who have fought for freedom. As I think of their names and I look back, I form my own personal Muster list to be added in my heart to the names that will be read later tonight.

I'd like to share my personal list with you. And, as I do so, I ask each of you to join with me in answering "here" as I call their names.

First, an artilleryman who fought in France in World War I—my dad, my hero Clayton Williams, class of 1915. I say, "Here." [At this point, Claytie choked up and brushed away tears.]

Next, an Aggie who shared the misery of those World War I trenches, who gave us the "Aggie War Hymn"—J.V. "Pinky" Wilson, class of 1920. I say, "Here."

Another soldier who fought in both World War I and World War II, and whose muster on Corregidor was the impetus for the worldwide Muster tradition—Maj. Gen. George Moore, class of 1908. I say, "Here."

Many Aggies served in World War II, and many were heroes. This soldier, one of seven Medal of Honor recipients, added to the mystique of the Aggie ring when, almost sixty years later, his class ring was returned to A&M from the German battlefield where he fell—Lt. Turney Leonard, class of 1942. I say, "Here."

While there were many Aggie heroes in World War II, none left a greater heritage than this one; the commander of the Rangers who scaled the heights of Point Du Hoc during the battle of the Normandy D-Day Invasion. The president of A&M who opened the gates to our future — Maj. Gen. James Earl Rudder, class of 1932. I say, "Here."

In the Korean War, we lost a great yell leader and an outstanding role model who I looked up to as an underclassman — Lt. Lew Jobe, class of 1952. I say, "Here."

I think of two Aggies whose remains were recently returned from Vietnam after so many years — Capt. Carl Long, class of 1966, and Lt. Donald Matocha, class of 1967. I say, "Here."

When I think of Aggies who served in Vietnam, I think of my roommate, of bravery, courage: ten helicopters coming in under fire to land their troops. The first seven were shot down. My roommate was number eight, the first to successfully land in that battle — Maj. Jack E. Custer, class of 1954. [Choking up again, he asked for help in saying "Here."]

And my cowboy horse trader, hard-of-hearing best friend — Lt. Marion Baugh, class of 1967. I say, "Here."

Aggies maintained their record of outstanding service in the Persian Gulf War. Three did not come home — Maj. Richard Price, class of 1974; Lt. Daniel Hull, class of 1981; and Capt. Thomas Bland Jr., class of 1986. I say, "Here."

And the Aggie tradition of service continues. Four Aggies have been killed in Southwest Asia and Iraq since the last Muster. Their names will be called later tonight [during the candlelit roll call for deceased Aggies].

These Aggies on my personal list, and so many, many more, have left us a legacy of service and courage that continues to this day. As we gather here tonight, the tree of liberty is again being nourished by the blood of patriots. To remain free and independent and to bring the sacred blessings of freedom and democracy to others half a world away, America once again battles a deadly and committed enemy. And, as in the past, the extensive use of the National Guard and Reserve troops helping fight this battle means that nearly everyone here tonight knows someone who is helping fight the war on terror.

Not since World War II has the home front been so united in support of our troops. Our most fervent hopes and prayers go with them as they stand in harm's way. And, as with all of America's conflicts since the Spanish-American War, the sons and daughters of Texas A&M have shouldered their patriotic responsibilities, picked up the gauntlet, and joined the fray. The fighting is vicious, the privations are great, and the sacrifices are many. But, like the Aggies before them, they serve proudly. They know some will not return. They understand this may be the price of keeping their nation free and their loved ones safe, but they're here.

Now I'd like a very special young lady to join me. This is Madison Walker of Bryan, Texas. Madison is eight years old and she goes to Harvey Mitchell Elementary. She's a competitive swimmer and an accomplished gymnast. Did I get all that right, Madison? [Kneeling down to speak eye to eye with the little girl.]

Now Madison, let me just tell you what I think any one of the thousands of Aggies serving us scattered all over the world would say to you if they were here tonight. They would say, "Madison, you go home tonight and you sleep in your bed . . . and you get up in the morning and go to school . . . and you go to gym class and you go to swimming class . . . and you study and learn all you can so that you can grow up to be a wonderful, responsible citizen in this world." And they would say to you, "Madison, don't you worry . . . because *we've got the watch.*"

[After thanking Madison for her appearance, he continued.]

You young Aggies in this audience tonight will soon have the watch. You will be challenged; you will be tested; you will be asked to give your all. This may not necessarily occur on the battlefield, but on the field of life. You may in your world be called to fight a lifesaving battle in the operating room or to advance great legal principles in the courtroom. You may find yourselves at war to save the family farm, or to save the company you work for, or to keep your children from drugs. Your battleground may be in the laboratory, the classroom, or on the factory floor. The battle may even be with your own conscience. Regardless of the fields of conflict, just as Aggies before you, you will be called to fight.

In these times of crisis, will you call on all the things you learned at Texas A&M? *Will you* remember that you're a Fightin' Texas Aggie, and damn proud of it? *Will you* summon the courage to do the right thing when it is easier not to? *Will you* find the strength to lead where others fear to tread, and *will you* employ the will to fight on when others abandon the cause?

Will you remember that you have the fire of the Aggie Spirit in your heart, the strength of Aggie heroes in your souls?

Muster has made it so . . . Muster, and Silver Taps, and the 12th Man, and the Aggie Code of Honor, and all the other great traditions of Texas A&M and all the values they stand for.

Muster, then, is about remembering ideals of service before self, of honor, of integrity, of loyalty, and perseverance. It's about renewing the ties that bind us to our school and to each other. It's about saying to the world that the values we hold are worth celebrating, even under enemy fire.

These things, to me, are the real meaning of Aggie Muster, and all the other ways in which we celebrate our uniqueness as Aggies. It is what brings us together year after year to stand for those who have left our ranks—and to drink once again from the well of Aggie Spirit. Muster is about people and it's about remembering, and my challenge to you is this:

Which one of you will be the next Earl Rudder? Who will become our next Rick Perry, our first Aggie governor? Who will be the next Mike Halbouty to find new oil fields and give back so much to Texas A&M? Who will be the next Bum Bright to build businesses, to lead our board of regents, and to give back millions to the school he loved? Who will be the next John Hagler, who excelled in the financial world and who gave us the Hagler building? Who will be the next Jack Brown, whose building, the chemical engineering building, will be dedicated in the morning? And this man was an oilman, an innovator, an explorationist, and a pioneer. And who will be the next "Head" Davis, a man for all seasons that we all knew and celebrated? And, yes, who will be the next John David Crow, who gave us such rich and wonderful memories from Kyle Field?

What will your contribution be to the future of Texas A&M?

The audience responded with a thunderous standing ovation. University president Bob Gates grabbed Claytie's arm when they left the stage that night and said: "Claytie, that was fantastic!" (Before the year was out, President Bush would tap Gates to replace Defense Secretary Donald Rumsfeld.)

The speaker was almost too relieved to speak—but at the same time confident of a job well done.

A young woman named Tammy Bartsch, class of '98, left that night to compose an e-mail to a man she never met. It said in part:

"I attended the Muster ceremony at Texas A&M last night and found your speech to be very meaningful. . . . Your personal 'roll call' was very touching. . . . I was sitting with the Matocha family, who lost an Aggie son last summer in a car accident. They were also there representing Donald Matocha, the Aggie that was killed in Vietnam, whose remains were finally brought home last summer. Thank you for mentioning Donald's name. I know their family appreciated that.

"I'm proud to have attended the same school as you, and all the other outstanding Aggies in this world. Thank you for representing A&M in such a positive light, and for giving one of the most thoughtful speeches I've heard.

"Take care and Gig 'em!"

And from Bob Parker, Claytie's longtime friend, business associate, mentor, and founder of Parker Drilling of Tulsa: "Claytie: I'm so proud of you. You nailed it."

Congratulatory messages poured in by the dozens. "I worked for four months off and on to come up with the best speech possible—and I believe I did," said Claytie, unaccustomed to saying good things about himself, and certainly not publicly. He was terrified that he might be thought pompous, pretentious, or hypocritical. Thus he savored the reaction to his Muster remarks, such as this handwritten note from Harry Green Jr. of College Station, Aggie class of '52:

"Dear Clayton:

"You are unique!

"Your Muster speech was wonderful. It was special in content and delivered extremely well and sincerely. Nelda and I feel so fortunate to have heard your inspiring remarks.

"Best wishes to you and Modesta."

One of the most moving handwritten letters came from Ann Baugh in Brownwood, Texas, the widow of Claytie's great friend, Marion Baugh.

"Yesterday I talked with a friend of mine whose daughter attends A&M," Ann wrote. "After attending the Muster, she called her mother, crying, and said she had just heard the 'most wonderful man' speak—you! She also said that she stood in line to speak to you but finally gave up because the line was so long. . . . You are still a wonderful inspiration to young people and have the ability to 'fire up' those Aggies. What a gift!!!"

Along that line, Rod Pittman, chairman of the Texas Water Development Board and a member of the Aggie class of '56, wrote to say he'd just received a phone call from his grandson, Jeremy Pittman, a junior at A&M at the time.

"Granddad, you would have been mighty happy with Mr. Williams's Muster speech—it really hit home with me and my buddies in the Corps," Pittman quoted his grandson as saying. "It reminded me of the days when I was very young and would come to Texas A&M with you and Grandmother—I don't know of any other place I would rather be than right here in the Texas Aggie Corps of Cadets. Mr. Williams reminded us what it's all about being a Texas Aggie. . . . We loved it!"

And then there was the note from Kimberly Harris, the Muster committee member who had introduced Claytie that special evening. The letter was so heartfelt that he immediately ordered it framed and hung on his office wall.

"I cannot tell you, Sir, what an honor it was to introduce you at the Muster ceremony," Kim, class of '06, said in a two-page, handwritten note. "I have never experienced a moment of greater pride and greater humility combined than the moment your speech ended and I witnessed over 12,000 people rise to their feet. No experience has made me feel more like a Texas Aggie (and damn proud to be one!) than watching how you affected every person in Reed Arena that night. If I am never able to attend another Aggie Muster, that moment will keep me 'mustering' in my heart forever."

Less than a year after his triumphant Muster appearance—and on the eve of one of his highest honors—Claytie was greeted at a black-tie Austin function by protesters harking back to the 1990 election. Lying in wait for him outside the entrance to the Austin Convention Center, four youngsters toted crudely fashioned signs proclaiming in effect that Claytie was an insensitive and despicable sexist lout. "Claytie Dishonors Women," said one. "Weather . . . Rape," reminded another. A third: "$$$$ Can't Buy Honor."

Asked what he thought of the protestors, Claytie rolled his eyes and replied: "Not too bad; at least they remembered me sixteen years later."

As his dad would say, heights one day, depths the next. . . .

And so it was that on March 4, 2006, Clayton Wheat Williams Jr. capped a lifetime of awards and honors with perhaps his most prestigious tribute ever: Texas History Maker of the Decade, so proclaimed by the Texas State Historical Association. His four fellow honorees included First Lady Laura Bush, Hall of Fame base-ball pitcher Roger Clemens, Houston philanthropist and former Lt. Gov. Bill Hobby, and novelist-playwright Horton Foote. With sleek black limousines discharging guests onto a red carpet, the black-tie crowd poured into the Austin Convention Center for a night of high-class revelry and high-dollar live and silent auctions—not to mention a dinner christened "Everything Texas" and "designed" by Texas celebrity chef Grady Spears.

With sponsorships ranging from $2,500 to $50,000, and some auc-tion items reaching six figures, the evening reaped a multimillion-dollar bounty for the TSHA. But even while embracing the glamour and glitter, Claytie and Modesta kept the evening a family-flavored affair. Dozens of longtime friends, employees, and business as-sociates filled four tables of ten, and a family table included sister Janet Pollard, eight members of her family, and lifetime family friend Jane Sibley. Joining Claytie and Modesta at the honoree table were Kelvie Muhlbauer, Jerry and Allyson Groner, Greg and Chim Welborn, Clayton Wade and Kristy Williams, and Jeff Williams with date Erin Dwyer.

J. P. Bryan, chief executive officer of Torch Oil Company of Houston and chairman of the historical association, introduced the five honorees as "extraordinary individuals . . . who consider it common to achieve the uncommon" and whose "courage and virtue are not words but a way of life." Their finest statements, he added, "are not in what they have said but in the lives they have lived."

Describing the quintet as the "five points of the star that make up the whole of our historical heritage," Bryan noted that Laura Bush was honored for education, Hobby for philanthropy, Clemens for sports, Foote for arts and literature, and Claytie for business. Mrs. Bush, a Midland native, was traveling in India and Pakistan with the president, and Clemens was participating in the new World Baseball Classic. Both addressed the group via video-tape, while Horton Foote personally accepted his award with elo-quent dignity.

As an oilman himself, Bryan captured the Clayton Williams flavor with a passion, introducing him as a legend in the energy business, an icon who has painted with bright colors and broad strokes on life's canvas. "Dull and boring may be a theme in many lives, but they are as foreign to Clayton as a day without laughter," he said, prompting vigorous applause. "Though he has all the complexities of a driven and successful entrepreneur, he is at his core simply a Texas original from the top of his Stetson to the bottom of his boots."

Calling him the last of the colorful breed of oilmen known as wildcatters, he said Claytie is willing to risk everything drilling for huge oil reserves while relying more on instinct than science.

"The wildcatter is going the way of the Western frontier, but Claytie is the notable exception," Bryan asserted. "He has coupled the fearlessness of the wildcatter with the technology of the day to build an enormously successful enterprise. Not hidebound by committees and corporate bureaucracy, Clayton Williams is not afraid to trust the instincts that have been insightful companions for these many years.

"He will rush in where lesser men fear to tread."

Citing what he called the "boyish charm" that has served him so well, Bryan said Claytie negotiates with the skills of a horse trader and can close a deal faster than a livestock auctioneer.

"Everybody in our industry has a story about Claytie—many of them apocryphal no doubt—but they emphasize the truth that people revere those who can make an otherwise conventional and mundane life into high adventure," Bryan said. "Though in business Clayton can be as tough as dry boot leather, with friends and family he is as soft as a small child's embrace. And to those causes he frequently and generously supports, he is as giving as a desert rain."

Bryan brought his audience to its feet for a rousing ovation when he suggested in closing that Claytie's perfect counterpart would not be a fellow wildcatter but the state's greatest cattleman, Charles Goodnight, first of the legendary trail drivers and the pioneer of the modern cattle industry. Insisting, correctly, that while Claytie's money is in the oil and gas business, his heart is on his ranches, Bryan said: "In their shared values, Goodnight and Claytie could have been Woodrow Call and Gus McRae of *Lonesome Dove*."

Futhermore, he said, he knows what Claytie is thinking when he rides across his ranches pondering projects to restore grasslands or introduce another species of bighorn sheep: "If only a band of Apaches would appear on the horizon . . . what a glorious sight it would be."

Then, speaking directly to the honoree at a table beneath the dais, Bryan added: "Claytie, Charles Goodnight, if he had known you, would have praised you as the right man to join with him on that last great trail drive."

Rising to deliver his response, Claytie paused to plant a world-class smooch on Modesta, then bounded up to the microphone and announced: "I should just shut up, take the award, and go sit down." When the laughter subsided, he continued to poke fun at himself. "Had I done the same in my political experience, I'd probably be your governor."

After the laughter faded, he said he was both honored and humbled to be compared with Goodnight. He then talked briefly of his own heritage, of his pioneering ancestors, including one who linked his own family by marriage to the frontiersman Daniel Boone. He reminisced about the tales handed down to him by his father and grandfather, recalling how both were splendid historians and writers. He recalled also that O. W. Williams was a Harvard-educated lawyer who arrived in Fort Stockton in 1883 and that his father, Clayton Sr., was born there in 1895.

"I know who I am. I know where I came from. And so I'm doubly honored to be here," he said, wrapping up his response. "Now, in the real world," he added in a lighthearted aside to Bryan, "I've got the best lease play going right now."

Bryan laughed — "I'll take a quarter."

Claytie started back to his table, then suddenly stopped, spun around, and returned to the microphone. "A little advice for those

Texas State Historical Association Award, 2006

of you with political aspirations," he deadpanned. "I suggest to you: never tell a joke!"

Three months after the TSHA honor, in the early summer of 2006, Claytie and Modesta flew to Ireland to attend a convention of the prestigious Shikar-Safari Club International and accept a couple more major awards and a ringing conservation tribute. Already the second woman in the world to get the so-called Super Slam of sheep, Modesta was awarded first place for taking the largest African crocodile ever, in 2005, an eighteen-foot, seven-inch trophy.

"Crocodile Destee," Claytie dubbed her at the Shikar-Safari Club award ceremony, where he received the Award of Merit for second place with a slightly smaller crocodile, a seventeen-foot, six-inch monster taken at the same time and place.

Earlier in 2006, the International Sheep Hunters Association bestowed on Modesta its top award as Super Slammer of the Year. Thus, said Claytie, she got a world record crocodile trophy and the outstanding sheep hunter of the year honor in the same year. It was not her first—in 1988 she took the world record Gansu Argali sheep in China.

"Not many people have two world records," Claytie observed proudly. "And no woman has two world records—particularly a good-looking sexy one."

September 17, 1983, was the first of several "red letter" days in pursuit of their big-horn quarry. That was the day they became only the second husband-and-wife team in the world recognized as "Superslammers" in the international realm of wild sheep hunting. It was also the day Modesta became the second woman in the world to complete the Super Slam. Their fourteen-year quest ended on a ranch in Colorado where, a minute apart, they each took a free-ranging Iranian Red Sheep, the last of twelve species required for a Super Slam. The first of the dozen species, a pair of Dall sheep, came in 1969 in Alaska.

Besides the continental United States, their quest had taken them to Alaska and throughout the world: Afghanistan, Pakistan,

Modesta and world-record crocodile, 2005

Turkmenistan, Mongolia, Nepal, Azerbaijan, Russia twice, Mexico, Canada, Spain, and much of Africa.

Although it requires twelve species of sheep to obtain the Super Slam, Claytie has now taken a total of twenty different species and Modesta twenty-one in the course of their global hunting adventures. When Claytie and Modesta took their twelfth sheep to complete the Grand Slam in 1983, they did so on the Bill Cox Ranch in Colorado. That experience would lead Claytie into an exciting and successful conservation campaign.

"Bill had bought these sheep from the New Mexico game department where they had come directly from Iran," Claytie said. "They were the only Red Sheep in free range available for hunting and were the only sheep we could take to complete our Super Slam of Wild Sheep."

Many other species of wild sheep existed but lived in Asia where Russia, China, Afghanistan, and other neighboring countries were closed for hunting.

The Iranian Red Sheep, found along the Iran-Iraq border, faced extinction in the early 1970s — a challenge ideally suited for Claytie.

Modesta and her world-record Ganzu Argali sheep, western China, 1988

"We became interested in trying to save this species," he said. "We purchased the remaining sheep from Bill Cox. We captured them using nets shot from the landing strut of a helicopter. It took three different trips and eight helicopter hunting days to capture those animals—two rams and five ewes. They were wild as hell!"

They were shipped to Claytie's High Lonesome Ranch in the Davis Mountains, where the elevation, rugged West Texas terrain, and sporadic rainfall are similar to those of the El Burz Mountains of western Iran.

"We built paddocks to raise and protect them from predators and increase their numbers," Claytie said. It would be a long-term, innovative commitment. He first attempted embryo transfer—he'd funded such research at Texas A&M—but found that what worked best to increase the wild sheep numbers was natural reproduction and predator control.

Desert Big Horn sheep, taken in Mexico by Claytie at age seventy-three

"Now," he says with considerable satisfaction, "the High Lonesome Ranch is inhabited by three hundred Red Sheep and two hundred Armenians as free-ranging animals. And today, sheep hunters come to hunt the magnificent little animals in pursuit of their own Super Slams."

And that is why Shikar-Safari International, besides honoring them for their trophy crocodiles, presented Claytie and Modesta the foundation's annual Conservation Award for saving the wild Iranian sheep by establishing them in the West Texas habitat of High Lonesome.

The successful rescue of the Armenian and Red Sheep populations was not an isolated conservation event for Claytie and his partner in such sheep projects, Rowdy McBride. McBride, a rather famous mountain-lion hunter and bioscientist, was able to acquire some Desert Bighorn Sheep from the San Diego Zoo. Additional efforts to acquire other Desert Bighorns from different zoos proved futile, and embryo transfer efforts failed, but Claytie's sheep campaign did not end there.

"The reestablishment of native species of wild desert sheep remains a lifelong objective to me," he said, although he was dealt a setback in October 2006 when a mountain lion climbed a containing fence and killed ten of the remaining sheep, leaving only four rams. "There's no hope for reproduction now, but I'm going to keep trying. I've had dry holes before and overcame them." By early 2007, Claytie already had a lead on some desert sheep in Mexico. "We will continue to work to return this species of wild sheep to private land in the Trans-Pecos area."

Claytie's conservation concerns date to the drought of the 1950s. "From 1950 to 1957, I watched with pain and chagrin as much of the land deteriorated badly. Bare spots became prevalent over much of the Pecos Region and particularly on the remains of the Clayton Williams Sr. ranch. After I became a landowner, I entered a lifetime battle against the invasive brush species of mesquite, catclaw, whitebrush, and the like. It's almost become part of my DNA to improve and restore the land.

"I'm sure when I'm gone," he added with that beguiling grin, "these brush species will breathe a sigh of relief and say, 'We're glad that little son of a bitch is outta here.'"

"Being who he is, is more important than him being in politics. He wouldn't have fit, ever."

31

By any measure, 2006 was a banner year personally and professionally for Claytie and his company: a year that presumably buried forever any haunting memories of bankruptcy and bank failures and the painful dispersal of many of his entrepreneurial treasures.

"Things are too good," he fretted facetiously. "That's why I'm worried; when and where is the next shoe going to drop?"

His Aggie Muster speech in 2005 had been a personal milestone, as were the Texas State Historical tribute and the Shikar-Safari awards that followed for both him and Modesta. The honors would spill over into the new year with his selection as the recipient of the 2007 Kupfer Distinguished Executive Award, named for 1954 A&M business administration graduate Harold F. Kupfer and recognizing professionalism, enthusiasm, and dedication to service. In campus ceremonies spread over two days, Claytie joined a renowned group of previous honorees ranging from Army Gen. Alexander Haig to the former Dallas Cowboys quarterback Roger Staubach; they included such familiar business luminaries as Michael Dell, Herb Kelleher, H. Ross Perot, Ray Hunt, Boone Pickens, and Richard Rainwater. His acceptance remarks were vintage—sprinkled with Claytieisms and self-deprecating stories that stressed the importance of entrepreneurship, integrity, salesmanship, risk-taking, and of course, an Aggie education.

Meanwhile, elder son Clayton Wade had moved from Alpine to Midland with wife Kristy and toddler Aubry and was learning the

Claytie and Modesta walking under a sabre arch formed by the Ross Volunteers during the Kupfer Award honors at Texas A&M, 2007

production end of the oil business working full-time for Clayton Williams Energy Inc. The couple's second son, Claytie and Modesta's seventh grandchild, was born in November 2006 and christened Chance Everett Wheat Williams. Sons-in-law Greg Welborn and Jerry Groner were blossoming in the oil patch, Greg in the land end of CWEI and Jerry with his own Midland-based company. Son Jeff took over the High Lonesome Ranch and became engaged to a young woman from Austin, Erin Lauren Dwyer.

Meanwhile, daughter Kelvie's September 30 marriage to Timothy Herron Cleverdon of Midland was an enchanting event for the entire family and provided Claytie still another son-in-law to terrify. ("I've mellowed," he swears.) Tim, who spent twenty years in oil and gas marketing, had launched his own company, called "Bee Busters." After learning of the earlier adventures of Claytie and sons-in-law Jerry and Greg, Tim approached his future father-in-law with caution. After a series of mostly sleepless nights, he had decided to seek Kelvie's hand in marriage in a face-off with Claytie at the Alpine ranch. But several attempts misfired. Finally, during the Christmas holidays of 2005, Tim caught him at the ranch and they sat down to chat.

"I did notice that he was unarmed—a good sign," Tim said. "A 'dramatic pause' occurred, which I took as my cue to begin." There was this exchange:

Tim: "Claytie, I'd like to talk to you about Kelvie and me."

Claytie: "I thought it might be something like that."

Tim: "But it's good news . . . and she's not pregnant!"

Claytie laughed.

Tim (stammering): "The bottom line is . . . I love Kelvie . . . and I think she loves me . . . and, uh, uh, I'd like to have your permission . . . and your blessing . . . to propose to her!"

Claytie: "That's great. I'd love to have ya. She's my baby."

Tim: "I know."

"He welcomed me with open arms," recalled Tim, sounding both surprised and relieved. "It was great." When Tim called Modesta with the news, she admitted she might just shed a joyful tear.

"Me, too!" said Tim.

Meanwhile, on the financial front, Claytie's expanding and encouraging exploration activities were invigorated by yearlong oil prices that flirted with $80 a barrel but mostly ranged from the low $60s to the mid-$70s while dipping briefly into the $50s in the fourth quarter. CWEI stock, which all but disappeared from the charts in the mid-'90s, bounced around in the $30 to $40 range much of the year and hit a record $55.33 in one quarter. Examining the zigzagging chart, someone remarked with acidic humor that it reflected Claytie's erratic history of personal fortunes—maybe as far back as when the town dogs wreaked havoc on his sheep.

Nevertheless, he hit another peak in 2006 with the sale of fancy real estate he bought in 1984 along Barton Creek off Austin's Loop 1, known locally as Mopac. Located on the southwestern fringe of the downtown area, the so-called Terrace included four buildings erected on the 111-acre prime business site. "I paid $6 million for those acres, damn near $54,000 an acre, but in 1984 I thought I could afford it."

Claytie said environmental concerns and a liberal-controlled Austin City Council precluded early plans for development and re-sale of the site. "And in '86 and '87 the Texas real estate market collapsed along with the oil business, and we were dead in the water."

Claytie said he had a franchise today "because Austin was so negative and so antigrowth for so long that virtually no prime office sites became available for development."

He held on for more than two decades, maintaining an uncharacteristic low profile in a hostile liberal city while borrowing and sending money to his chief operating officer, Paul Latham. His point man in the Austin real estate venture performed his customary financial magic.

Difficulties obtaining entitlements were so overwhelming at one time that Claytie considered giving the land to Texas A&M with a proviso that the Aggies construct a 150-foot arm on the site. Atop that arm, he grinned, would be a maroon-and-white hand with the middle finger extended in consummate defiance to all in Austin who had frustrated his development schemes.

Never happened, fortunately, but not because of decorum on Claytie's part. In the summer of 2006, Latham helped arrange a sales package for the buildings that produced a nearly $70 million profit. Almost as impressive, the potential profit and development fees on four future Terrace buildings were estimated at more than $50 million.

"Paul did a brilliant job. My only contribution was borrowing the money to keep sending to him as he needed it."

That and staying out of Austin.

"As bad as Ann Richards beat me in Austin," he drawled, "I don't go there without an armed guard."

In the spring of 2006, Claytie was visibly and deeply saddened to hear that Ann had been diagnosed with esophageal cancer, and wrote her: "Modesta and I are sorry to learn you've had some health problems and we have put you in our prayers. I think back warmly to the campaign we had and I regret only that you and I didn't have a little more time together."

He blamed that estrangement on handlers of the opposing campaigns and said he'd like to see her after her recovery: "When you get your feet back on the ground, give me a call. I'll come in and we can have a fun lunch talking about the fun things of our campaigns."

Ann responded a few days later, saying: "Dear Clayton, thanks for the good wishes from you and Modesta. I feel confident I will be successful in beating this cancer."

That friendly exchange between two philosophically opposite political rivals appeared in the *Midland Reporter-Telegram* five months later when Ann succumbed to her illness in mid-September at age seventy-three. Describing her as "a great Texan," Claytie told the *Reporter-Telegram* he long had admired and respected her personally, adding: "I met Ann before I got into politics and I thought she was a very witty, charming person. [Ours] was a strong battle between a man and a woman with very different concepts, and I always felt my battle was with the media more than with Ann. The Democrats have lost a good spokesman and a fine leader for their cause."

On July 2, 2006, Claytie wrote a letter to cheer up his old friend Billy Clayton, the former Texas House Speaker who was seriously ill in a Lubbock hospital. The letter read, in part:

> I've been reflecting over my life and the very important part you've played in it. You were involved in helping raise debenture money in Austin for ClayDesta Communications. You were very definitely involved and led the way when we fought AT&T and eventually defeated them at the last minute in conference. You were involved in the incident that led up to me taking my cowboys to ride up to have a press conference on the Capitol steps, which probably turned the tide along with your leadership.

You were certainly involved in my race for governor. Without your encouragement, I would not have done it. Maybe I shouldn't love you so much; BUT it was the grandest event of my life and you were a major part of it. . . .

Not long after spending two weeks relaxing, exercising, and fishing at their old Wyoming ranch, where they retained visiting privileges following the sale, Claytie and Modesta headed back to Tanzania in August 2006. Modesta was nursing ribs broken in a freak fall at the High Lonesome Ranch and didn't hunt, but Claytie took a trophy lion and excitedly vowed to bag him another, a black-maned cat, on a pending African excursion. He did so in early November.

In between safaris, Claytie and Modesta spent hours reminiscing with friends, family members, and employees about ranching and wildcatting, about work and play, family and friendship, politics and fate—and about life, both the good and the not-so-good, with emphasis on the former. He recalled the day at Happy Cove Ranch when, in despair and desperation, he dropped to his knees and turned his life over to the Lord. During those difficult moments, he remembered embracing the words of the Serenity Prayer: "Lord, grant me the serenity to accept the things I cannot change, the courage to change the things I can, and the wisdom to know the difference."

And his life has been many times blessed, he said.

"It's fun to have my kids involved in the company, and in the farming and ranching," he noted, adding that he personally thrives on the balance between the oil business and ranching, building gas pipelines and working cows.

He and Modesta also shared their thoughts on hunting, particularly how their global adventures have been so important in so many ways during their forty-plus years together.

"Modesta and I are healthy, and we've managed to save up enough money and time to hunt intermittently through the year

Claytie and lion, 2006

with at least one major trip of at least three weeks," he said. Such trips serve a multitude of purposes beyond the sheer enjoyment of the hunt itself. "Sometimes I've left here frustrated, disgusted, tired, grumpy, and upset. I just needed to get away to clear my head. I can sleep nights when I'm hunting, because I don't have all the customary worries. I come back rested and I can accomplish more in a few days than I can sometimes in two months."

So, he rationalized, with his mind and body rested, the time off actually made him money. "Even if it didn't, I convinced myself it did."

Beyond the therapeutic and financial rewards, the hunts also contribute indirectly to their healthy lifestyle. Sheep hunting in particular is so physically demanding that it compels them both to work out year-round to stay in tip-top condition. "Whenever I can, I go to the ranch to exercise," Claytie said. "I like to climb to the top of that mountain at Happy Cove a couple of days a week. It lets me function for days at a higher level."

Writing once in a publication called *The Hunting Heritage,* Modesta touched on the more esoteric benefits of the couple's global wild-game hunting.

"The hunts have been such a big part of our lives that we display our memories around us throughout the house," she said, referring to the mounted trophies that decorate their home, their ranch, and their offices. "Each time we look at an animal, we remember a different person, place, or circumstance that was either pleasant or in some cases not so pleasant, but certainly one that is embedded in our minds and in our hearts forever."

She called these hunting trips "our time": "When you are in a foreign country, it's nice to have your best friend, hunting companion, and lover . . . all rolled up into one, with you."

Claytie conceded that he'd slowed down a bit in his seventy-fifth year, but not much, which he demonstrated rather gallantly on October 8, 2006. With a spirited boost from Modesta, Claytie celebrated his seventy-fifth birthday with another impressive climb, this time at Beaver Creek in the Rocky Mountains of Colorado. And he finished in a snowstorm, no less. Besides Claytie and Modesta, the climbing party again included Richard and Denise Kelly and David Ligon, all survivors of the Guadalupe Peak quest five years earlier, along with newcomers Pat and Martha Reesby, the Reesbys' college-age daughter Laura, and Ligon's Corpus Christi crony Bob Crow. Seven of the nine reached the eleven-thousand-foot summit ahead of Claytie and Ligon, exchanging congratulatory high-fives as the storm intensified. All wore special T-shirts beneath their climbing gear that read, "In overdrive at 75; Summit Celebration." On the back was a highway-shaped sign that said: "CAUTION: Claytie Crossing." After a short wait atop the mountain, the summit seven climbed into a waiting Suburban and started down the mountainside in search of the laggard duo.

As they rounded the first corner, they spotted Claytie.

"Stop!" Modesta told the driver. "He's going to make it, and I'm going to hike the rest of the way with him."

When Claytie saw her, he began *running* toward her.

"Keep in mind," recalled Denise, "that this was after four miles of uphill climbing and in what was now a snowstorm. It was obvious that she continues, after forty-plus years of marriage, to give him the energy and drive and motivation to keep going. It was a sweet moment to watch them embrace and then continue the climb to the summit together."

Once again, Claytie had achieved his goal, although this time it was Modesta who provided the flourish. "I think it's true that very few people could do today what I do at my age," he said. "That's some genetics, but also exercise and determination."

Retirement? Never.

Partial retirement? "Being partially retired is like being a little bit pregnant, isn't it?"

Continuing in his reflective and philosophical mood, Claytie offered his opinion on a wide range of topics and concerns, including the loss of the governor's election. He says he most regrets the notion that he let his supporters down by losing, and the missed opportunity to create a boot camp in the Big Bend for dealing with young drug offenders, emphasizing not punishment but rehabilitation.

Those who know him well are adamant that he would have been a good governor, an entertaining and unifying and fiscally responsible governor, and Claytie himself takes a measure of satisfaction in that he did bring tens of thousands of new converts into the Republican Party. "Looking back, I believe that I contributed something of value to the people," he said. At the same time, he shares to some extent the concerns of friends and family that the governorship would have had a destructive, perhaps devastating, impact on his business empire and perhaps even his personal life. Sister Janet Pollard put it this way: "That night I was crushed and brokenhearted, but later I was very glad he wasn't governor. He has a gift that's more important. . . . Being who he is, is more important than him being in politics. He wouldn't have fit, ever."

Eldest daughter Kelvie agrees, saying flatly: "If elected, he would have been in trouble constantly."

Awarded the rank of Eagle Scout in 1946, Clayton Williams gives much of the credit for his personal and business successes to tenets he learned as a Boy Scout, including dutiful service to God and country, focus on helping other people, personal commitment to physical, mental, and moral improvement, and dedication to other laws and principles ranging from trustworthiness and loyalty to cleanliness and reverence. These fundamental devotions were later reinforced through his embrace of the Jaycee Creed, which exhorts faith in God and the brotherhood of man, a fundamental belief that economic justice can best be won through free enterprise and government based on law, and respect for both the treasure of human personality and service to humanity.

These are the principles Claytie has held most dear, that have underlain each of the twenty-three business entities he has established and the various honors and prizes he has received. Some of the more notable of these range from the Distinguished Service Award of the American Association of Petroleum Landmen (1979), to the Distinguished Alumni Award of the Association of Former Students of Texas A&M University (1981), his induction into the Hall of Honor of the Texas A&M Corps of Cadets (1998), the Foy Proctor Memorial Cowman's Award of Honor from the Haley Museum (2004), his induction into the Petroleum Museum Hall of Fame (2005), his selection as Muster Speaker for the main campus of Texas A&M University (2005), and his designation as the Texas State Historical Association Businessman of the Decade (2006), among many others.

As he wandered reflectively through the triumphs and turbulence of his lifetime, Claytie paused only fleetingly to delve into certain regrets. The forced sale of Clajon Gas remained foremost among his business misgivings, and the falling-out with high school teammate and banker Karl Butz lingered as a poignant personal loss. As he said on several occasions—most recently while relaxing over drinks with friends and writers on an October 2006 night—the split was in essence a misunderstanding. It was also a cruelly ironic misunderstanding because the quarrel and confusion actually occurred between Butz and Jamie Winkel, the company executive negotiating a business deal on Claytie's behalf who later died in the 1990 plane crash.

High atop Claytie's philosophical list is the importance of self-worth, especially as it applies to his children and grandchildren. "They may inherit some money but unless they have a job, unless they're contributing, unless they feel they're of value as a person, the money will ruin them over time," he asserted. "Many inheritors don't have that; they don't do anything because they don't have to. One of the worst things people can do is to give their children enough money that they don't have to work. Mine are probably gonna have that, but the work ethic is pretty strongly ingrained in our family.

"You *have* to contribute something to feel good about yourself. You *have* to be of value."

In that context, reputation is so vitally important also, he said. Friends and foes alike still marvel that when countless numbers of his colleagues were going broke or filing for bankruptcy protection, Claytie was paying off $500 million in debts during the run-up to the governor's race. That included once making a $21 million interest payment in a *single* three-month quarter. After the election, they note, he spurned bankruptcy while spearheading one of the most remarkable comebacks in oil-patch history—and he was able to borrow or raise money to do so because of his reputation for integrity.

Although Claytie caught flak from some because of his fondness for solving disputes with his fists, he takes pride in his reputation as a brawler. "I've not been intimidated ever from fighting people," he said, speaking both literally and figuratively and including both

bullies and business rivals. That goes back to his high school days. "I was small but a pretty tough linebacker, a pretty tough little toot. It was kind of my world fighting people bigger than me, usually bullies. I didn't always win, but I won enough to keep me going. Fighting was just what you did, and Dad taught me to box and encouraged me to fight."

And then there's the issue of ego and successful entrepreneurship. "I've made lots of mistakes," Claytie says, "but one of the reasons I didn't go broke when a lot of people did in the bust of the '80s was that I didn't let my ego get in the way of facing reality." He dealt with adversity then and later by reluctantly selling off cherished assets such as Clajon, ClayDesta Plaza, and the Wyoming ranch—and emerged a survivor despite brushes with bankruptcy and financial ruin. While stressing that self-esteem can override good judgment and even sanity in some instances, he said: "It takes ego and self-confidence to build something. It takes that extra self-confidence to get through the bumps on the way up. That same ego, when out of control, can bring the business right back down. Ego is a double-edged sword."

Looking back on seventy-five riotous years, Claytie sees an exciting mix of hard work and great fun, building pipelines and drilling wells one day and branding calves and working cows the next—all embellished with a spectacular marriage in which he and Modesta raised kids and traveled widely while frequently working side by side in the office, on the ranch and farm, and even in the oil patch. "She worked cattle, branded calves, made evening beer runs on the pipeline . . . everything. We've done a lot of things together, and that's one reason we've had a good marriage, a unique marriage." Even in reflection, Claytie can't stay too serious too long. "The negative is, she's a better shot than I am now. But what a wonderful, wonderful experience my life has been. And it ain't over yet."

On Monday morning, January 8, 2007, after reveling in a holiday hunting trip near San Antonio, Claytie returned to his Midland office unaware that his dear friend Billy Clayton had died over the weekend. He was a fellow Aggie and West Texan: the former Texas House Speaker who rushed to Claytie's aid during his telecommunication skirmishes in Austin; the canny Democrat who convinced Claytie to run for governor; who convinced him that Texas, and Texans, *all Texans,* Democrat and Republican, needed his unbridled candor and bountiful talents; the friend for whom he and Davis Ford had recently flown to Lubbock to tender their earnest concern and sickbed support.

Awaiting Claytie that same morning was a mountain of mail. A letter on top, handwritten on small, lined, yellow paper, caught his eye. It was dated January 1.

Denise Kelly stood by as Claytie read.

"I'll be damned!" Claytie said.

Denise fought back a tear as "a smile as big as Texas" brightened up his face.

It was a letter from Buddy Butz, expressing the high value that he continued to place on their old friendship and his poignant regret that he had never acknowledged his complete forgiveness regarding the disruptive pipeline incident of so many years ago. Butz closed the brief letter with the hope for continued blessings in all things for Claytie and his family.

"I'll be damned! Isn't that neat? I'm a little shocked . . . a little flabbergasted. How long has it been?"

"Nineteen eighty-seven," Denise said.

"I guess that's right," he said. "Twenty years."

Claytie could hardly contain himself at the thought of a friendship rekindled: an old friend and confidant, born in the same hospital bed four days apart, Panthers football teammate, and banker to his greatest successes.

One January morning. Two friends. Billy Clayton and Buddy Butz. Great heartache at losing one. Great happiness at finding the other. Claytie's relentless, lifelong roller coaster rattled on, careening once more through the heights and depths.

"The Lord," Claytie told a writer friend minutes after reading the Butz letter, "does indeed work in mysterious ways."

Recognitions

From day one, Claytie stressed to me that the secret to whatever success he's enjoyed is no secret at all. "I have always surrounded myself with bright, talented, and conscientious people," he said. Looking back over his fifty years in the oil and gas business and his other endeavors, he cited "just a handful" of the friends, associates, and employees who played important roles during the pivotal business cycles of his life.

"In the pre-Giddings years, roughly two decades," he said, "the group included the Weavers and Dow Puckett, my dad and uncle, J. C. Williams, and all the shareholders in the Scope and other royalty companies. And certainly my early partner Johnny May and his family. There were different bankers such as Clayton Puckett, Charles Frazier, Tom Stevens, and particularly Karl 'Buddy' Butz. There were landowners and oil drillers like Ralph Burkholder, John and Johnny Dorr; dealers like Ned Marrow, Jack Blake, Gary Burnett, Stan Beard, and many, many others. There were great employees like Bill Haverlah, Clint Atkins, Wayne Roye, Doc Malone, Bernie Scott, J. L. Davis, Sandy Jones, Lana Loyd, Wynona Riggs, Pilo Perales, Jim Shepherd, and Dick Morton. There were also great friends and teachers like Ted Gray, and good friends like Charlie Moody and Cleo and Mike Costello at Sarah's Café.

"Of the many ventures, projects, and activities that I've taken over a lifetime, one of the most satisfying was the acquisition of the Alpine [Happy Cove] Ranch. Along with the ranch, came Guadalupe 'Chappo' Ramirez and later, his son James. What a pleasure it has been to me to go to the ranch, work on projects, work cattle, and always have these two solid men there to help me every step of the way. Chappo is as much of a workaholic as I and he was by my side through many, many ranch projects. Another great satisfaction has come through working with my dear friend Frank Velasco as we put

together and developed the irrigated Fort Stockton farms, which today produce 16,780 tons of alfalfa hay a year."

Claytie told me repeatedly that none of the giant strides forward
during the Giddings boom would have been possible without Bob
Lyon and Travis Lynch and their team of gas buyers, as well as Bob's
presiding over administration and contracts. He went on to salute
Bill Haverlah for his lease acquisitions; Charlie Moody, for his pipeline building; Jack Bradford and Dave Greenlee, for their well drilling; Wally Raschall, for his building the gas plants; Clint Atkins, for
his early oversight; and Quatie Wolfshohl, for overseeing all Clajon
activities.

"In later years, there were friends and employees such as Sam
Pfiester, Pat Reesby, Paul Latham, Mel Riggs, and Kelly Beckham in
oil and gas; Nancy Carpenter, Martin Sullivan, Clay Cowart, James
Ramirez, and Paul Henderson in agriculture; Ray Ramirez, the estate manager; and, especially, my right arm and loyal, capable assistant for twenty years, Denise Kelly. I am certain that Paul, Mel, my
son-in-law Greg Welborn, John Kennedy, and Sam Lyssy will all be
key players as we continue to grow."

Most recently, Greg took over the land operations from son-in-
law Jerry Groner, who started his own company, and son Clayton
Wade moved from Alpine to Midland to work full-time for CWEI
and learn the producing end of the oil business. Son Jeff is a farm
and ranch manager who manages the High Lonesome Ranch, and
daughter Kelvie works part-time in real estate.

Finally, in Claytie's mind and heart, there will always be a special place for the five men, friends as well as colleagues, who died in
the company plane crash in 1990: Bob Smith, Randy Kidwell, Jamie
Winkel, Aaron Giebel, and Ken Mardis.

Author's Acknowledgments

As may be expected in an ambitious endeavor such as this, I have so many people and publications to thank for their contributions to this book that it is impossible to name them all.

Foremost, I owe particular gratitude to my editor Michael Blackman, a longtime Fort Worth friend and colleague whose talent, wisdom, humor, and patience got us through some perilous moments with the charmingly volatile subject of this book.

Those same attributes apply also to Denise Kelly, Claytie's effervescent and tireless executive assistant, and to Davis Ford, a member of Claytie's corporate board of directors as well as a member of the advisory council of Texas A&M University Press. Denise was the "go-to gal" for virtually every aspect of this book, from selecting photographs to arranging and deciphering interviews, all the while contributing substantially to the text and tone by sharing her own experiences in—and observations on—the tantalizing and turbulent world of Clayton Wheat Williams Jr.

With wise counsel and finesse, Davis Ford helped the book's serpentine journey from inception to publication, overcoming all manner of stumbling blocks along the way. He's a unique mix of Aggie and Longhorn, and this journey required a bunch of Aggie and no small amount of Longhorn.

As a latecomer to the book project, Claytie's eldest daughter, Kelvie Cleverdon, was invaluable as both a tireless researcher and a delightful storyteller.

Many of my former colleagues in the Texas press corps were most helpful, particularly John Gravois, formerly of the *Houston Post* and now political editor of the *Fort Worth Star-Telegram,* and Kaye Northcott, who covered the 1990 governor's election for the *Star-Telegram.* I am grateful also to the dozens of state, national, and international newspapers and magazines whose reporting of the campaign provided such incisive, provocative, and entertaining accounts that I felt compelled to quote them frequently and shamelessly. Truth be told, I did so a little proudly, having worked hand-in-hand with many of the newspaper editors, reporters, and photographers during four decades as a roving Texas correspondent for the Associated Press. In this regard, a special thanks also to Michael Levy, publisher of *Texas Monthly,* and several of his staff members whom I'm proud to call friends as well as colleagues.

I want to recognize several of the major Texas and West Texas dailies, starting with the *Midland Reporter-Telegram,* its publisher Charles Spence, and editor Gary Ott. Through their coverage of the energy industry, ranching, and Claytie's political and philanthropic activities, they have served up an abundance of compelling material. Texas is indeed blessed to have major city newspapers such as the *Dallas Morning News, Fort Worth Star-Telegram, Houston Chronicle, Austin American-Statesman, El Paso Times,* and *San Antonio Express-News,* all of whose reporting I drew on from time to time. Though now history, I'd be remiss if I didn't also mention the late *Dallas Times Herald, Houston Post,* and *San Antonio Light.* Admittedly biased, I doubt that any state has finer regional newspapers than West Texas, many of which contributed substantially to this effort.

Although now out of print, S. D. Myres's superbly edited and researched *Pioneer Surveyor—Frontier Lawyer,* the personal narrative of O. W. Williams published in 1966 by Texas Western Press, was a rich source of information about Claytie's remarkable grandfather, as was the book's lively introduction by author C. L. Sonnichsen.

Writing this biography brought me into contact with scores of Claytie's friends, employees, and family members, which made the project as enjoyable as it was deeply rewarding. Claytie's top executives, Paul Latham and Mel Riggs, went beyond the norm in providing solid and insightful business, financial, and legal information and advice. And I'm not sure we could have pulled this off without the day-to-day assistance and smiling encouragement of Modesta's executive assistant, Carolyn Sandlin, and the dynamic Fort Stockton duo, Wynona Riggs and Nancy Carpenter. My heartfelt thanks go to all of you for your generous help and support, and most of all for your friendship.

All together, I've conducted more than two hundred interviews, totaling several hundred hours, with this remarkable circle of Claytie contacts. Claytie *really* never wanted a "fluff" biography, but he did want me to recognize and express the important meaning to his life of many of the personal relationships, experiences, and principles that have shaped him. Plans are under way to someday deposit the tapes and transcripts of these interviews in an appropriate archive open to the public.

Finally, I owe special thanks to my wife, Sondra, who rode through the heights and depths of this enterprise with unflagging patience and good humor and assurances that the end was out there . . . somewhere.

My only serious regret was my failure to interview Ann Richards personally. I did contact the former governor prior to the March 2006 announcement of her illness, yet we did not get an opportunity to talk before her death later in the year. However, authors Mike Shropshire and Frank Schaefer did graciously permit me to quote from their excellent biography, *The Thorny Rose of Texas,* published by Birch Lane Press in 1994.

In nearly five decades of chronicling everything Texas, nothing quite prepared me for the Claytie and Modesta adventure — and that's what it has been: an adventure. I didn't climb the mountains with them, but I interviewed him in cars, planes, boats, and Jeeps; at homes, offices, and bars; at farms and deer camps; and at ranches scattered from Alpine to Wyoming. They really are bigger than life, and sometimes Claytie is just as perplexing. But his contributions to this book were unvarnished and probably unprecedented for an "authorized" biography, and I'm richer for the experience.

Photo Credits

Unless otherwise noted, photographs are from the personal collection of Clayton W. Williams Jr.

Cover image and fronticepiece are © by Danny Turner, Danny Turner.com.

Photos on pp. viii, 21, 22, 123, 124, 125 by Stan Beard; pp. 126, 224, 290, 389 by Denise Kelly; p. 389 by Rowdy McBride; p. 345 by Larry Mitchell; p. 105 by Kathleen Jo Ryan; pp. 74, 84, 100, 118, 207, 212, 215 by Modesta Williams.

Photos on p. 285 courtesy Associated Press; pp. 315, 402 courtesy Hendershot Photography; p. 254 courtesy *Midland Reporter-Telegram;* p. 168 courtesy Sam Hollis Photography; p. 399 courtesy Schott's Photography; p. 167 courtesy *Texas Business;* p. 268 courtesy *Texas Monthly;* p. 369 courtesy *The Battalion.*

Index

Note. Italic page numbers indicate material in figures. When the name "Williams" appears in the index with no given name, it refers to Clayton W. Williams Jr.

Hitt, Michael, 199
Hobby, Bill, 379
Horn, Paul, 160
Houston Chronicle, 166, 292
Houston Livestock Show, 245
Houston Post, 199, 200, 241–242, 262, 271
Huckaby, J. B., 46
Huckaby, Robert, 46
Hull, Daniel, 373
Hunnicutt, Jim, 177
Hunt, Herbert, 367
Hunt, Ray, 388
Hunter's Africa, 179–183
hunting
    benefits and therapeutic value of hunting, 393–395
    big game in Botswana (1997), 40, 46–47
    the "Cactus Caper," 209
    deer camp at Matrix ranch, 101, 109, 144–145, 146
    deer hunting with father, 1944, *44*
    deer hunting with Jerry Groner, 209
    on Gataga Mountain, 216
    international hunting trips, 157–158, 338, 347–348, *349,* 383–384, 393
    with John May, 64
    with Kelvie, 211–213
    lion hunt in Tanzania, 2006, 393, *394*
    Modesta's world record African crocodile, 383, *384*
    in Pakistan, 233
    quail hunting with Modesta's mother, 92
    Sullivan ranch, 194
    See also sheep hunting
The Hunting Heritage, 395
Hyde, Sandy, 89

insurance sales, 58–60
International Brangus Breeders Association, 127
International Sheep Hunters Association, Super Slammer of the Year award for Modesta, 383

Jacoby, Mary, 272, 273
Jaycees (Fort Stockton Junior Chamber of Commerce), 78, 92–93, 95–96, 117, 175, 397
Jobe, Lew, 373
Johnson, Boris, 245
Johnson, Lyndon, 272
joke about rape
    apology and explanation by Williams, 266–267
    political and media reactions, 266, 267–270, 298
    reaction of family, 264, 266–267
    reporters' reactions to overhearing joke, 263–266
    Williams's telling of joke, 263
Jones, David, 172
Jones, Jill, 111
Jones, Punk, 136
Jones, Sandy, 107–108, 110–112, 141–142, 178, 235
Jones Ranch, 322, 325–326
    See also Marfa, TX

Kelleher, Herb, 388
Kelly, C. J., 101, 108–109
Kelly, Denise (née Garrett)
    activity during Williams's September 2001 hunting trip, 350–351, 352–353
    climbing Beaver Creek Mountain, 395
    climbing Guadalupe Peak, 355–359
    date of hire, 17, 177

McCarthy, Joe, 286

McClure, Jessica (Baby Jessica), 248

McCrory, Mary, 272

McDonald, Chuck, 282

McFarland Group of Botswana, 180

McKissack, Howard, 83

McKissick, John, 284

McMurtry, Larry, 29, 272

Means of Ascent (Caro), 272–273

Melson, Ann, 368

Mentone, Texas, 131, 135, 136–137, 159

   See also Gataga #2 gas well

Mercantile-M Bank, 114

Meriwether, Jimmy (father of Betty Williams), 77, 80

Merrick, Robert J., 69–70

Merrick #1 well, 70–71, 73

Michener, James, 21–23, *22*, 120–121

Midland home, 34, 158

Midland Petroleum Club, 169

Midland Reporter-Telegram

   American Academy of Achievement award, 176

   Chicora, 33–34

   ClayDesta Center, 342–343

   ClayDesta Communications, 219–220

   death of Ann Richards, 392

   Gary Ott column on Williams, 306

   Guadalupe Mountains National Park, 356

   Hunter's Africa, 179

   Midland oil and business leaders, 175

   thirty-sixth wedding anniversary, 342

   Williams as Aggie, 159

M-I Drilling Fluids, 336

Milam, Joe

   'Bustin Rocks' commercials in Williams campaign, 240–241, 255, 343

   as campaign adviser for Williams, 236, 240–241

   commercial for ClayDesta Communications, 220–221, 223, 227, 343

   on sale of ClayDesta Communications, 227

military experience

   cadet life at Texas A&M, 47–52, *53, 54,* 82

   in Mineral Springs, 57–59

   U.S. Army basic training, 56–57

military history of Graham and Williams families, 15, 33, 35

Miller, Jarvis, 164

Mills, Doc, 370

Mitchell, Mike, 115

Mobil-Sibley #1 well (Sibley #1), 71–72, 73

Monroe, Carolee, 145

Monroe, John, 144–145

Monroe, Stephanie, 145

Moody, Bill, 81

Moody, Charlie, 154, 194

Moore, Betty, 22

Moore, George, 372

Moore, Hinson, 258–259

Moore, Joe Hiram, *22,* 22–23

Moore, Tom, 320

Muhlbauer, Kelvie (née Williams). *See* Cleverdon, Kelvie

Muhlbauer, Michael Clayton, 210, *215*

Muhlbauer, Mike, 208

Myres, S. D., 24, 25

Nabors Drilling, 336

NAPE (North American Prospect Expo), 362, 366

National Transportation Safety Board (NTSB), 251, 253

Natural Gas Policy Act (NGPA), 148, 189

Nauman, Jack, 144

description by Denise Kelly, 17
description by *Odessa American,*
    17, 19
marriage, 33–34
picture with children, 1935, *18*
reaction to son's joke about rape,
    266–267
son's gubernatorial campaign, 256,
    310, *312*
Williams, Chicora Modesta (Chim).
    See Welborn, Chicora Modesta
Williams, Clayton Wade
    adoption, 205
    as baby, 215
    birth of son Aubry, 213, 365
    birth of son Chance, 389
    Clayton Williams Energy Inc.,
        388–389
    college graduation and marriage,
        365
    on growing up with Williams, 205,
        365
    horse trading, 215
    involvement with drugs and re-
        habilitation, 12, 195, 205, 238,
        364–365
    photo with Williams and brother
        Jeff, *207*
    on Sullivan Ranch, 194
    Texas State Historical Association
        Award banquet, 2006, 379
Williams, Clayton Wheat, Sr.
    at 1983 cattle sale, 21, *21*
    Animal Tales of the West, 32
    boyhood, 30, 381
    deer hunting with son, 1944, *44*
    description by daughter, 17, 19–
        20, 32
    description by son, 20, 378
    description of son, 20
    education, 30–31, *31*
    History of West Texas, 55
    Never Again, 15

occupations, 15, 31–32
oil business, 19, 32
Permian Basin Petroleum Hall of
    Fame induction, 19
at Scott Pollard's wedding, 16–17
signing book at Fort Stockton, *168*
speech by son at 2005 Aggie Mus-
    ter, 372
terminal illness and death, 20–
    21, 172
Texas A&M University Press and, 15
*Texas' Last Frontier: Fort Stockton
    and the Trans-Pecos, 1861-1895,*
    22, 168
Williams, Jack, 23
Williams, Janet. *See* Pollard, Janet
Williams, Jefferson Wheat Gataga
    (Jeff)
    adoption, 205, 216
    African hunting trip, 40
    Fort Stockton ranch, 205
    High Lonesome Ranch, 389
    on love in parent's marriage, 216
    photo with Williams and brother
        Clayton Wade, *207*
    on Sullivan Ranch, 194
    Texas State Historical Association
        Award banquet, 2006, 379
Williams, Jesse, 35
Williams, Jessie Caleb (J. C.), 24,
    30–31
Williams, Kelvie. *See* Cleverdon,
    Kelvie
Williams, Kristy, 213, 365, 379, 388
Williams, Modesta
    actions during Gataga #2 blowout,
        134–135, 136–137
    attack by pet deer, 338–341
    birth of daughter Chim, III, 205
    childhood, 89–90
    "Chipped Tooth Caper," 142–144
    on Clajon success and Clayton Wil-
        liams, 81–82

ISBN-13: 978-1-58544-634-6
ISBN-10: 1-58544-634-3